PIANO
AND KEYBOARD
CHORDS
MADE EASY

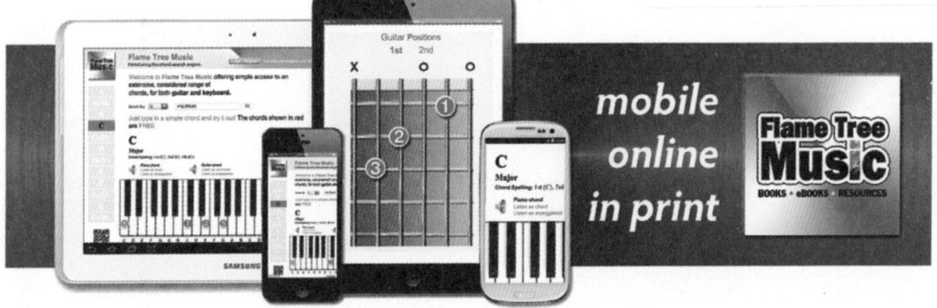

Publisher and Creative Director: Nick Wells
Project, design and media integration: Jake Jackson
Website and software: David Neville with Stevens Dumpala and Steve Moulton
Editorial: Laura Bulbeck, Emma Chafer and Esme Chapman

Special thanks to: Jane Ashley, Frances Bodiam, Helen Crust, Christine Delaborde, Stephen Feather, Sara Robson, Chris Herbert, Polly Prior, Gail Sharkey, Mike Spender and Birgitta Williams.

First published 2013 by
FLAME TREE PUBLISHING
Crabtree Hall, Crabtree Lane
Fulham, London SW6 6TY
United Kingdom

www.flametreepublishing.com

Music information site: www.flametreemusic.com

15 17 16
5 7 9 10 8 6 4

The CIP record for this book is available from the British Library.

Jake Jackson is a writer and musician. He has created and contributed to over 20 practical music books, including *Reading Music Made Easy*, *Play Flamenco* and *Piano and Keyboard Chords*. His music is available on iTunes, Amazon and Spotify amongst others.

ISBN: 978-0-85775-799-9

Printed in China

PIANO
AND KEYBOARD
CHORDS MADE EASY

SEE IT HEAR IT

COMPREHENSIVE SOUND LINKS

JAKE JACKSON

FLAME TREE
PUBLISHING

Contents

A
A♯/B♭
B
C
C♯/D♭
D
D♯/E♭
E
F
F♯/G♭
G
G♯/A♭

FREE ACCESS on smartphones including iPhone & Android

Using any QR code app scan and **HEAR** the chord (e.g. this is C Major)

A
A♯/B♭
B
C
C♯/D♭
D
D♯/E♭
E
F
F♯/G♭
G
G♯/A♭

Piano Chords

An Introduction

Your attitude towards the idea of a chord book for the keyboard depends on your musical tradition. However in almost any musical tradition, where a keyboard sits at the heart of the engine room of the band, chords provide the building blocks for composition and arrangement.

It's true that we can't all be Alicia Keys or Billy Joel, but a basic understanding of how a keyboard works, how its sounds can structure a song, how piano chords can both provide the backbone of a song and inspiration for solo work, will add colour and life to any band sound. Just listen to any music on the radio, the internet, the TV, in the mass market X-factor finals or the musicological extravanganzas of a Jools Holland show, and you'll find a keyboard somewhere in the mix. In the fantasy rock songs of Queen, Freddie Mercury's piano stands loud and proud; in the intricate and scintillating rock of Muse, multi-instrumentalist Matt Bellamy wields the piano like a demon weapon, driving their songs forward.

The piano stylings of the early Harlem school of piano – from Jelly Roll Morton and Duke Ellington, through Fats Waller to Thelonius Monk, Art Tatum, Herbie Hancock and Chick Corea – jazz, that truly great American art form which embraced the powerful simplicities of chord structures and used the keyboard to explore and embrace music and to draw in generations of listeners and audiences with their big, wide sounds. For the rest of us, for whom virtuoso performances are something to dream of and work towards, we can learn and plan in the knowledge that understanding chords is fundamental to arranging successful music.

FREE ACCESS on smartphones including iPhone & Android

Using any QR code app scan and **HEAR** the chord (e.g. this is C Major)

The piano can be a potent and versatile instrument, even in the hands of a beginner. Understanding the structure of the chords themselves and building a knowledge of how these work on a keyboard will help develop a good musical ear, and show you how to create the harmonies, melodies, echoes and textures that are essential to every good song.

I write mostly on the guitar, but when arranging for a band, or for a recording, its the keyboard that takes over. For years I've used various software sequencing programs, from **Cubase** to **LogicPro** to **Music Studio** now on **iPad**, to create soundscapes from keyboard sounds. Building engines of chords, organising progressions of music, adding new colours and flavours by flattening a fourth, or adding a ninth can alter the texture and the feel of a song. A shift of rhythm, a move from single chords to arpeggios in the third verse, the use of fatter major chords in the chorus... all can be experimented with on screen, as well as by any competant keyboard player.

So, this new book offers the left and right hand positions for **10 chords per key**, *and* through the power of mobile technology you can **hear** how the chord is meant to sound by using a **smartphone** and any **free QR reader app**. Connected to the flametreemusic.com website you can listen to each chord on the piano, keyboard, and the guitar too. **Good Luck!**

Jake Jackson, London.

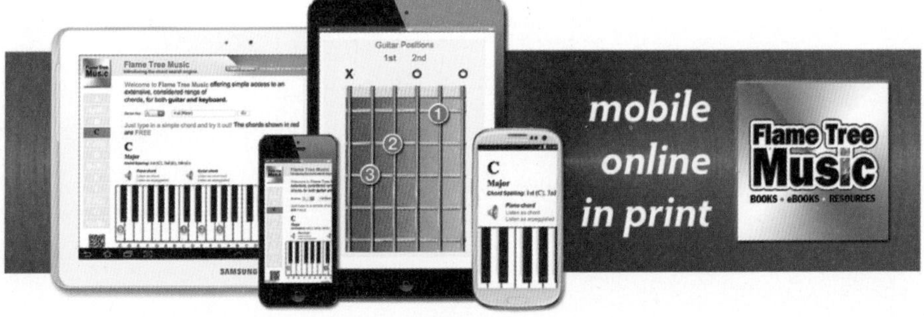

FREE ACCESS on smartphones including iPhone & Android

Using any QR code app scan and **HEAR** the chord (e.g. this is C Major)

Chord Diagrams

A Quick Guide

The chord diagrams are designed for quick access and ease of use. You can flick through book using the tabs on the side, then use the finger positions and keyboard to help you make the chord.

The chord on the **left** page is for the **left hand**, on the **right** page, the chord is for the **right hand**. Each chord is provided with a *Chord Spelling* to help you check each note. This is a great way to learn the structure of the sounds you are making and will help with melodies and solo work.

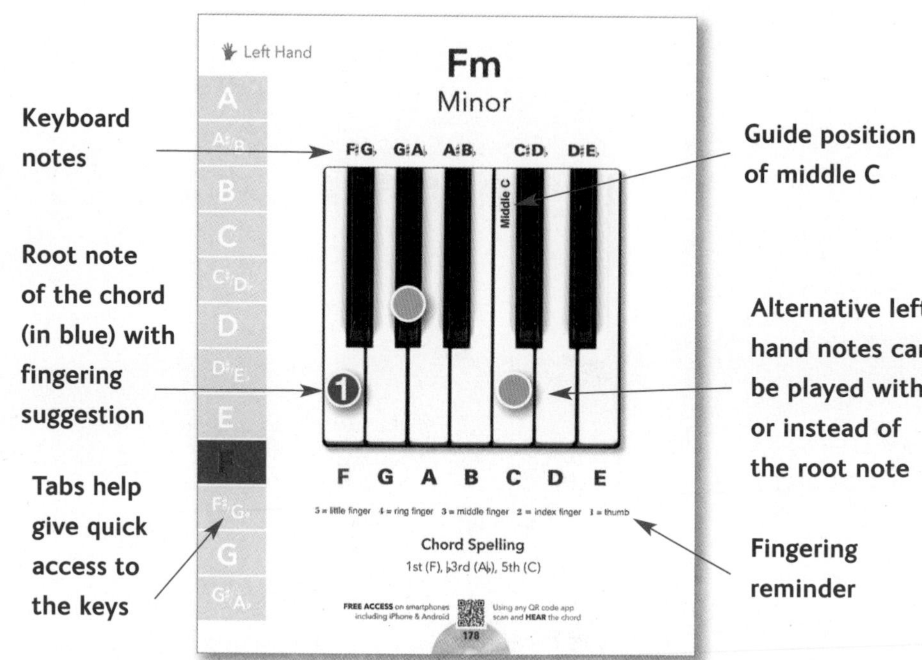

FREE ACCESS on smartphones including iPhone & Android

Using any QR code app scan and **HEAR** the chord (e.g. this is C Major)

Chord Title: Each chord is given a short and complete name, so the short name C°7 is properly known as C Diminished 7th.

Right Hand Fingerings: ❶ is the thumb ❷ is the index finger ❸ is the middle finger ❹ is the ring finger ❺ is the little finger

Left Hand Fingerings: ❶ is the little finger ❷ is the ring finger ❸ is the middle finger ❹ is the index finger ❺ is the thumb

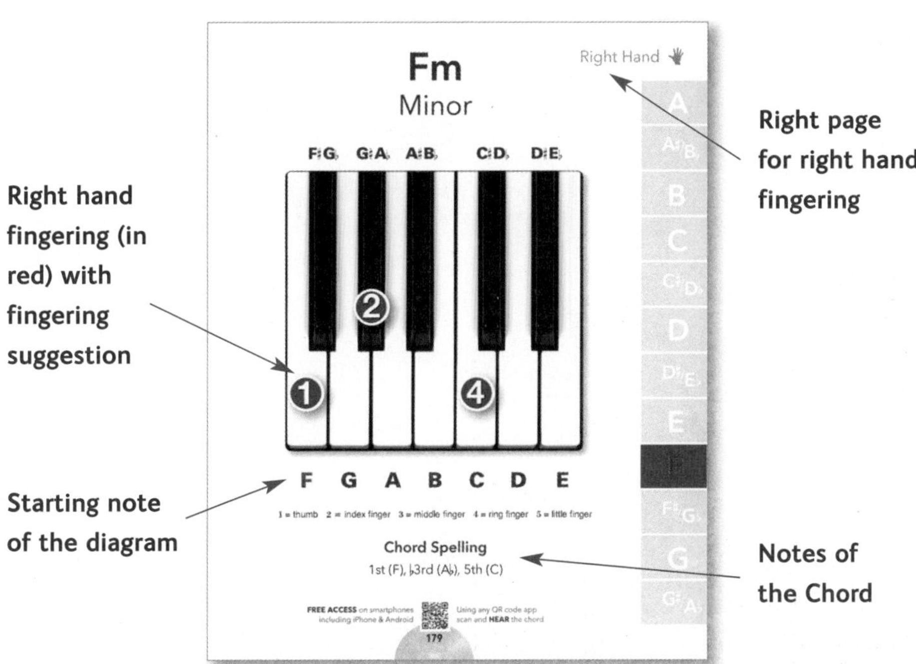

FREE ACCESS on smartphones including iPhone & Android

Using any QR code app scan and **HEAR** the chord (e.g. this is C Major)

The Sound Links
A Quick Guide

Requirements: a camera and internet ready smartphone (eg. **iPhone**, any **Android** phone (e.g. **Samsung** Galaxy), N**okia Lumia**, or **camera-enabled tablet** such as the **iPad** Mini). The best result is achieved using a WIFI connection.

1. Download any **free QR code reader**. An app store search will reveal a great many of these, so obviously its is best to go with the ones with the highest ratings and don't be afraid to try a few before you settle on the one that works best for you. Tapmedia's QR Reader app is good, or ATT Scanner (used below) or QR Media. Some of the free apps have ads, which can be annoying.

2. Find the chord you want to play, look at the diagram then check out the **QR code** at the base of the page.

FREE ACCESS on smartphones including iPhone & Android  Using any QR code app scan and **HEAR** the chord

76

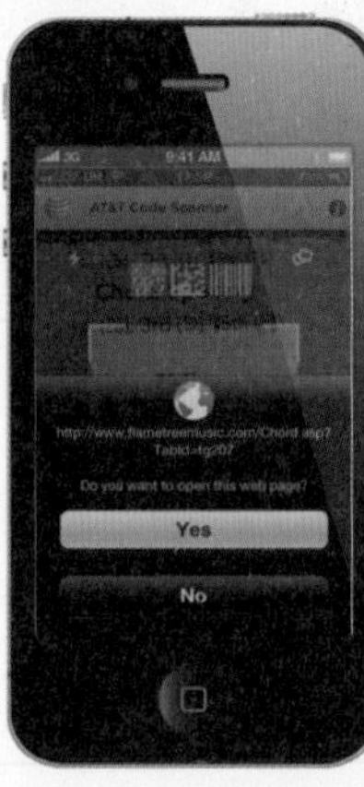

3. On your smartphone, open the app and **scan** the **QR code** at the base of any particular chord page.

4. The QR reader app will take you to a browser, then the specific chord will be displayed on the flametreemusic.com website.

FREE ACCESS on smartphones including iPhone & Android  Using any QR code app scan and **HEAR** the chord (e.g. this is C Major)

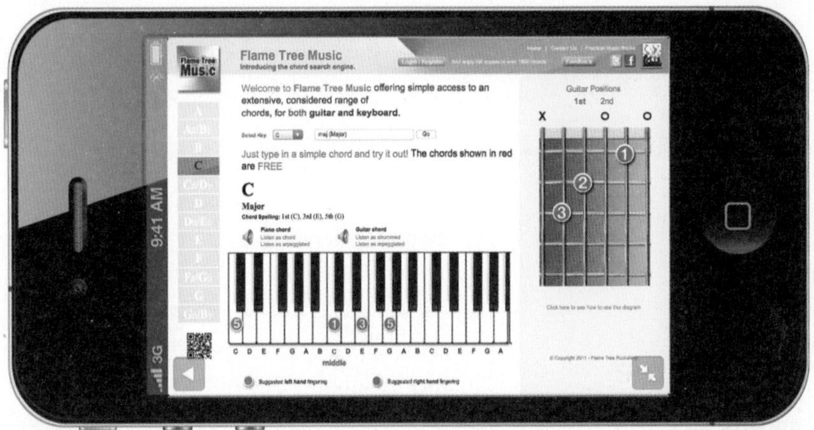

5. Using the usual pinch and zoom techniques, you can focus on four sound options.

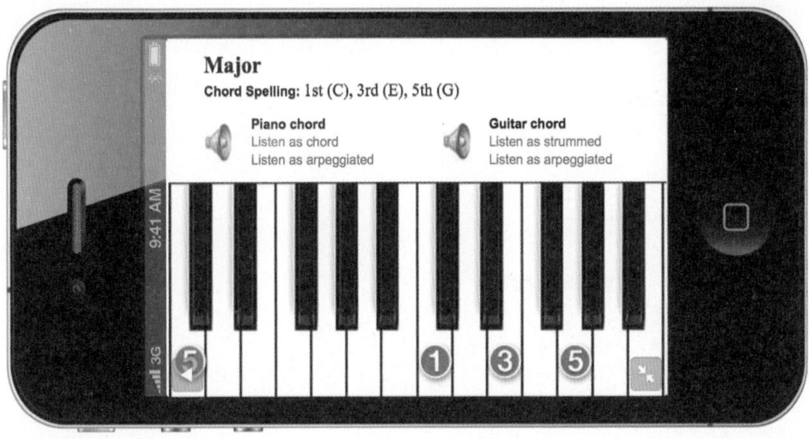

6. Click the sounds! Both piano and guitar audio is provided. This is particularly helpful when you're playing with others.

The QR codes give you direct access to all the chords. You can access a much wider range of chords if you register and subscribe.

The Website

flametreemusic.com

The Flame Tree Music web site is designed to make searching for chords very easy. It complements our range of print publications and offers easy access to chords online and on the move, through tablets, smartphones, desktop computers and books.

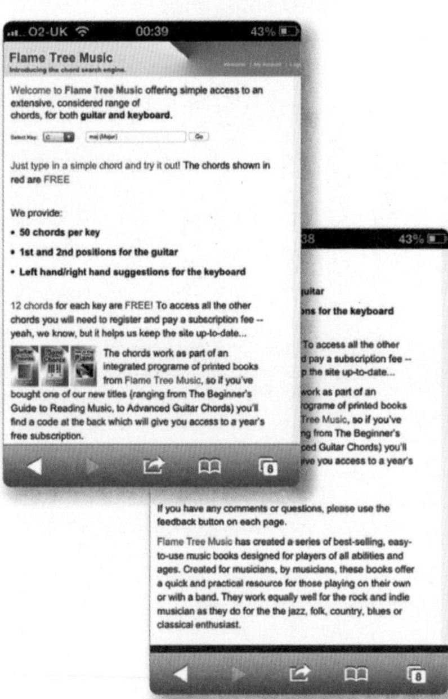

1. The site offers access to chord diagrams and finger positions for both the guitar and the piano/keyboard, presenting a wide range of sound options to help develop good listening technique, and to assist you in identifying the chord and each note within it.

2. The site offers 12 **free** chords, those most commonly used in a band setting or in songwriting.

3. A subscription is available for those who would like access to the full range of chords, **50** for **each key**.

FREE ACCESS on smartphones including iPhone & Android

Using any QR code app scan and **HEAR** the chord (e.g. this is C Major)

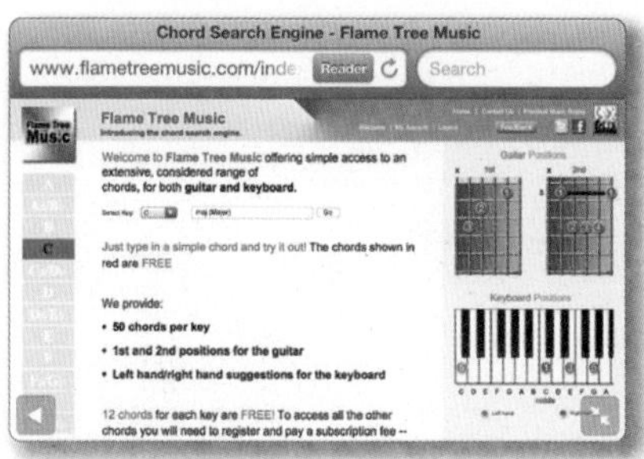

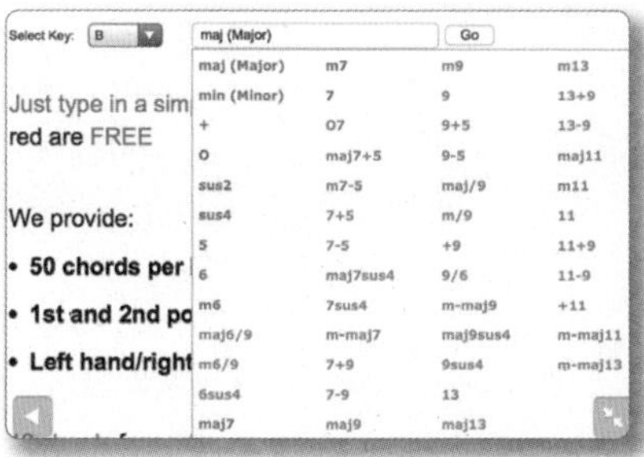

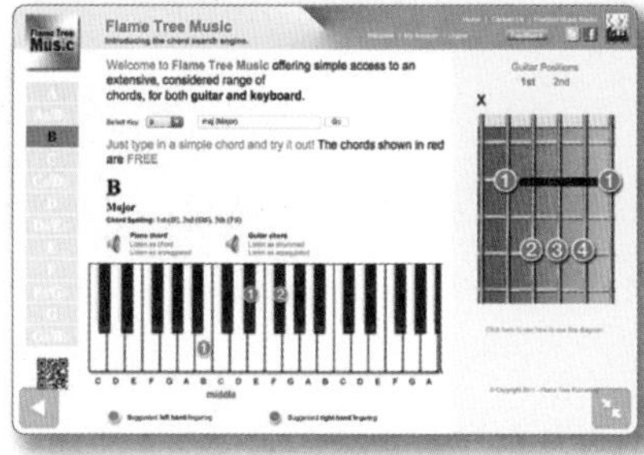

4. Guitar chords are shown with **first** and **second positions.**

5. For the keyboard, **left**- and **right-hand positions** are shown. The keyboard also sounds each note.

6. Choose the key, then the chord name from the drop down menu. Note that the **red chords** are available **free**. Those in blue can be accessed with a subscription.

7. Once you've selected the chord, press **GO** and the details of the chord will be shown, with chord spellings, keyboard and guitar fingerings.

8. Initially, the first position for the guitar is shown. The second position can be selected by clicking the text above the chord diagram.

9. Sounds are provided in four easy-to-understand configurations.

We are constantly developing the web site, so further features will be added, including resources, scales and modes.

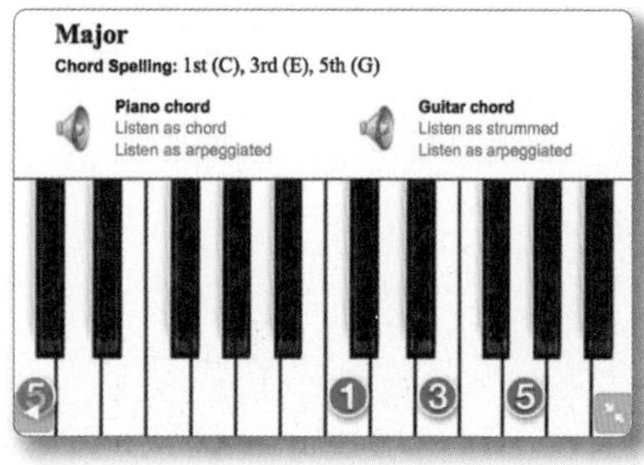

FREE ACCESS on smartphones including iPhone & Android  Using any QR code app scan and **HEAR** the chord (e.g. this is C Major)

The Chords

FREE ACCESS on smartphones including iPhone & Android

Using any QR code app scan and **HEAR** the chord (e.g. this is C Major)

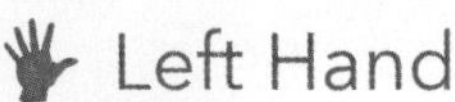

A
Major

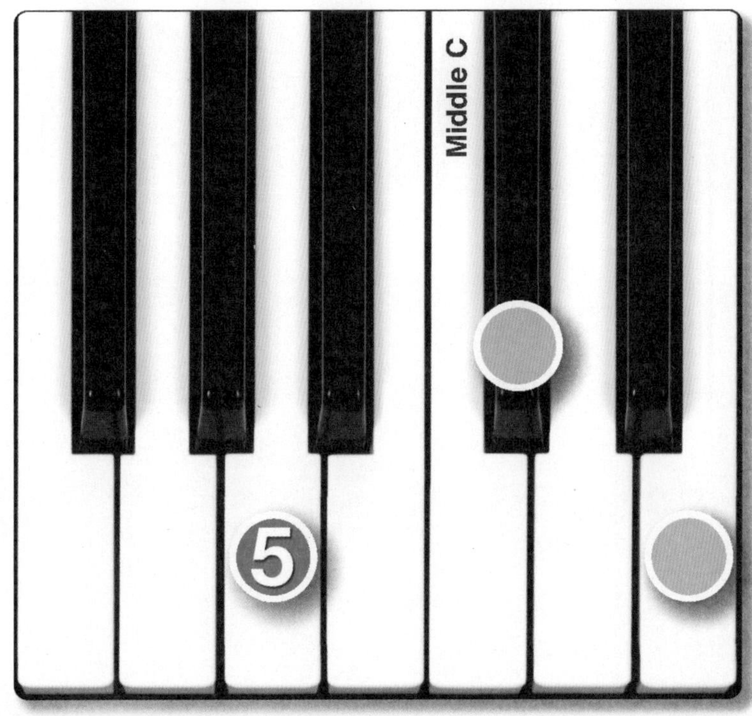

5 = little finger 4 = ring finger 3 = middle finger 2 = index finger 1 = thumb

Chord Spelling

1st (A), 3rd (C♯), 5th (E)

FREE ACCESS on smartphones including iPhone & Android

Using any QR code app scan and **HEAR** the chord

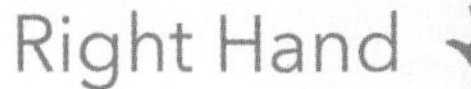

A
Major

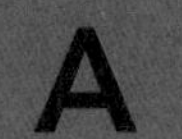

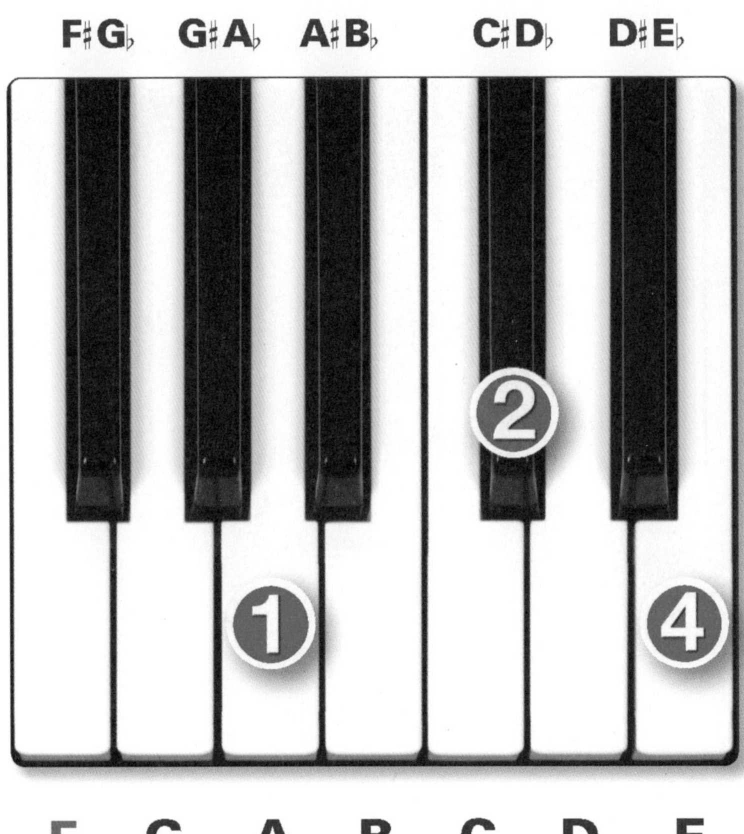

1 = thumb 2 = index finger 3 = middle finger 4 = ring finger 5 = little finger

Chord Spelling

1st (A), 3rd (C♯), 5th (E)

FREE ACCESS on smartphones including iPhone & Android

Using any QR code app scan and **HEAR** the chord

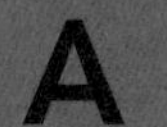

Am
Minor

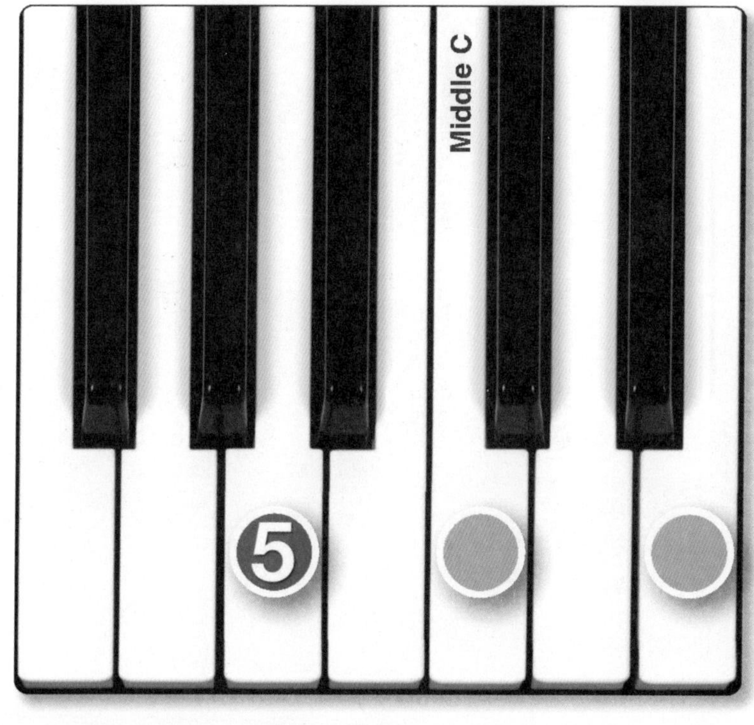

5 = little finger 4 = ring finger 3 = middle finger 2 = index finger 1 = thumb

Chord Spelling

1st (A), ♭3rd (C), 5th (E)

FREE ACCESS on smartphones including iPhone & Android

Using any QR code app scan and **HEAR** the chord

Am
Minor

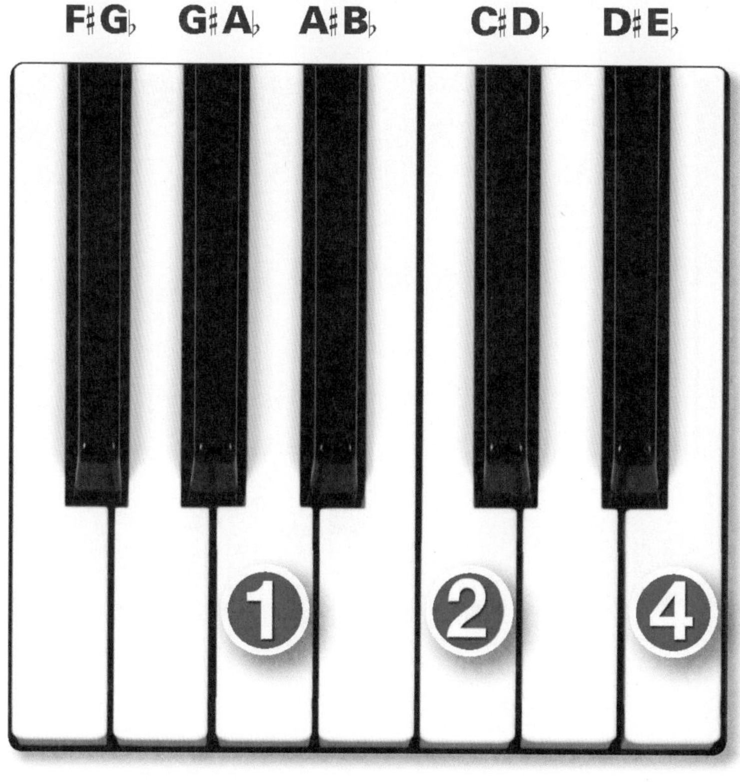

F G A B C D E

1 = thumb 2 = index finger 3 = middle finger 4 = ring finger 5 = little finger

Chord Spelling

1st (A), ♭3rd (C), 5th (E)

FREE ACCESS on smartphones including iPhone & Android

Using any QR code app scan and **HEAR** the chord

A+
Augmented Triad

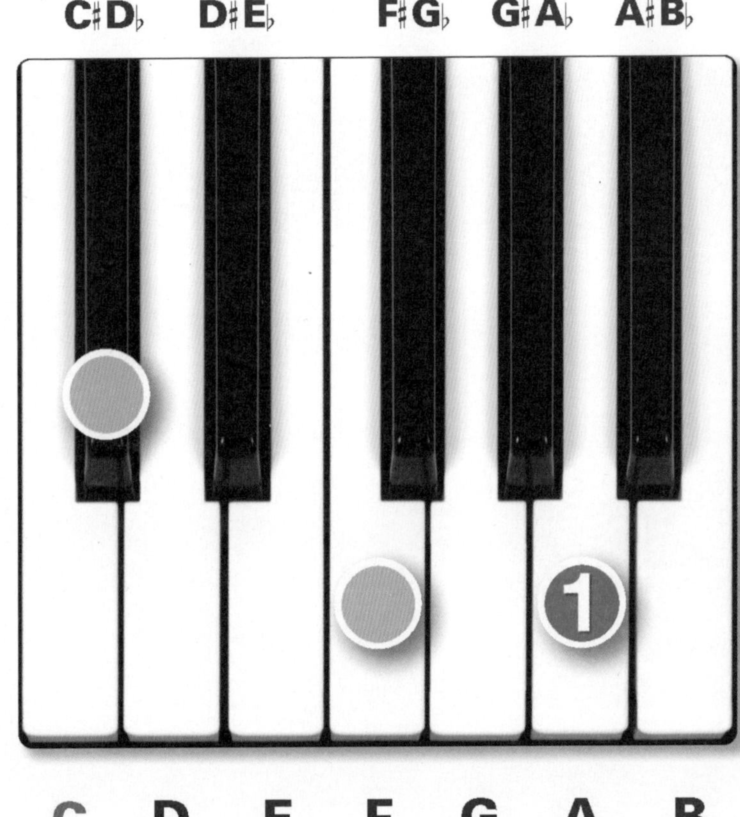

5 = little finger 4 = ring finger 3 = middle finger 2 = index finger 1 = thumb

Chord Spelling

1st (A), 3rd (C♯), ♯5th (E♯)

FREE ACCESS on smartphones including iPhone & Android  Using any QR code app scan and **HEAR** the chord

A+
Augmented Triad

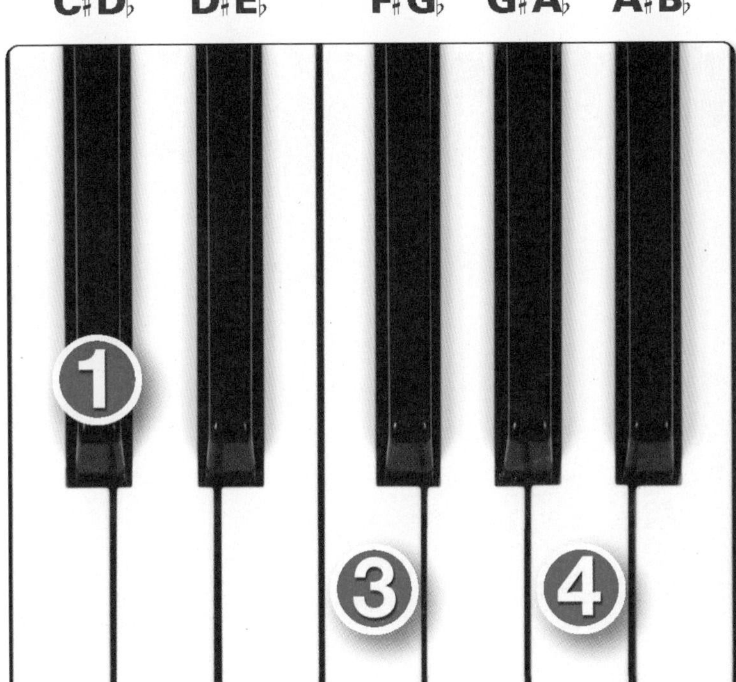

1 = thumb 2 = index finger 3 = middle finger 4 = ring finger 5 = little finger

Chord Spelling

1st (A), 3rd (C♯), ♯5th (E♯)

FREE ACCESS on smartphones including iPhone & Android

Using any QR code app scan and **HEAR** the chord

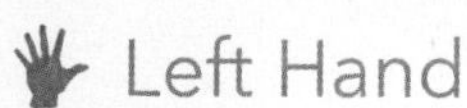

A
A♯/B♭
B
C
C♯/D♭
D
D♯/E♭
E
F
F♯/G♭
G
G♯/A♭

A°

Diminished Triad

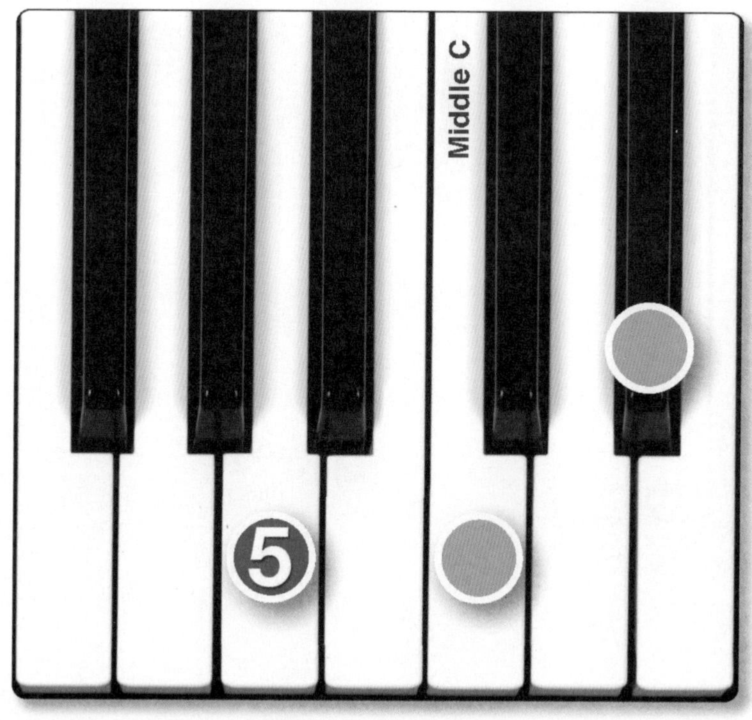

5 = little finger 4 = ring finger 3 = middle finger 2 = index finger 1 = thumb

Chord Spelling

1st (A), ♭3rd (C), ♭5th (E♭)

FREE ACCESS on smartphones including iPhone & Android

Using any QR code app scan and **HEAR** the chord

A°

Diminished Triad

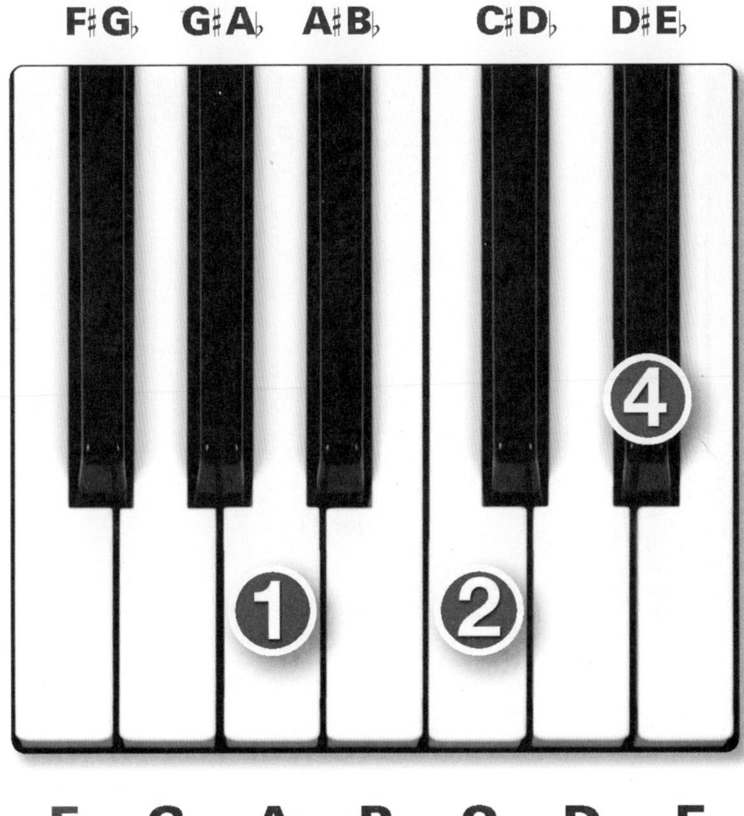

1 = thumb 2 = index finger 3 = middle finger 4 = ring finger 5 = little finger

Chord Spelling

1st (A), ♭3rd (C), ♭5th (E♭)

FREE ACCESS on smartphones including iPhone & Android

Using any QR code app scan and **HEAR** the chord

A6

Major 6th

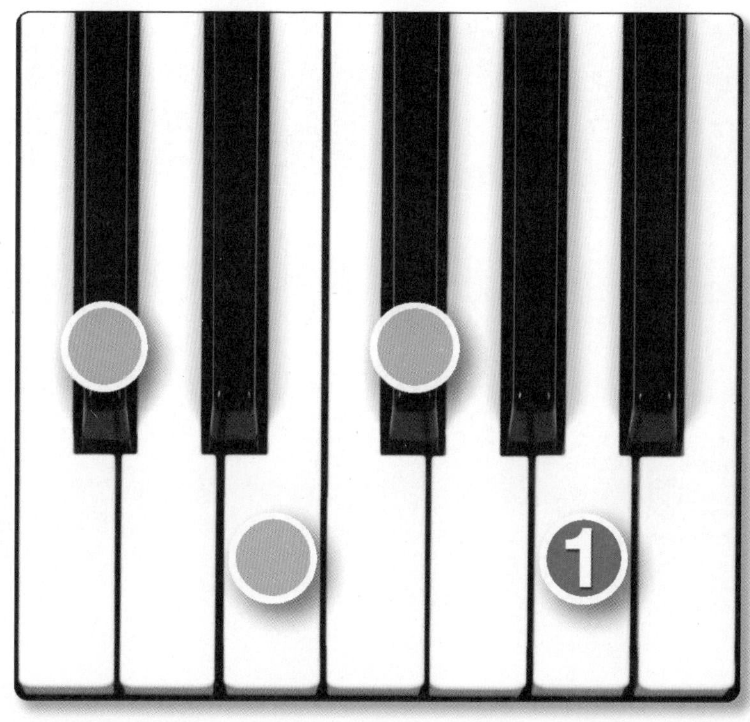

5 = little finger 4 = ring finger 3 = middle finger 2 = index finger 1 = thumb

Chord Spelling

1st (A), 3rd (C♯), 5th (E), 6th (F♯)

FREE ACCESS on smartphones including iPhone & Android

Using any QR code app scan and **HEAR** the chord

A6
Major 6th

1 = thumb 2 = index finger 3 = middle finger 4 = ring finger 5 = little finger

Chord Spelling

1st (A), 3rd (C♯), 5th (E), 6th (F♯)

FREE ACCESS on smartphones including iPhone & Android

Using any QR code app scan and **HEAR** the chord

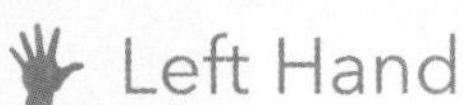

Am6

Minor 6th

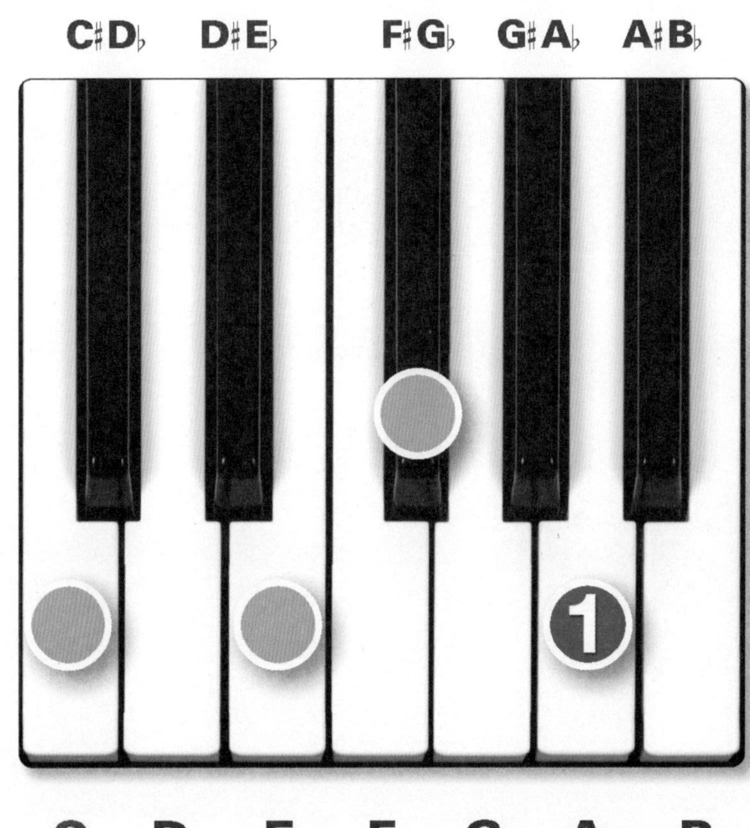

5 = little finger 4 = ring finger 3 = middle finger 2 = index finger 1 = thumb

Chord Spelling

1st (A), ♭3rd (C), 5th (E), 6th (F♯)

FREE ACCESS on smartphones including iPhone & Android  Using any QR code app scan and **HEAR** the chord

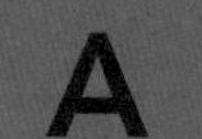

Am6
Minor 6th

C♯D♭ D♯E♭ F♯G♭ G♯A♭ A♯B♭

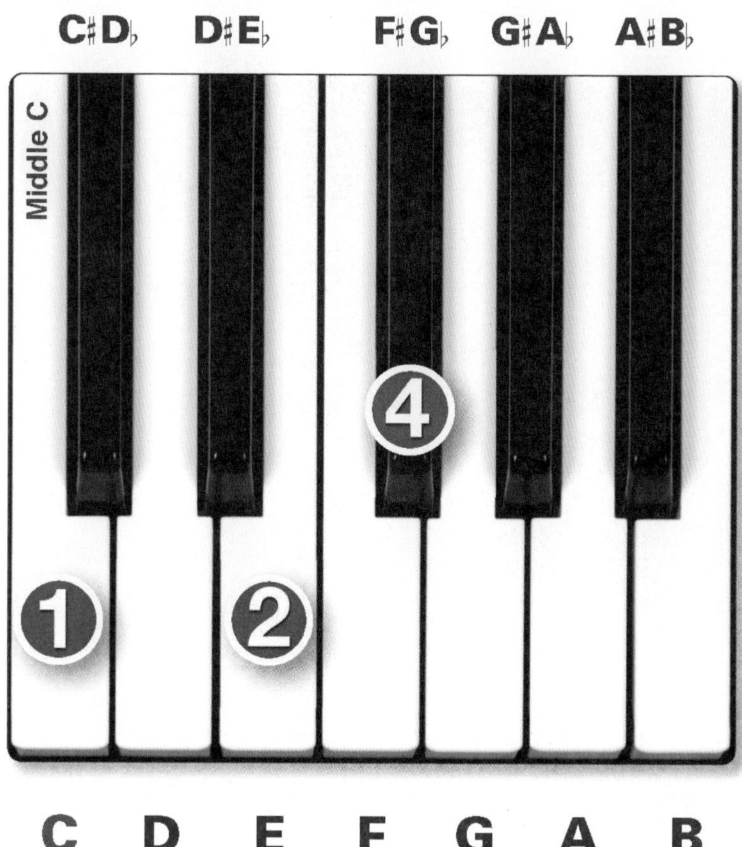

C D E F G A B

1 = thumb 2 = index finger 3 = middle finger 4 = ring finger 5 = little finger

Chord Spelling

1st (A), ♭3rd (C), 5th (E), 6th (F♯)

FREE ACCESS on smartphones including iPhone & Android

Using any QR code app scan and **HEAR** the chord

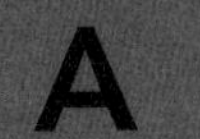

Amaj7

Major 7th

C♯D♭ D♯E♭ F♯G♭ G♯A♭ A♯B♭

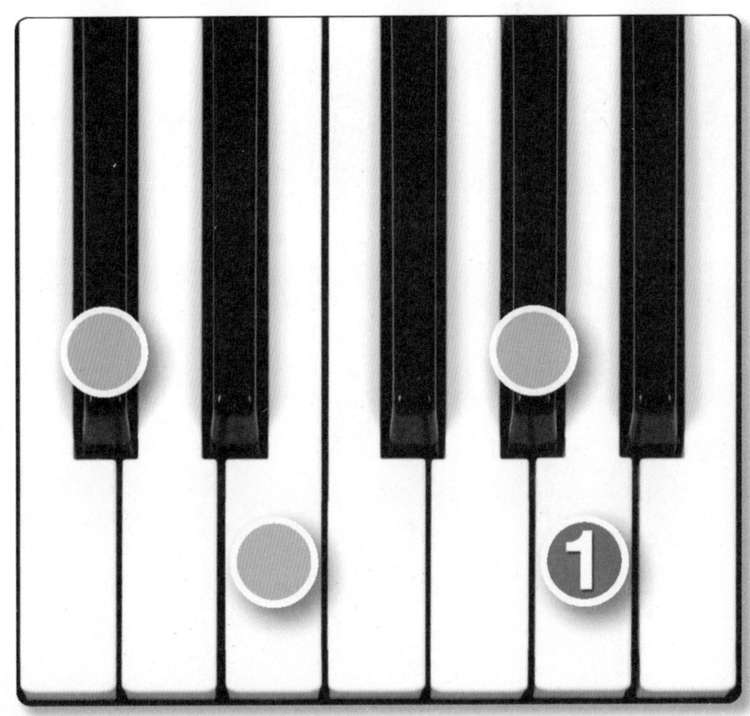

C D E F G A B

5 = little finger 4 = ring finger 3 = middle finger 2 = index finger 1 = thumb

Chord Spelling

1st (A), 3rd (C♯), 5th (E), 7th (G♯)

FREE ACCESS on smartphones including iPhone & Android

Using any QR code app scan and **HEAR** the chord

Amaj7
Major 7th

C♯D♭ D♯E♭ F♯G♭ G♯A♭ A♯B♭

Middle C

1 4 2

C D E F G A B

1 = thumb 2 = index finger 3 = middle finger 4 = ring finger 5 = little finger

Chord Spelling

1st (A), 3rd (C♯), 5th (E), 7th (G♯)

FREE ACCESS on smartphones including iPhone & Android

Using any QR code app scan and **HEAR** the chord

Left Hand

Am7

Minor 7th

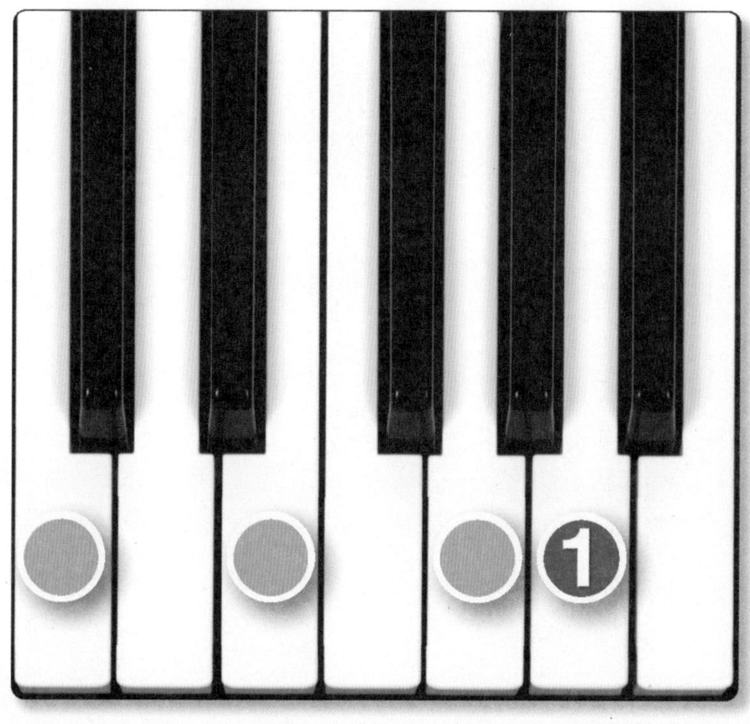

5 = little finger   4 = ring finger   3 = middle finger   2 = index finger   1 = thumb

Chord Spelling

1st (A), ♭3rd (C), 5th (E), ♭7th (G)

FREE ACCESS on smartphones including iPhone & Android

Using any QR code app scan and **HEAR** the chord

Am7

Minor 7th

C♯D♭ D♯E♭ F♯G♭ G♯A♭ A♯B♭

Middle C

1 2 4

C D E F G A B

1 = thumb 2 = index finger 3 = middle finger 4 = ring finger 5 = little finger

Chord Spelling

1st (A), ♭3rd (C), 5th (E), ♭7th (G)

FREE ACCESS on smartphones including iPhone & Android

Using any QR code app scan and **HEAR** the chord

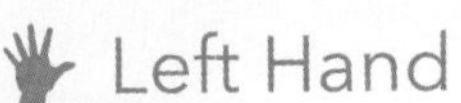

A

A♯/B♭

B

C

C♯/D♭

D

D♯/E♭

E

F

F♯/G♭

G

G♯/A♭

Amaj9

Major 9th

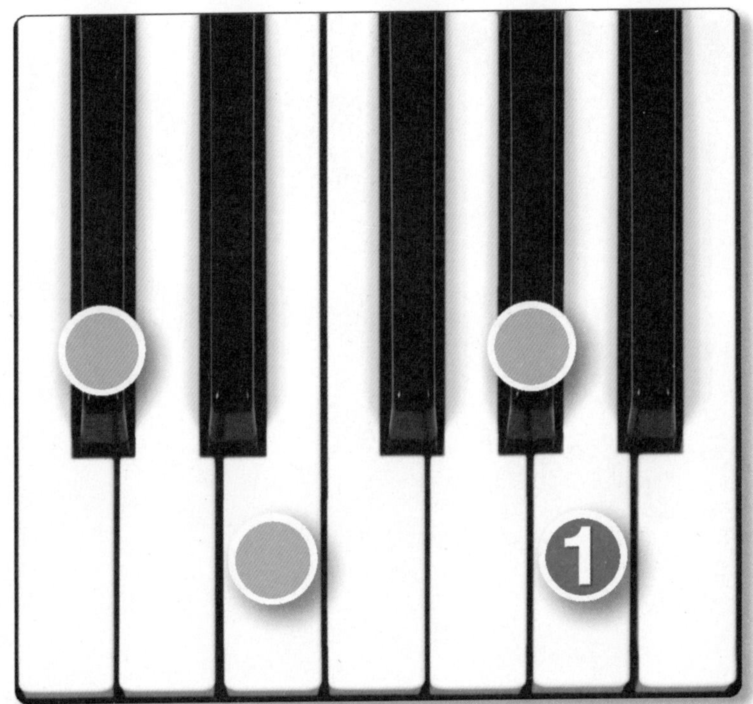

5 = little finger 4 = ring finger 3 = middle finger 2 = index finger 1 = thumb

Chord Spelling

1st (A), 3rd (C♯), 5th (E), 7th (G♯), 9th (B)

FREE ACCESS on smartphones including iPhone & Android

Using any QR code app scan and **HEAR** the chord

Amaj9

Major 9th

C♯D♭ D♯E♭ F♯G♭ G♯A♭ A♯B♭

1 4

2 5

C D E F G A B

1 = thumb 2 = index finger 3 = middle finger 4 = ring finger 5 = little finger

Chord Spelling

1st (A), 3rd (C♯), 5th (E), 7th (G♯), 9th (B)

FREE ACCESS on smartphones including iPhone & Android  Using any QR code app scan and **HEAR** the chord

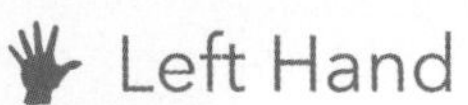

A

A#/B♭

B

C

C#/D♭

D

D#/E♭

E

F

F#/G♭

G

G#/A♭

Am9

Minor 9th

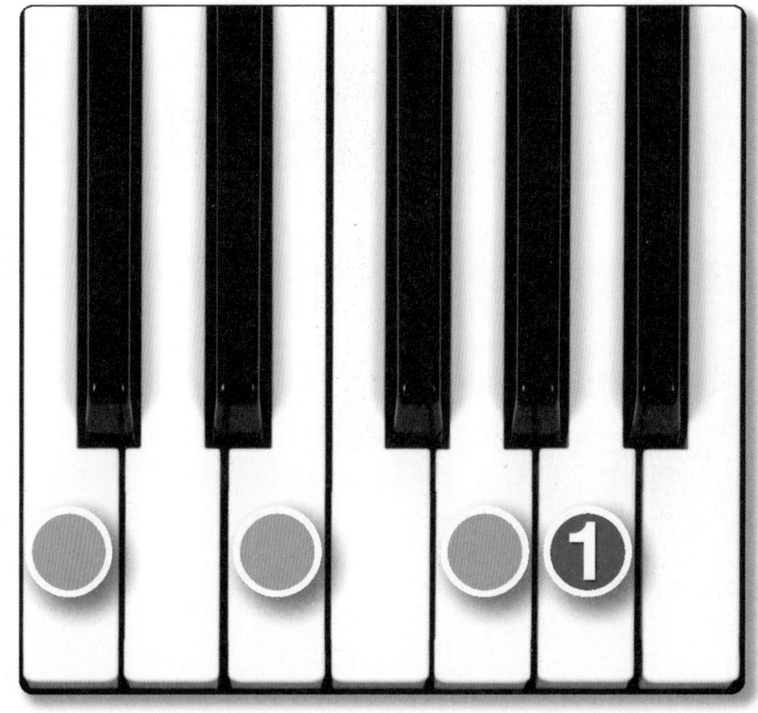

5 = little finger 4 = ring finger 3 = middle finger 2 = index finger 1 = thumb

Chord Spelling

1st (A), ♭3rd (C), 5th (E), ♭7th (G), 9th (B)

FREE ACCESS on smartphones including iPhone & Android  Using any QR code app scan and **HEAR** the chord

Am9

Minor 9th

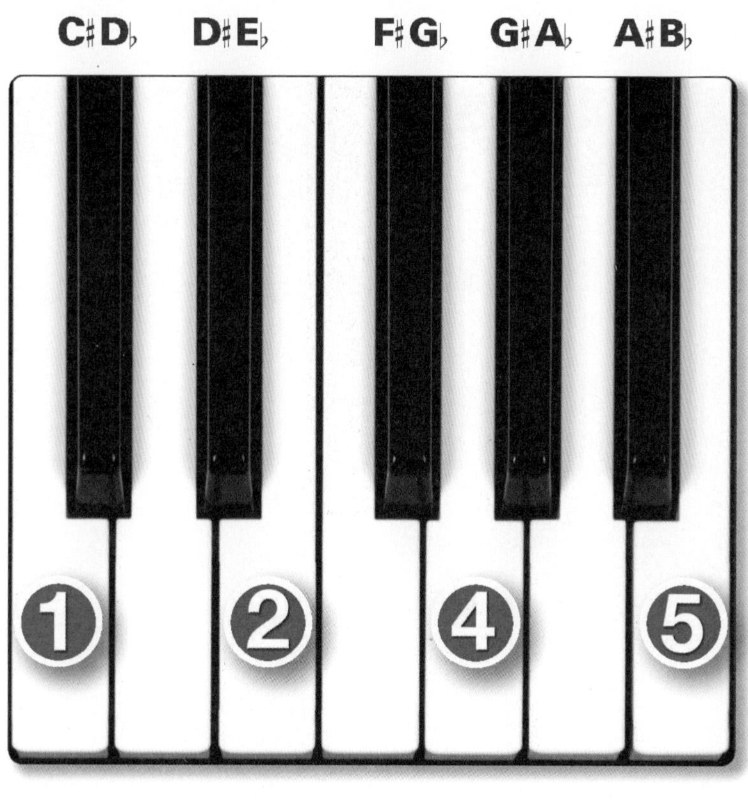

C D E F G A B

1 = thumb 2 = index finger 3 = middle finger 4 = ring finger 5 = little finger

Chord Spelling

1st (A), ♭3rd (C), 5th (E), ♭7th (G), 9th (B)

FREE ACCESS on smartphones including iPhone & Android  Using any QR code app scan and **HEAR** the chord

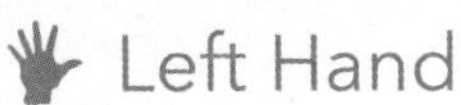

A♯/B♭
Major

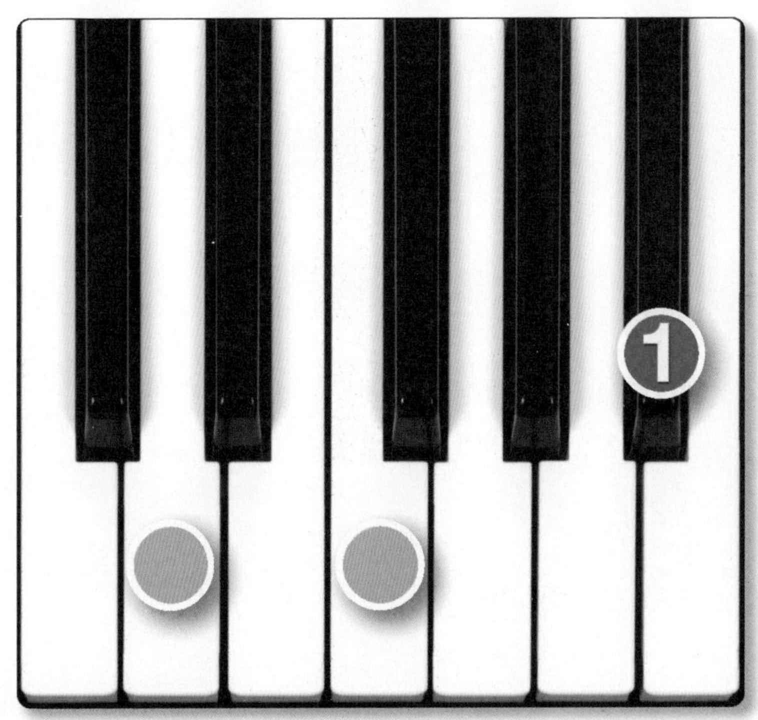

5 = little finger 4 = ring finger 3 = middle finger 2 = index finger 1 = thumb

Chord Spelling

1st (B♭), 3rd (D), 5th (F)

FREE ACCESS on smartphones including iPhone & Android

Using any QR code app scan and **HEAR** the chord

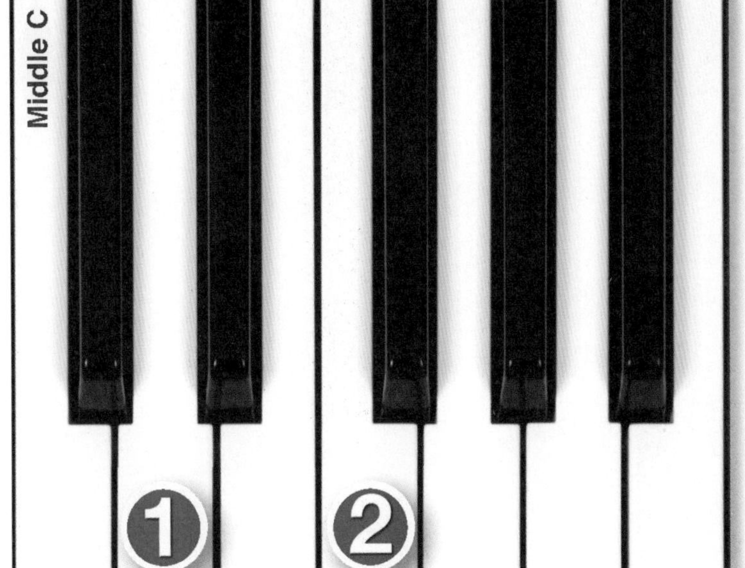

1 = thumb 2 = index finger 3 = middle finger 4 = ring finger 5 = little finger

Chord Spelling

1st (B♭), 3rd (D), 5th (F)

FREE ACCESS on smartphones including iPhone & Android

Using any QR code app scan and **HEAR** the chord

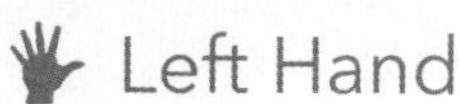

A♯/B♭m
Minor

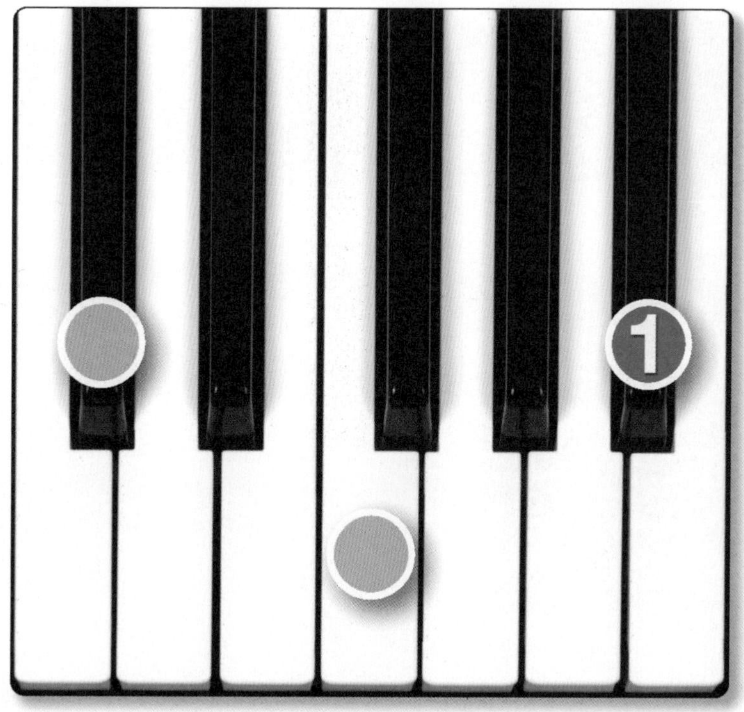

5 = little finger 4 = ring finger 3 = middle finger 2 = index finger 1 = thumb

Chord Spelling

1st (B♭), ♭3rd (D♭), 5th (F)

FREE ACCESS on smartphones including iPhone & Android  Using any QR code app scan and **HEAR** the chord

A♯/B♭m
Minor

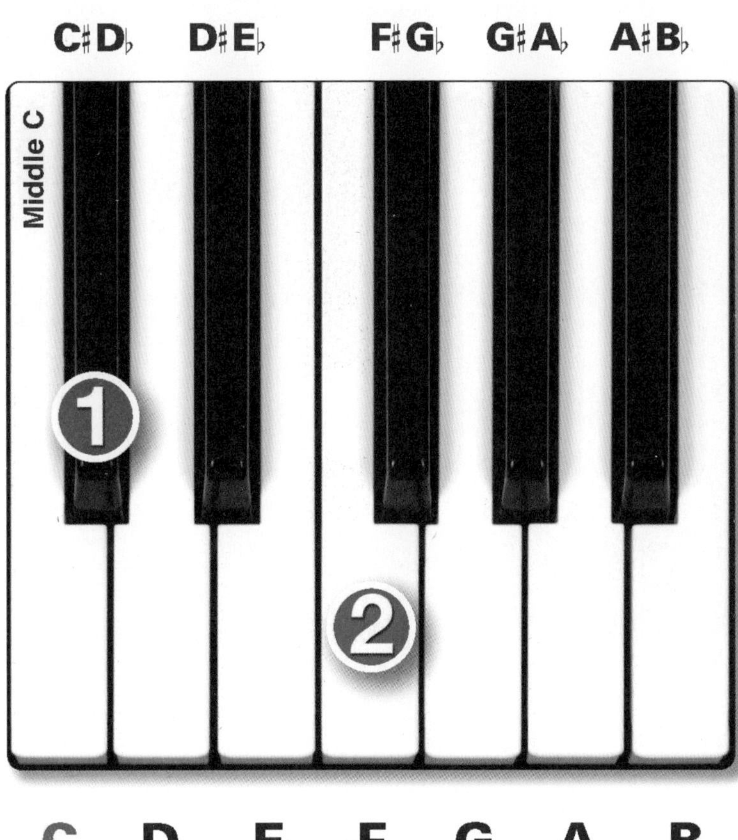

1 = thumb 2 = index finger 3 = middle finger 4 = ring finger 5 = little finger

Chord Spelling

1st (B♭), ♭3rd (D♭), 5th (F)

FREE ACCESS on smartphones including iPhone & Android

Using any QR code app scan and **HEAR** the chord

A♯/B♭+
Augmented Triad

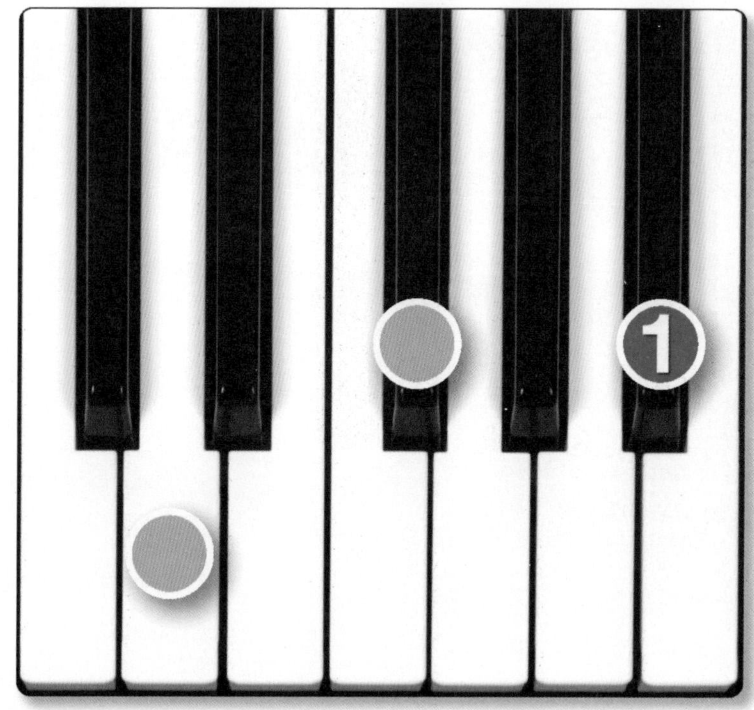

5 = little finger 4 = ring finger 3 = middle finger 2 = index finger 1 = thumb

Chord Spelling

1st (B♭), 3rd (D), ♯5th (F♯)

FREE ACCESS on smartphones including iPhone & Android

Using any QR code app scan and **HEAR** the chord

A♯/B♭+
Augmented Triad

1 = thumb 2 = index finger 3 = middle finger 4 = ring finger 5 = little finger

Chord Spelling

1st (B♭), 3rd (D), ♯5th (F♯)

FREE ACCESS on smartphones including iPhone & Android  Using any QR code app scan and **HEAR** the chord

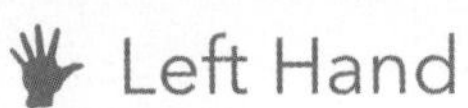

A
A♯/B♭
B
C
C♯/D♭
D
D♯/E♭
E
F
F♯/G♭
G
G♯/A♭

A♯/B♭°
Diminished Triad

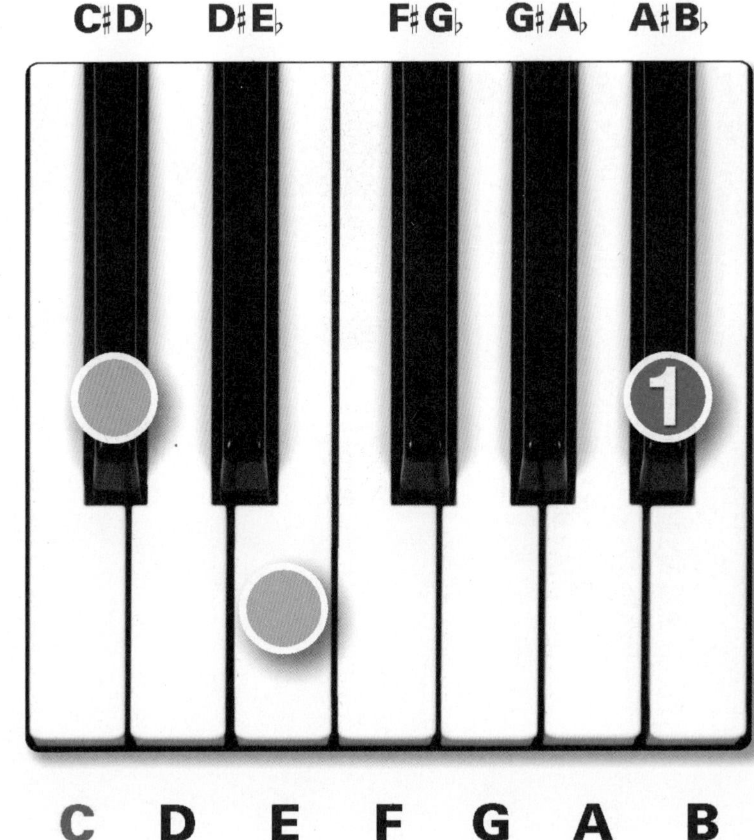

5 = little finger 4 = ring finger 3 = middle finger 2 = index finger 1 = thumb

Chord Spelling

1st (B♭), ♭3rd (D♭), ♭5th (F♭)

FREE ACCESS on smartphones including iPhone & Android  Using any QR code app scan and **HEAR** the chord

A♯/B♭°
Diminished Triad

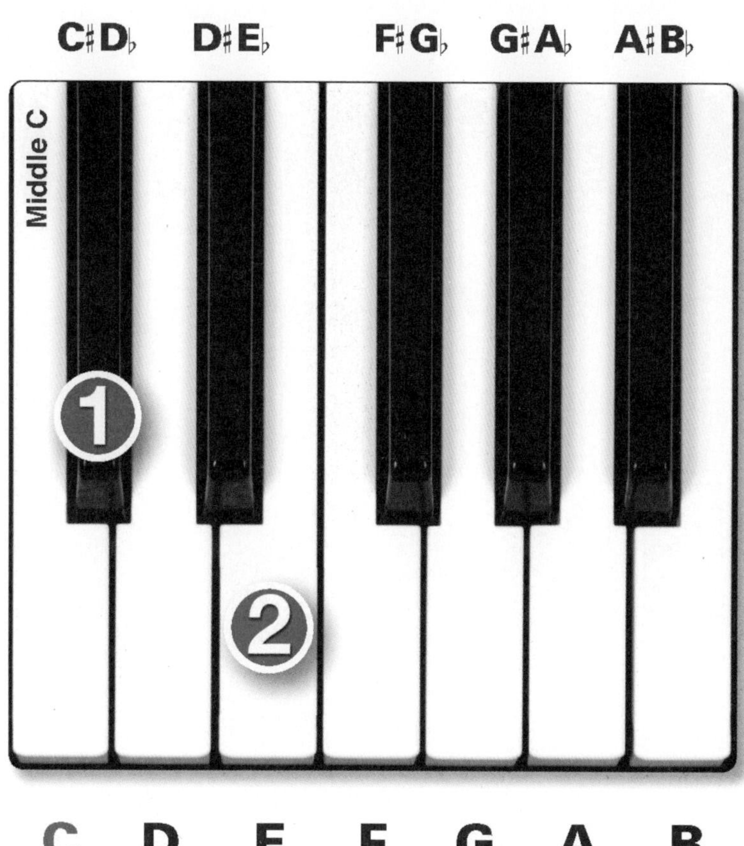

1 = thumb 2 = index finger 3 = middle finger 4 = ring finger 5 = little finger

Chord Spelling

1st (B♭), ♭3rd (D♭), ♭5th (F♭)

FREE ACCESS on smartphones including iPhone & Android  Using any QR code app scan and **HEAR** the chord

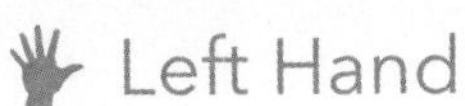

A♯/B♭6
Major 6th

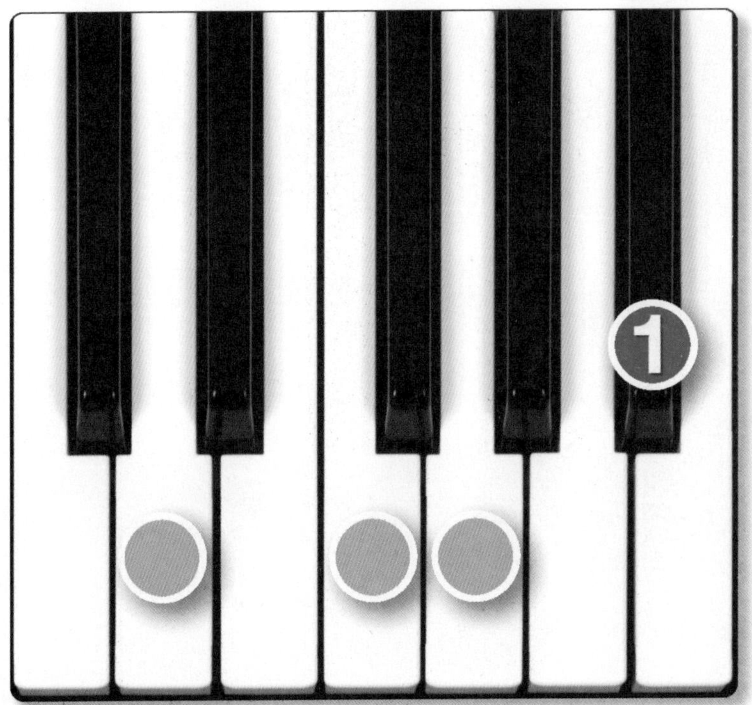

5 = little finger 4 = ring finger 3 = middle finger 2 = index finger 1 = thumb

Chord Spelling

1st (B♭), 3rd (D), 5th (F), 6th (G)

FREE ACCESS on smartphones including iPhone & Android

Using any QR code app scan and **HEAR** the chord

A♯/B♭6
Major 6th

1 = thumb 2 = index finger 3 = middle finger 4 = ring finger 5 = little finger

Chord Spelling

1st (B♭), 3rd (D), 5th (F), 6th (G)

FREE ACCESS on smartphones including iPhone & Android

Using any QR code app scan and **HEAR** the chord

A♯/B♭m6

Minor 6th

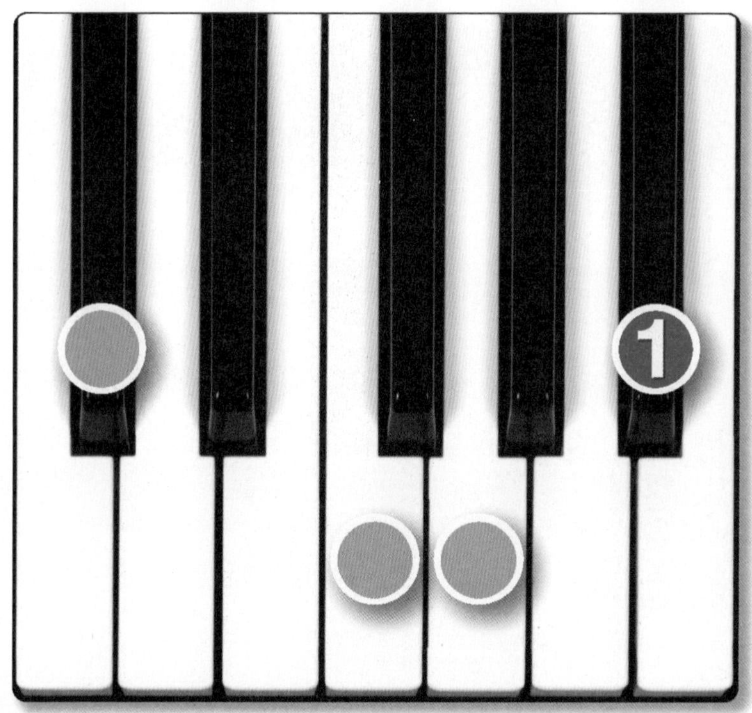

5 = little finger 4 = ring finger 3 = middle finger 2 = index finger 1 = thumb

Chord Spelling

1st (B♭), ♭3rd (D♭), 5th (F), 6th (G)

FREE ACCESS on smartphones including iPhone & Android

Using any QR code app scan and **HEAR** the chord

Right Hand 

A♯/B♭m6

Minor 6th

C♯D♭ D♯E♭ F♯G♭ G♯A♭ A♯B♭

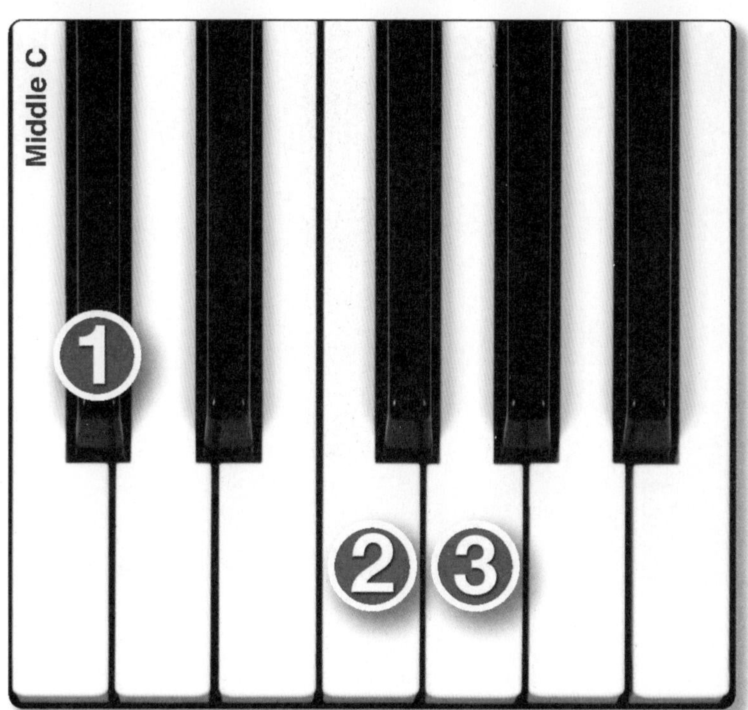

C D E F G A B

1 = thumb 2 = index finger 3 = middle finger 4 = ring finger 5 = little finger

Chord Spelling

1st (B♭), ♭3rd (D♭), 5th (F), 6th (G)

FREE ACCESS on smartphones including iPhone & Android

Using any QR code app scan and **HEAR** the chord

A♯/B♭maj7

Major 7th

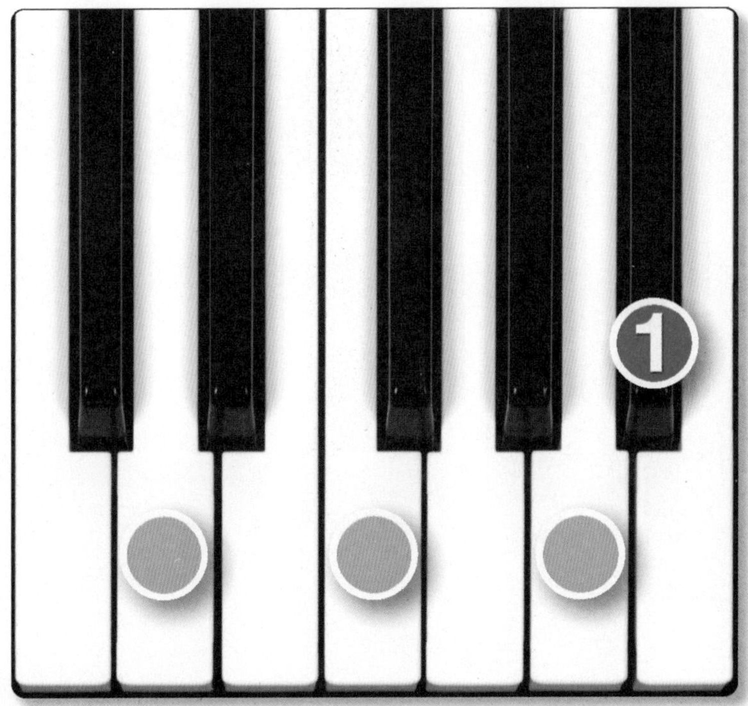

5 = little finger 4 = ring finger 3 = middle finger 2 = index finger 1 = thumb

Chord Spelling

1st (B♭), 3rd (D), 5th (F), 7th (A)

FREE ACCESS on smartphones including iPhone & Android

Using any QR code app scan and **HEAR** the chord

A♯/B♭maj7
Major 7th

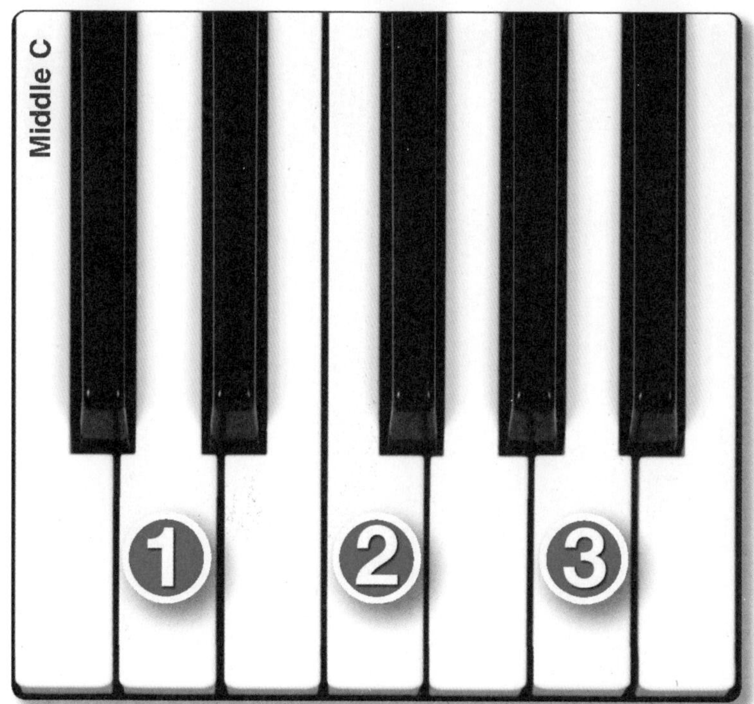

1 = thumb 2 = index finger 3 = middle finger 4 = ring finger 5 = little finger

Chord Spelling

1st (B♭), 3rd (D), 5th (F), 7th (A)

FREE ACCESS on smartphones including iPhone & Android

Using any QR code app scan and **HEAR** the chord

A♯/B♭m7

Minor 7th

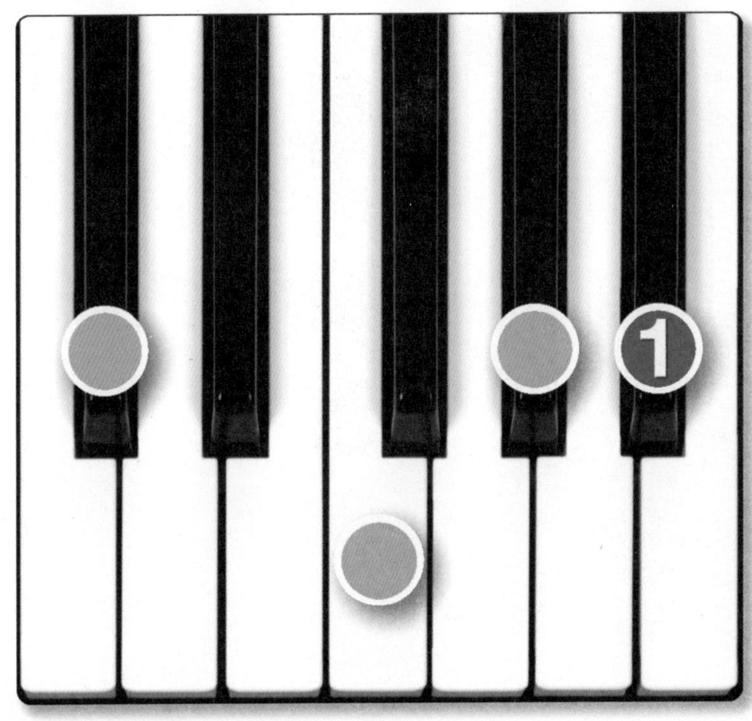

5 = little finger 4 = ring finger 3 = middle finger 2 = index finger 1 = thumb

Chord Spelling

1st (B♭), ♭3rd (D♭), 5th (F), ♭7th (A♭)

FREE ACCESS on smartphones including iPhone & Android

Using any QR code app scan and **HEAR** the chord

A♯/B♭m7

Minor 7th

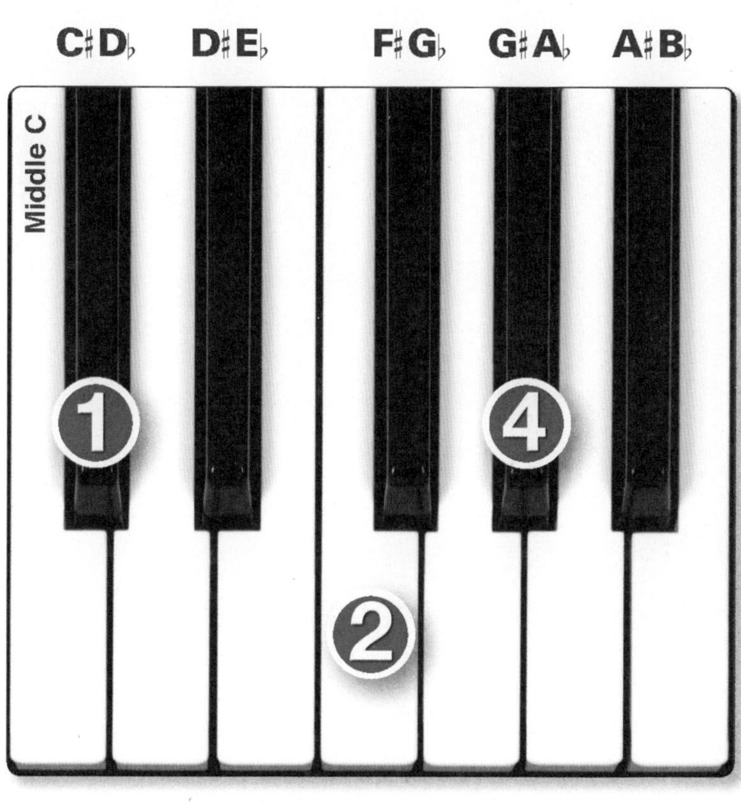

C D E F G A B

1 = thumb 2 = index finger 3 = middle finger 4 = ring finger 5 = little finger

Chord Spelling

1st (B♭), ♭3rd (D♭), 5th (F), ♭7th (A♭)

FREE ACCESS on smartphones including iPhone & Android

Using any QR code app scan and **HEAR** the chord

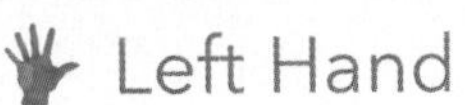

A♯/B♭maj9

Major 9th

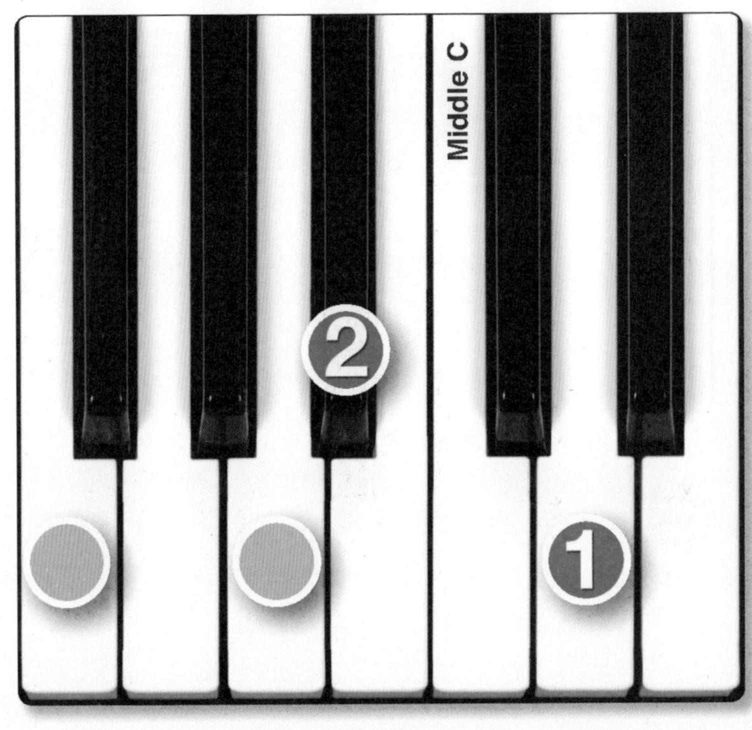

5 = little finger 4 = ring finger 3 = middle finger 2 = index finger 1 = thumb

Chord Spelling

1st (B♭), 3rd (D), 5th (F), 7th (A), 9th (C)

FREE ACCESS on smartphones including iPhone & Android  Using any QR code app scan and **HEAR** the chord

A♯/B♭maj9
Major 9th

Right Hand 

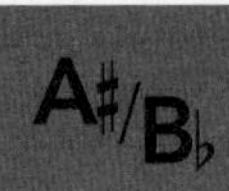

F G A B C D E

1 = thumb 2 = index finger 3 = middle finger 4 = ring finger 5 = little finger

Chord Spelling

1st (B♭), 3rd (D), 5th (F), 7th (A), 9th (C)

FREE ACCESS on smartphones including iPhone & Android  Using any QR code app scan and **HEAR** the chord

A
B
C
C♯/D♭
D
D♯/E♭
E
F
F♯/G♭
G
G♯/A♭

A♯/B♭m9

Minor 9th

5 = little finger 4 = ring finger 3 = middle finger 2 = index finger 1 = thumb

Chord Spelling

1st (B♭), ♭3rd (D♭), 5th (F), ♭7th (A♭), 9th (C)

FREE ACCESS on smartphones including iPhone & Android  Using any QR code app scan and **HEAR** the chord

A♯/B♭m9
Minor 9th

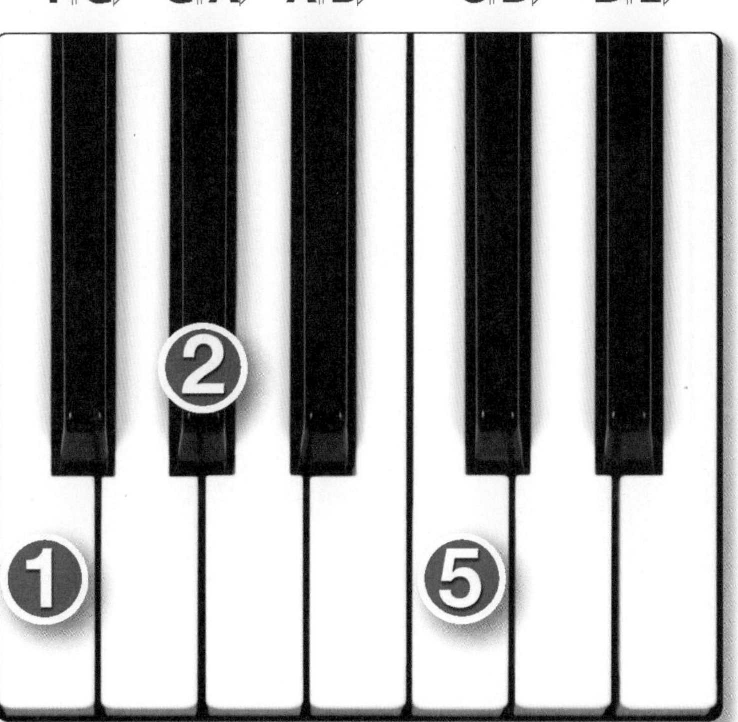

F G A B C D E

1 = thumb 2 = index finger 3 = middle finger 4 = ring finger 5 = little finger

Chord Spelling

1st (B♭), ♭3rd (D♭), 5th (F), ♭7th (A♭), 9th (C)

FREE ACCESS on smartphones including iPhone & Android  Using any QR code app scan and **HEAR** the chord

B

Major

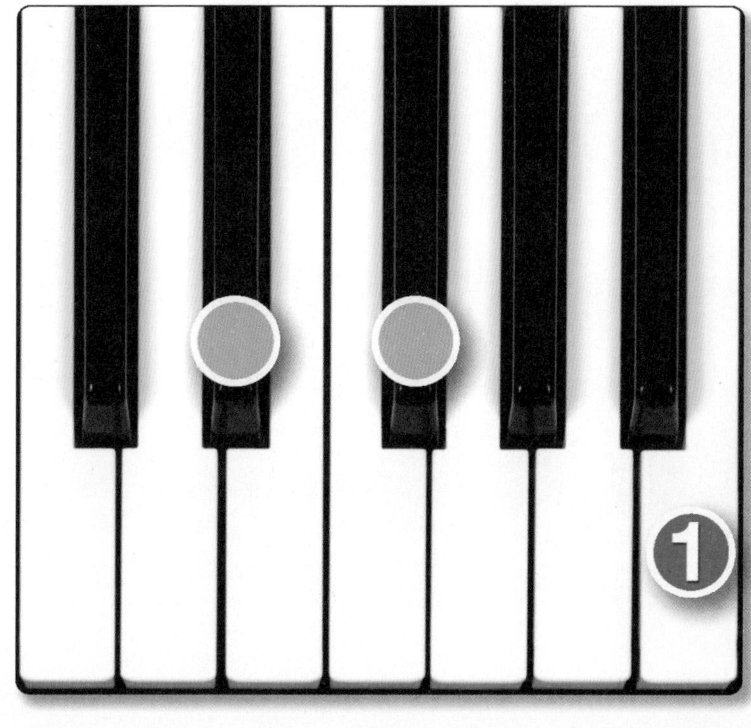

5 = little finger 4 = ring finger 3 = middle finger 2 = index finger 1 = thumb

Chord Spelling

1st (B), 3rd (D♯), 5th (F♯)

FREE ACCESS on smartphones including iPhone & Android

Using any QR code app scan and **HEAR** the chord

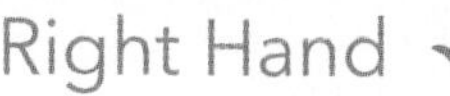

B

Major

1 = thumb 2 = index finger 3 = middle finger 4 = ring finger 5 = little finger

Chord Spelling

1st (B), 3rd (D♯), 5th (F♯)

FREE ACCESS on smartphones including iPhone & Android

Using any QR code app scan and **HEAR** the chord

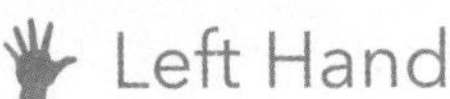

Bm

Minor

C♯D♭ D♯E♭ F♯G♭ G♯A♭ A♯B♭

1

C D E F G A B

5 = little finger 4 = ring finger 3 = middle finger 2 = index finger 1 = thumb

Chord Spelling

1st (B), ♭3rd (D), 5th (F♯)

FREE ACCESS on smartphones including iPhone & Android

Using any QR code app scan and **HEAR** the chord

Bm

Minor

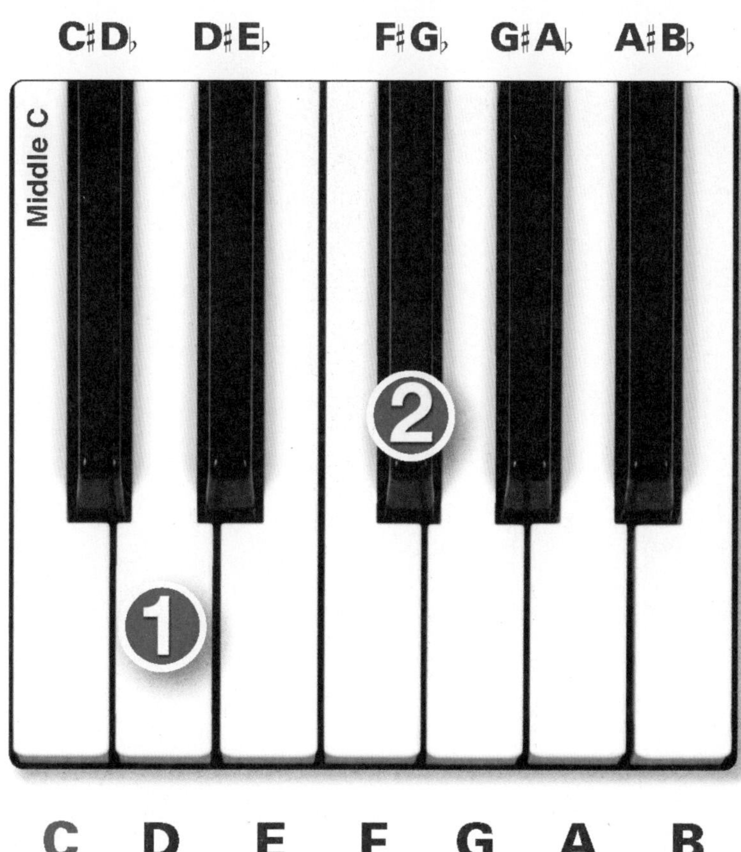

1 = thumb 2 = index finger 3 = middle finger 4 = ring finger 5 = little finger

Chord Spelling

1st (B), ♭3rd (D), 5th (F♯)

FREE ACCESS on smartphones including iPhone & Android

Using any QR code app scan and **HEAR** the chord

B+

Augmented Triad

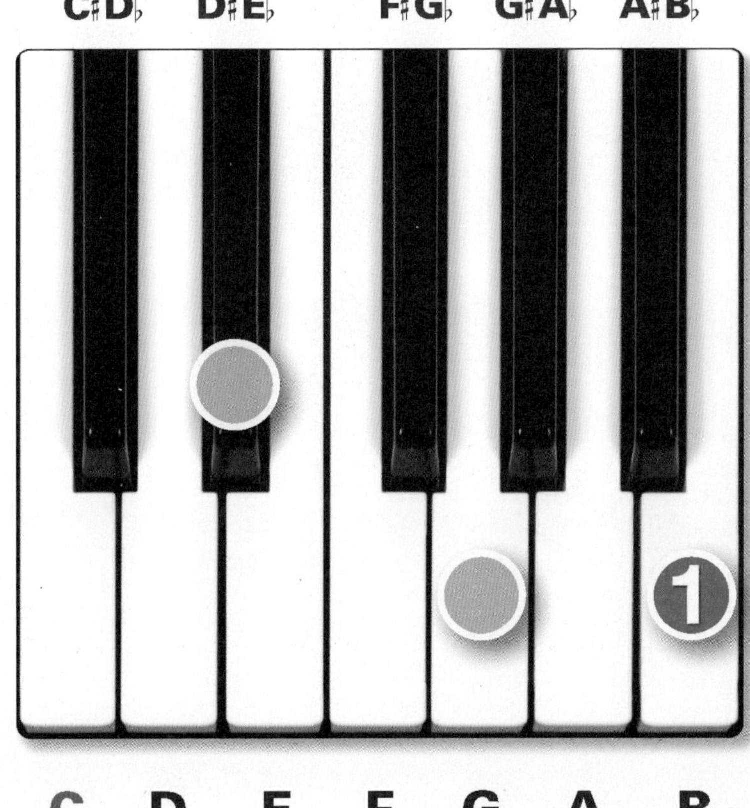

5 = little finger 4 = ring finger 3 = middle finger 2 = index finger 1 = thumb

Chord Spelling

1st (B), 3rd (D♯), ♯5th (Fx)

FREE ACCESS on smartphones including iPhone & Android

Using any QR code app scan and **HEAR** the chord

B+

Augmented Triad

1 = thumb 2 = index finger 3 = middle finger 4 = ring finger 5 = little finger

Chord Spelling

1st (B), 3rd (D♯), ♯5th (Fx)

FREE ACCESS on smartphones including iPhone & Android

Using any QR code app scan and **HEAR** the chord

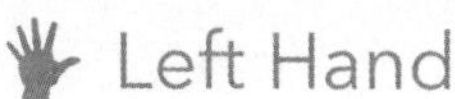

B°

Diminished Triad

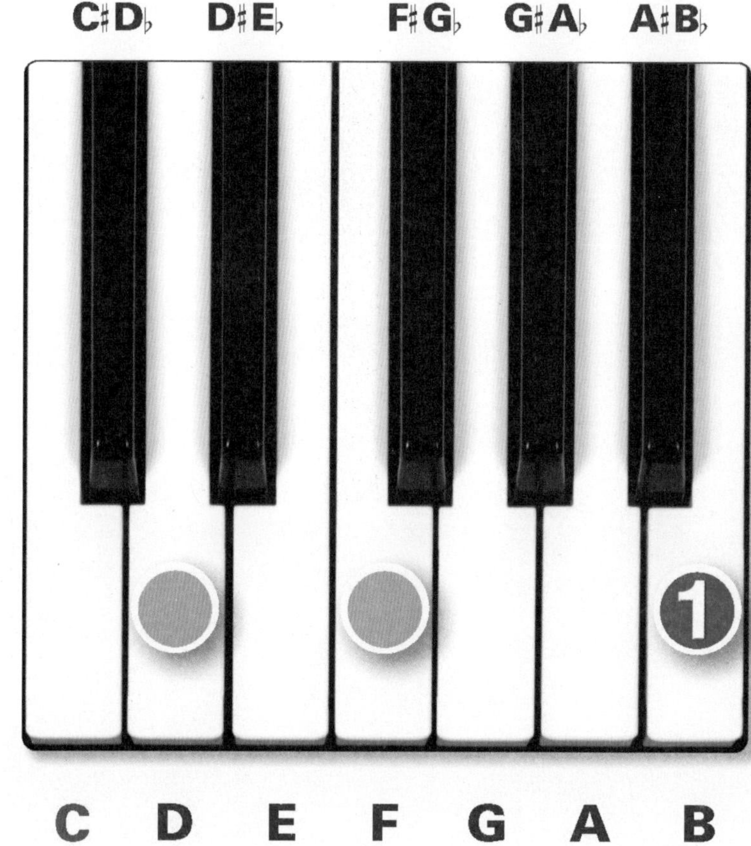

5 = little finger   4 = ring finger   3 = middle finger   2 = index finger   1 = thumb

Chord Spelling

1st (B), ♭3rd (D), ♭5th (F)

FREE ACCESS on smartphones including iPhone & Android

Using any QR code app scan and **HEAR** the chord

B°

Diminished Triad

Right Hand

A
A♯/B♭
B
C
C♯/D♭
D
D♯/E♭
E
F
F♯/G♭
G
G♯/A♭

1 = thumb 2 = index finger 3 = middle finger 4 = ring finger 5 = little finger

Chord Spelling

1st (B), ♭3rd (D), ♭5th (F)

FREE ACCESS on smartphones including iPhone & Android

Using any QR code app scan and **HEAR** the chord

B6

Major 6th

5 = little finger 4 = ring finger 3 = middle finger 2 = index finger 1 = thumb

Chord Spelling

1st (B), 3rd (D♯), 5th (F♯), 6th (G♯)

FREE ACCESS on smartphones including iPhone & Android  Using any QR code app scan and **HEAR** the chord

B6

Major 6th

1 = thumb 2 = index finger 3 = middle finger 4 = ring finger 5 = little finger

Chord Spelling

1st (B), 3rd (D♯), 5th (F♯), 6th (G♯)

FREE ACCESS on smartphones including iPhone & Android  Using any QR code app scan and **HEAR** the chord

Bm6

Minor 6th

C♯D♭ D♯E♭ F♯G♭ G♯A♭ A♯B♭

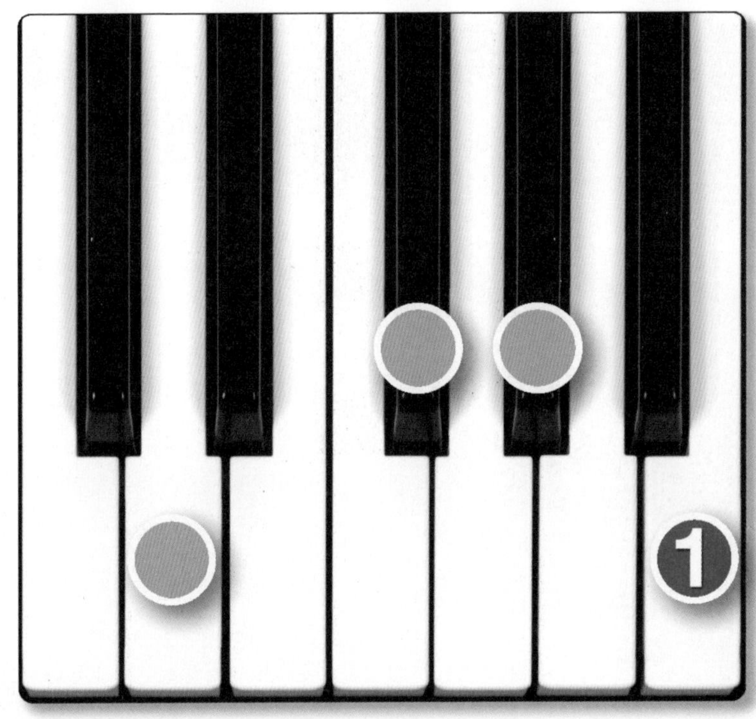

C D E F G A B

5 = little finger 4 = ring finger 3 = middle finger 2 = index finger 1 = thumb

Chord Spelling

1st (B), ♭3rd (D), 5th (F♯), 6th (G♯)

FREE ACCESS on smartphones including iPhone & Android

Using any QR code app scan and **HEAR** the chord

Bm6

Minor 6th

Right Hand 

1 = thumb 2 = index finger 3 = middle finger 4 = ring finger 5 = little finger

Chord Spelling

1st (B), ♭3rd (D), 5th (F♯), 6th (G♯)

FREE ACCESS on smartphones including iPhone & Android  Using any QR code app scan and **HEAR** the chord

Bmaj7

Major 7th

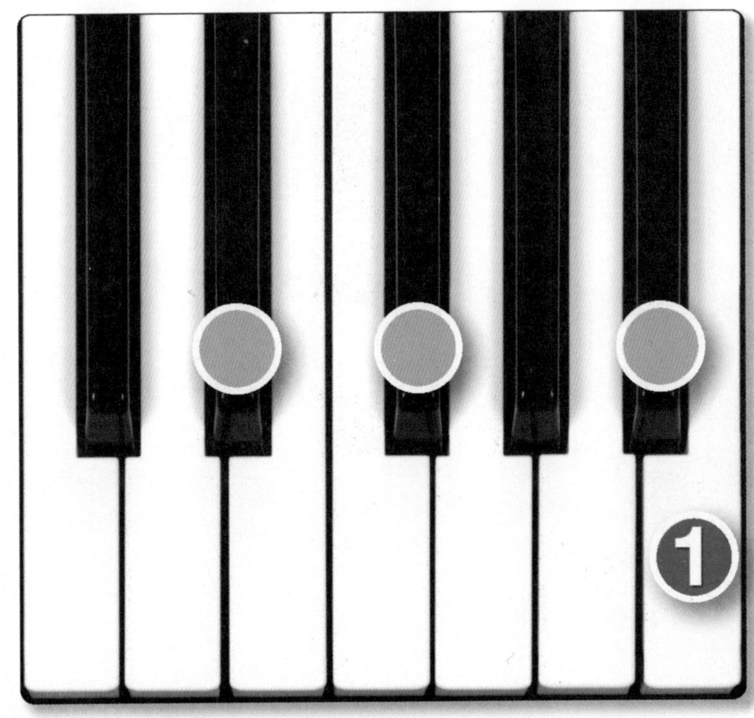

5 = little finger 4 = ring finger 3 = middle finger 2 = index finger 1 = thumb

Chord Spelling

1st (B), 3rd (D♯), 5th (F♯), 7th (A♯)

FREE ACCESS on smartphones including iPhone & Android

Using any QR code app scan and **HEAR** the chord

Bmaj7

Major 7th

1 = thumb 2 = index finger 3 = middle finger 4 = ring finger 5 = little finger

Chord Spelling

1st (B), 3rd (D♯), 5th (F♯), 7th (A♯)

FREE ACCESS on smartphones including iPhone & Android

Using any QR code app scan and **HEAR** the chord

Bm7

Minor 7th

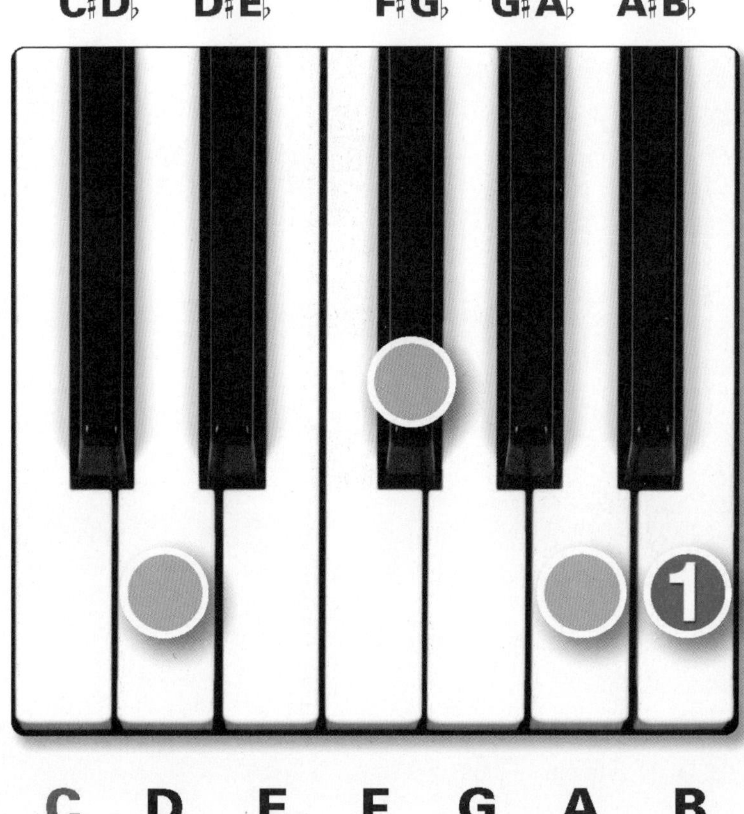

5 = little finger 4 = ring finger 3 = middle finger 2 = index finger 1 = thumb

Chord Spelling

1st (B), ♭3rd (D), 5th (F♯), ♭7th (A)

FREE ACCESS on smartphones including iPhone & Android

Using any QR code app scan and **HEAR** the chord

Bm7

Minor 7th

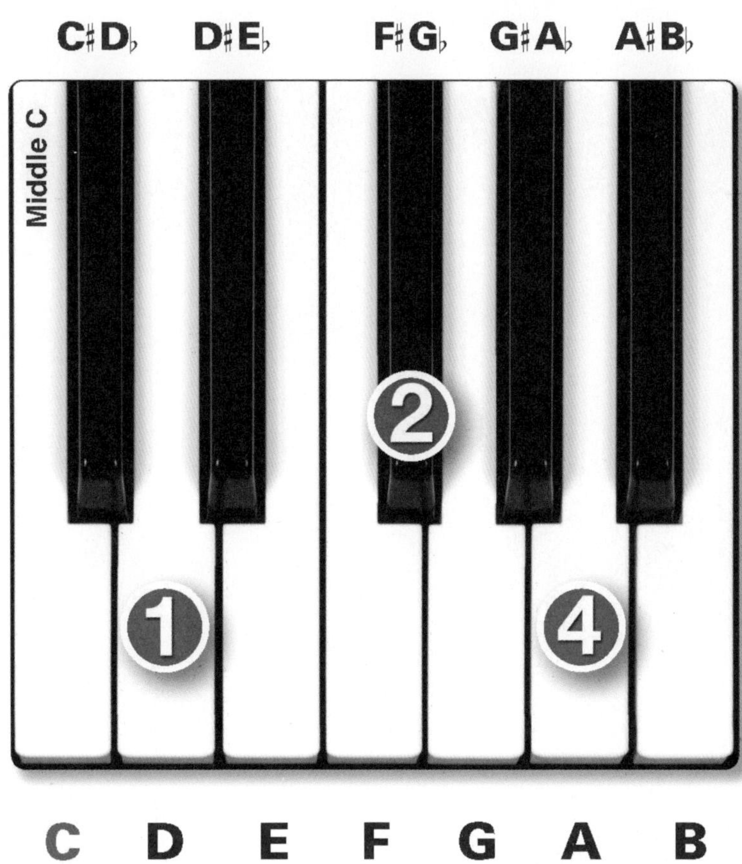

1 = thumb 2 = index finger 3 = middle finger 4 = ring finger 5 = little finger

Chord Spelling

1st (B), ♭3rd (D), 5th (F♯), ♭7th (A)

FREE ACCESS on smartphones including iPhone & Android  Using any QR code app scan and **HEAR** the chord

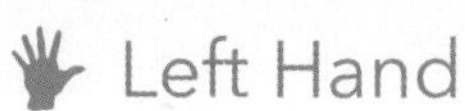

Bmaj9

Major 9th

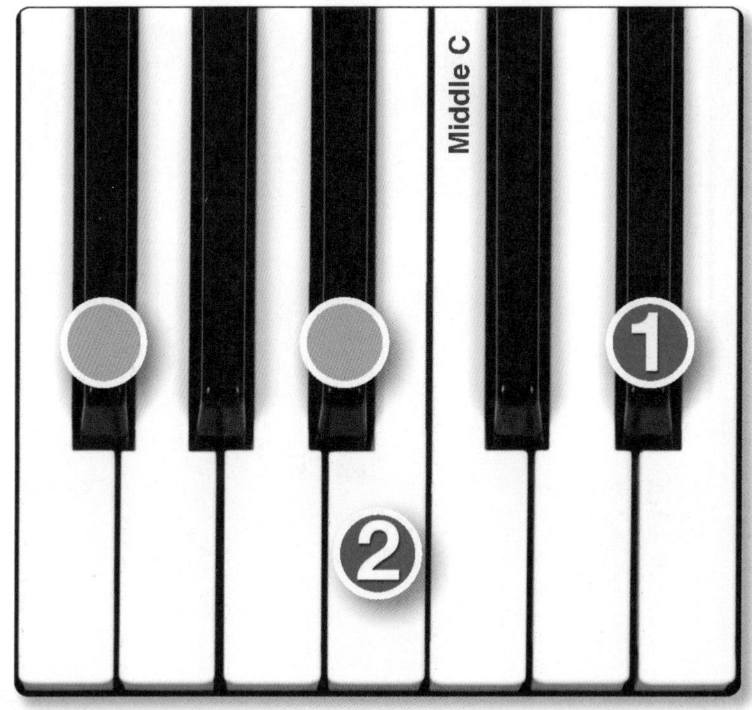

5 = little finger 4 = ring finger 3 = middle finger 2 = index finger 1 = thumb

Chord Spelling

1st (B), 3rd (D♯), 5th (F♯), 7th (A♯), 9th (C♯)

FREE ACCESS on smartphones including iPhone & Android  Using any QR code app scan and **HEAR** the chord

Right Hand 

Bmaj9

Major 9th

1 = thumb 2 = index finger 3 = middle finger 4 = ring finger 5 = little finger

Chord Spelling

1st (B), 3rd (D♯), 5th (F♯), 7th (A♯), 9th (C♯)

FREE ACCESS on smartphones including iPhone & Android  Using any QR code app scan and **HEAR** the chord

Bm9

Minor 9th

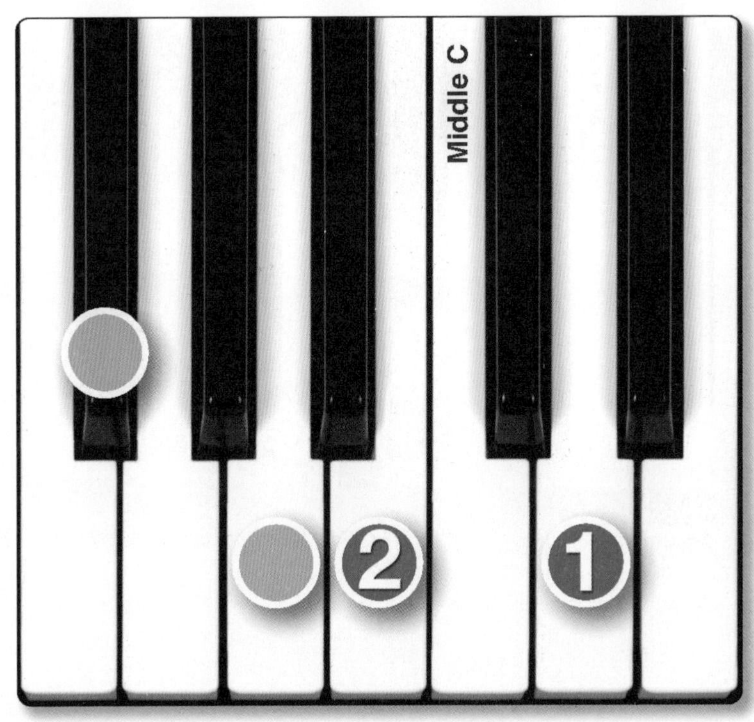

5 = little finger 4 = ring finger 3 = middle finger 2 = index finger 1 = thumb

Chord Spelling

1st (B), ♭3rd (D), 5th (F♯), ♭7th (A), 9th (C♯)

FREE ACCESS on smartphones including iPhone & Android  Using any QR code app scan and **HEAR** the chord

Bm9

Minor 9th

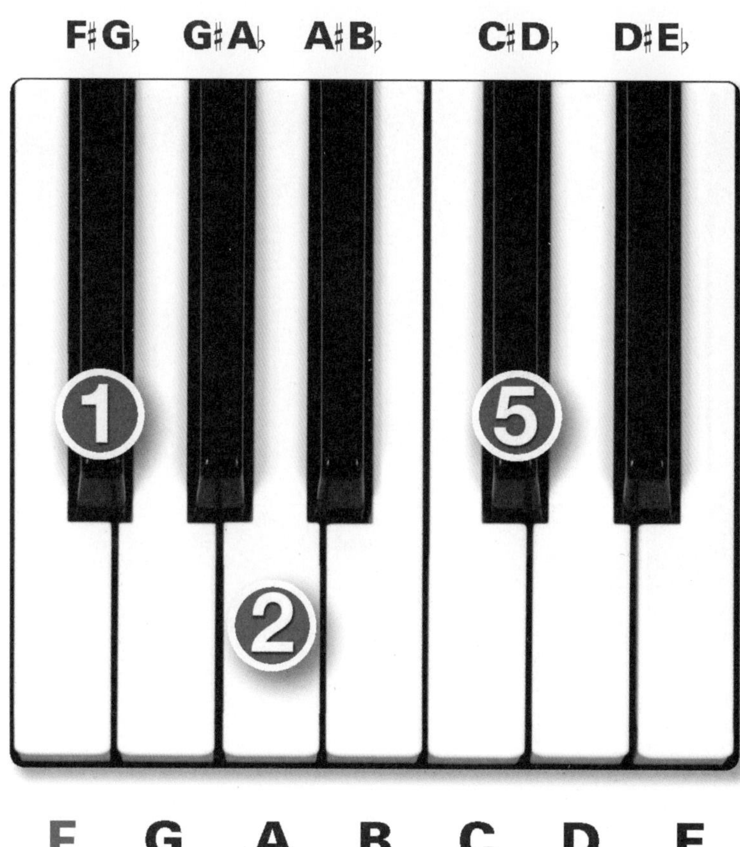

F G A B C D E

1 = thumb 2 = index finger 3 = middle finger 4 = ring finger 5 = little finger

Chord Spelling

1st (B), ♭3rd (D), 5th (F♯), ♭7th (A), 9th (C♯)

FREE ACCESS on smartphones including iPhone & Android

Using any QR code app scan and **HEAR** the chord

C
Major

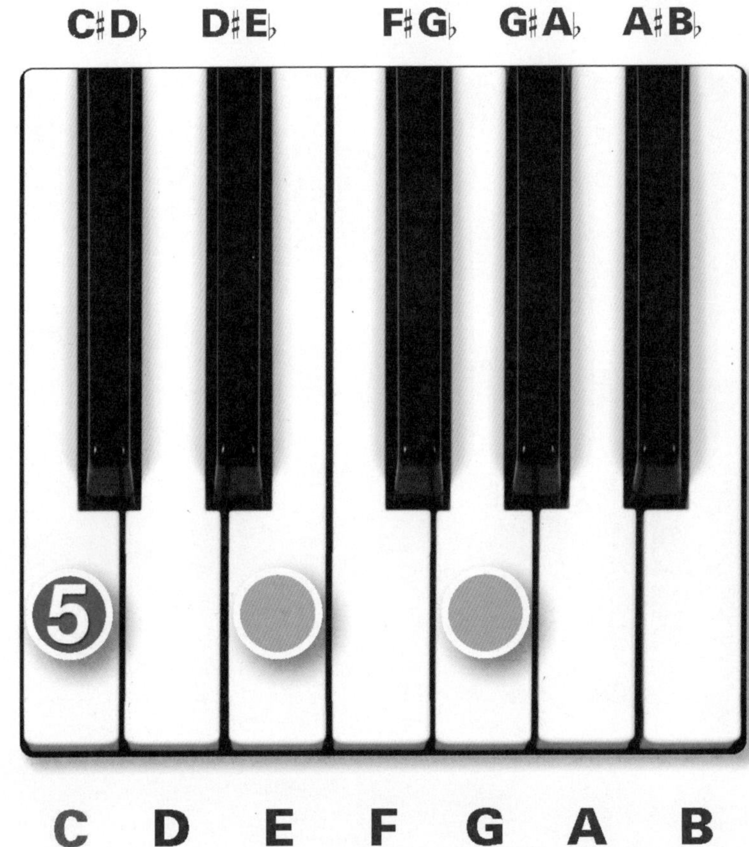

5 = little finger 4 = ring finger 3 = middle finger 2 = index finger 1 = thumb

Chord Spelling

1st (C), 3rd (E), 5th (G)

FREE ACCESS on smartphones including iPhone & Android  Using any QR code app scan and **HEAR** the chord

 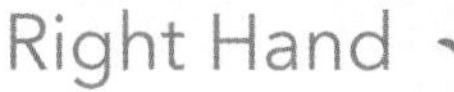

C

Major

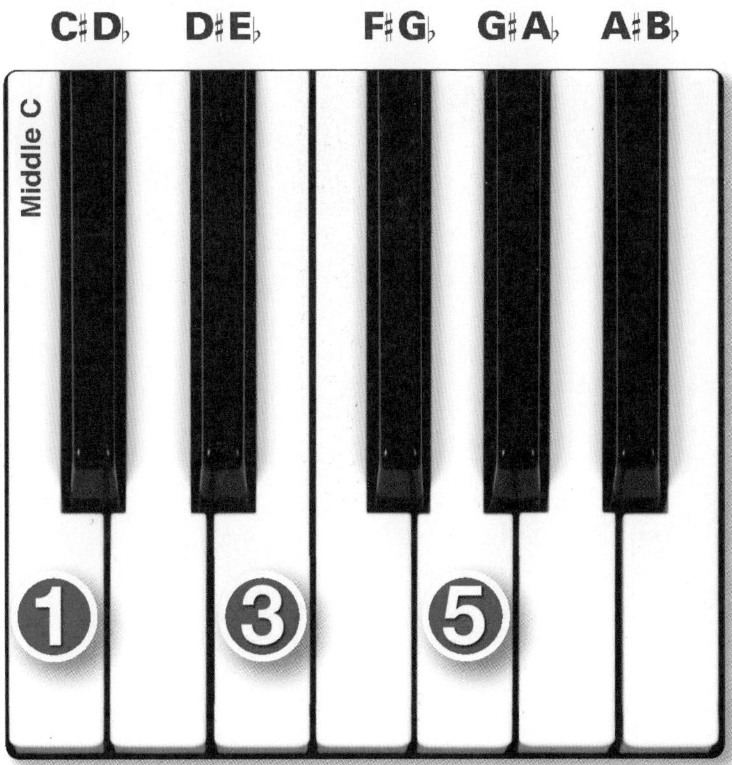

C D E F G A B

1 = thumb 2 = index finger 3 = middle finger 4 = ring finger 5 = little finger

Chord Spelling

1st (C), 3rd (E), 5th (G)

FREE ACCESS on smartphones including iPhone & Android  Using any QR code app scan and **HEAR** the chord

Cm

Minor

C♯D♭ D♯E♭ F♯G♭ G♯A♭ A♯B♭

C D E F G A B

5 = little finger 4 = ring finger 3 = middle finger 2 = index finger 1 = thumb

Chord Spelling

1st (C), ♭3rd (E♭), 5th (G)

FREE ACCESS on smartphones including iPhone & Android

Using any QR code app scan and **HEAR** the chord

Cm

Minor

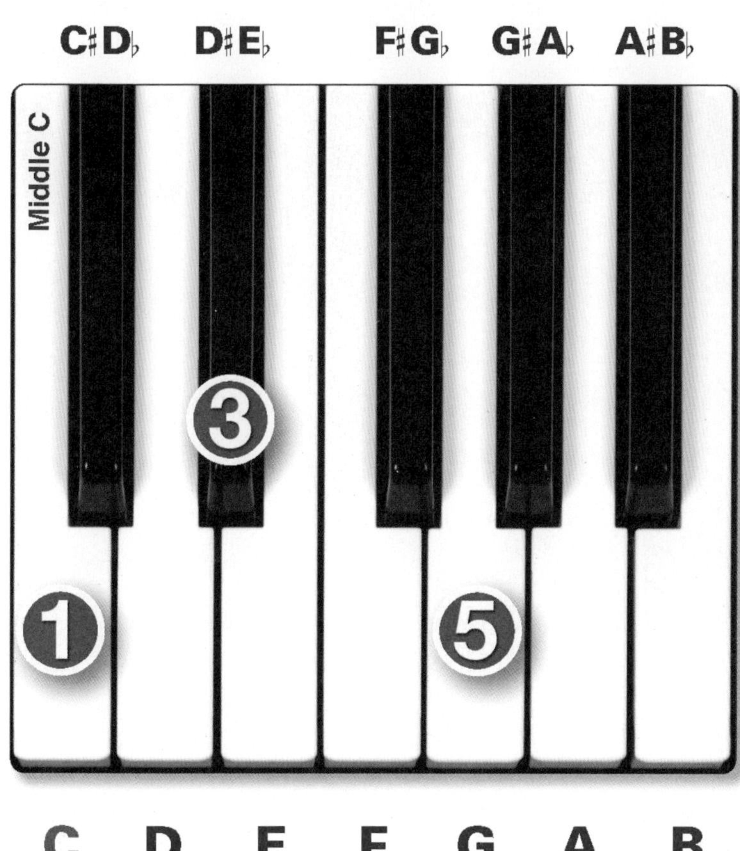

1 = thumb 2 = index finger 3 = middle finger 4 = ring finger 5 = little finger

Chord Spelling

1st (C), ♭3rd (E♭), 5th (G)

FREE ACCESS on smartphones including iPhone & Android

Using any QR code app scan and **HEAR** the chord

C+

Augmented Triad

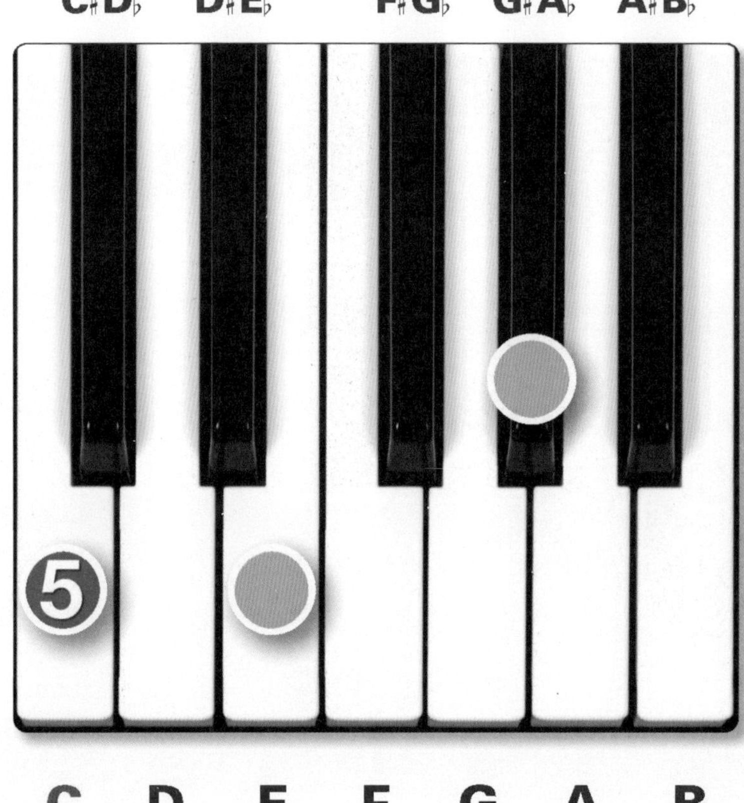

5 = little finger 4 = ring finger 3 = middle finger 2 = index finger 1 = thumb

Chord Spelling

1st (C), 3rd (E), ♯5th (G♯)

FREE ACCESS on smartphones including iPhone & Android  Using any QR code app scan and **HEAR** the chord

C+
Augmented Triad

1 = thumb 2 = index finger 3 = middle finger 4 = ring finger 5 = little finger

Chord Spelling

1st (C), 3rd (E), ♯5th (G♯)

FREE ACCESS on smartphones including iPhone & Android

Using any QR code app scan and **HEAR** the chord

C°

Diminished Triad

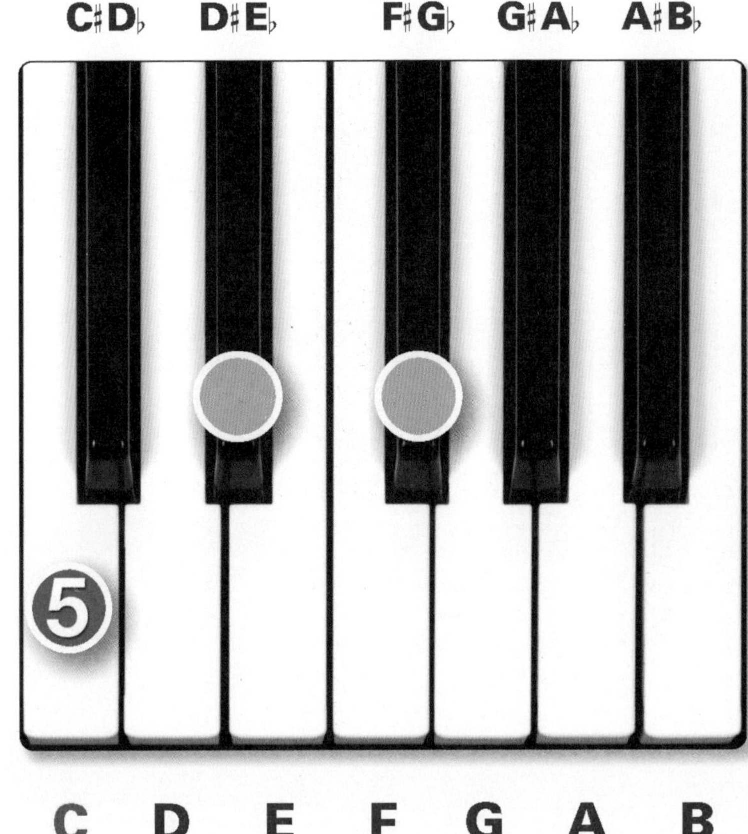

5 = little finger 4 = ring finger 3 = middle finger 2 = index finger 1 = thumb

Chord Spelling

1st (C), ♭3rd (E♭), ♭5th (G♭)

FREE ACCESS on smartphones including iPhone & Android  Using any QR code app scan and **HEAR** the chord

C°

Diminished Triad

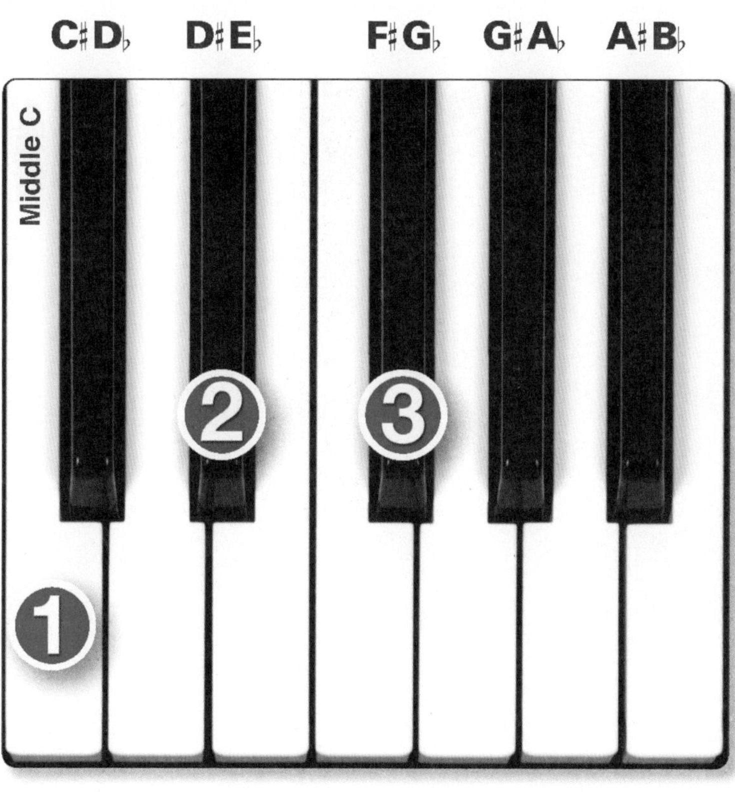

1 = thumb 2 = index finger 3 = middle finger 4 = ring finger 5 = little finger

Chord Spelling

1st (C), ♭3rd (E♭), ♭5th (G♭)

FREE ACCESS on smartphones including iPhone & Android

Using any QR code app scan and **HEAR** the chord

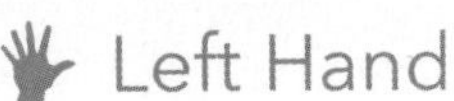

C6

Major 6th

C♯D♭ D♯E♭ F♯G♭ G♯A♭ A♯B♭

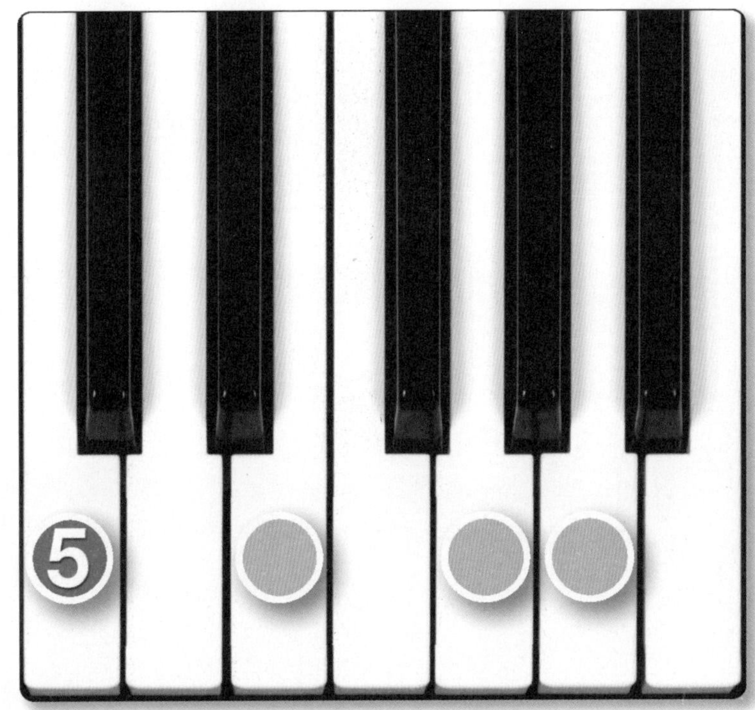

C D E F G A B

5 = little finger 4 = ring finger 3 = middle finger 2 = index finger 1 = thumb

Chord Spelling

1st (C), 3rd (E), 5th (G), 6th (A)

FREE ACCESS on smartphones including iPhone & Android

Using any QR code app scan and **HEAR** the chord

C6

Major 6th

Right Hand 

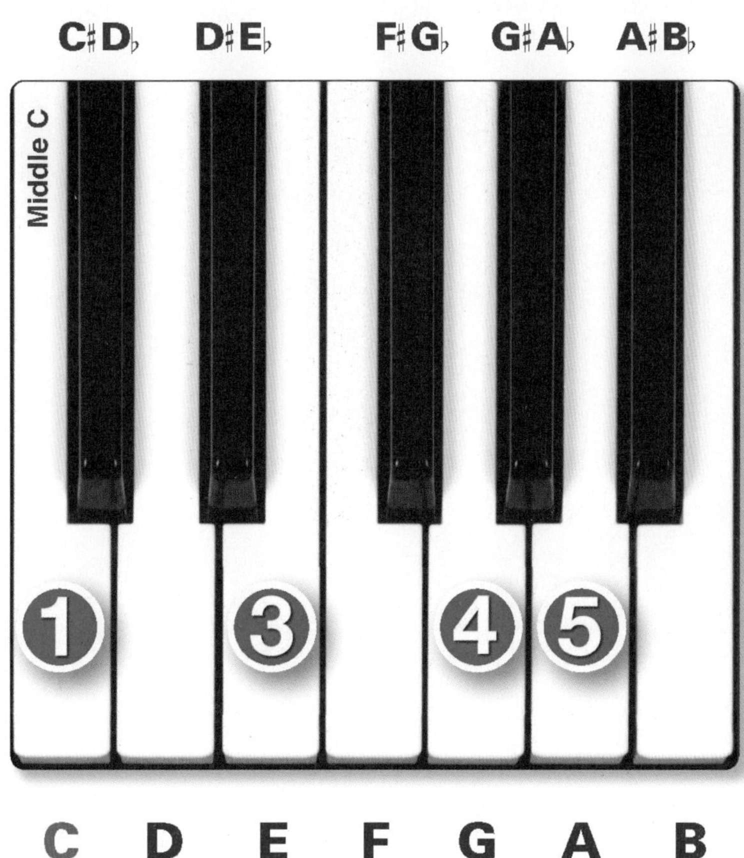

C D E F G A B

1 = thumb 2 = index finger 3 = middle finger 4 = ring finger 5 = little finger

Chord Spelling

1st (C), 3rd (E), 5th (G), 6th (A)

FREE ACCESS on smartphones including iPhone & Android  Using any QR code app scan and **HEAR** the chord

A
A♯/B♭
B
C
C♯/D♭
D
D♯/E♭
E
F
F♯/G♭
G
G♯/A♭

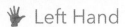

Cm6

Minor 6th

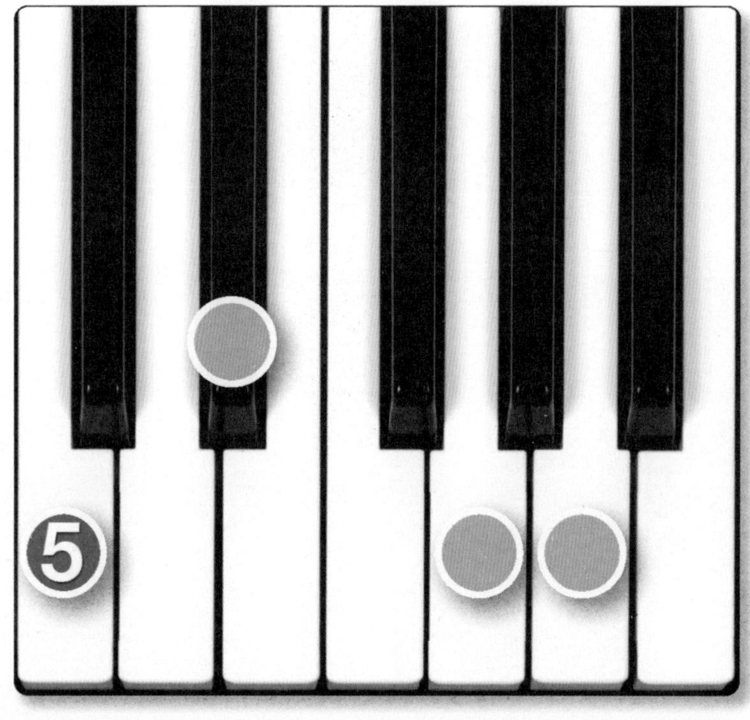

5 = little finger 4 = ring finger 3 = middle finger 2 = index finger 1 = thumb

Chord Spelling

1st (C), ♭3rd (E♭), 5th (G), 6th (A)

FREE ACCESS on smartphones including iPhone & Android

Using any QR code app scan and **HEAR** the chord

Cm6

Minor 6th

1 = thumb 2 = index finger 3 = middle finger 4 = ring finger 5 = little finger

Chord Spelling

1st (C), ♭3rd (E♭), 5th (G), 6th (A)

FREE ACCESS on smartphones including iPhone & Android

Using any QR code app scan and **HEAR** the chord

A
A♯/B♭
B
C
C♯/D♭
D
D♯/E♭
E
F
F♯/G♭
G
G♯/A♭

Cmaj7

Major 7th

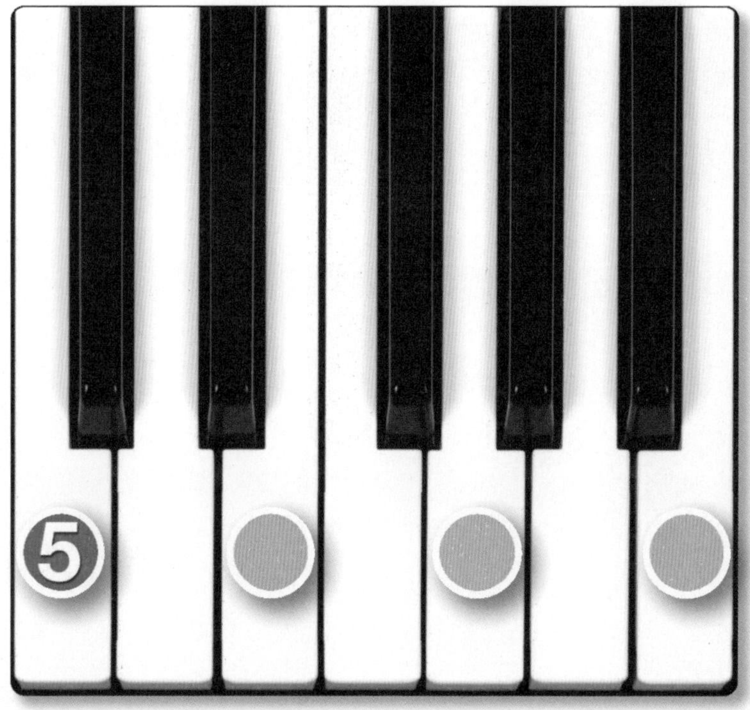

5 = little finger 4 = ring finger 3 = middle finger 2 = index finger 1 = thumb

Chord Spelling

1st (C), 3rd (E), 5th (G), 7th (B)

FREE ACCESS on smartphones including iPhone & Android

Using any QR code app scan and **HEAR** the chord

Cmaj7

Major 7th

1 = thumb 2 = index finger 3 = middle finger 4 = ring finger 5 = little finger

Chord Spelling

1st (C), 3rd (E), 5th (G), 7th (B)

FREE ACCESS on smartphones including iPhone & Android  Using any QR code app scan and **HEAR** the chord

Cm7

Minor 7th

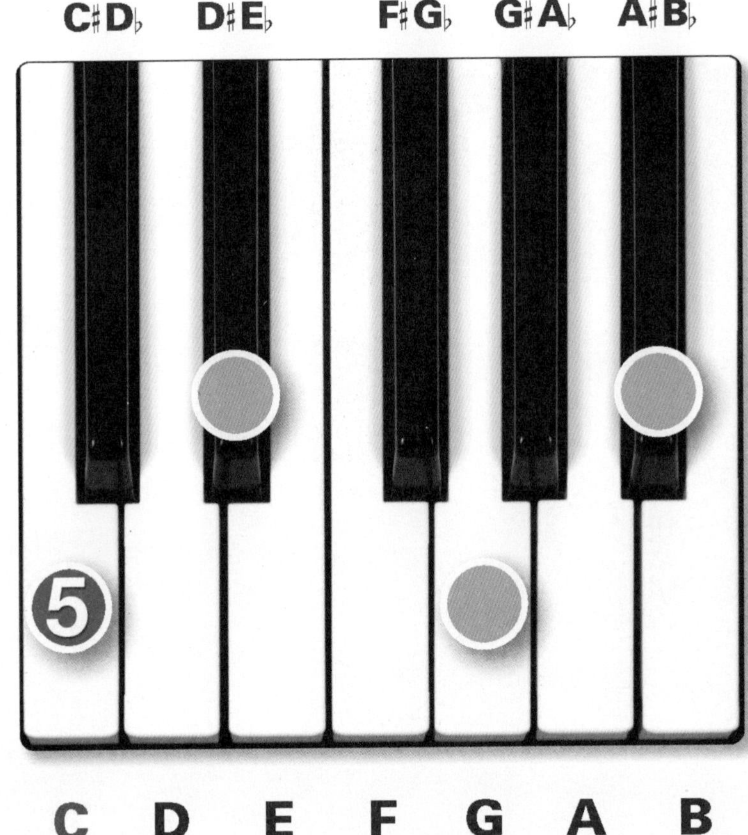

5 = little finger 4 = ring finger 3 = middle finger 2 = index finger 1 = thumb

Chord Spelling

1st (C), ♭3rd (E♭), 5th (G), ♭7th (B♭)

FREE ACCESS on smartphones including iPhone & Android

Using any QR code app scan and **HEAR** the chord

Cm7

Minor 7th

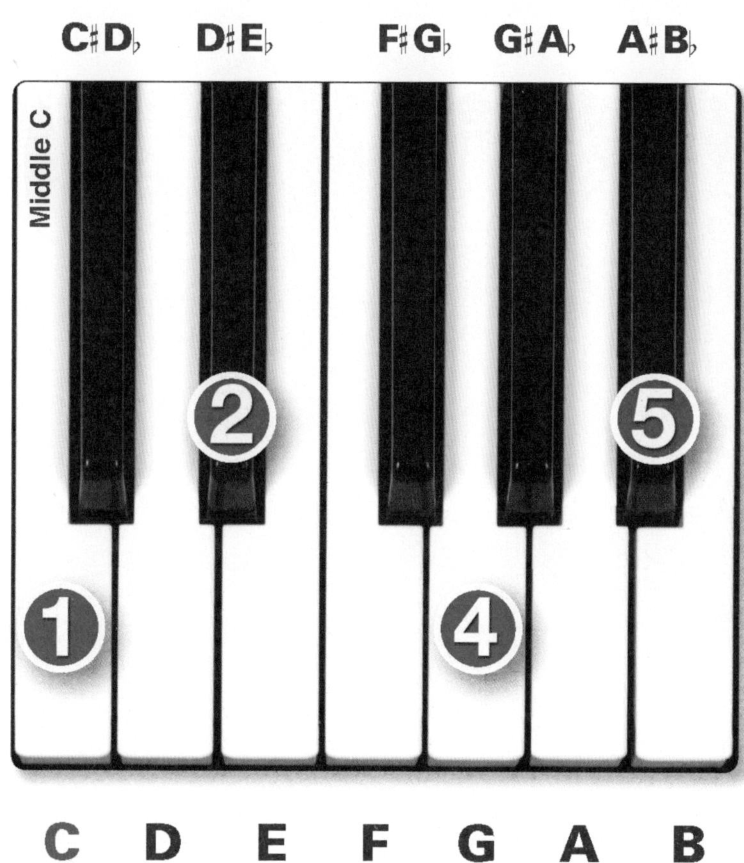

1 = thumb 2 = index finger 3 = middle finger 4 = ring finger 5 = little finger

Chord Spelling

1st (C), ♭3rd (E♭), 5th (G), ♭7th (B♭)

FREE ACCESS on smartphones including iPhone & Android

Using any QR code app scan and **HEAR** the chord

Cmaj9

Major 9th

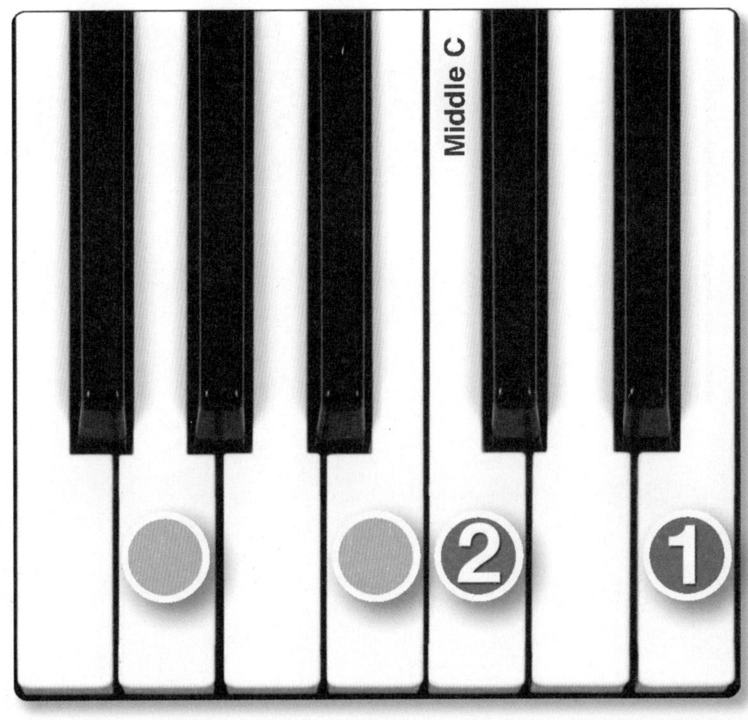

5 = little finger 4 = ring finger 3 = middle finger 2 = index finger 1 = thumb

Chord Spelling

1st (C), 3rd (E), 5th (G), 7th (B), 9th (D)

FREE ACCESS on smartphones including iPhone & Android

Using any QR code app scan and **HEAR** the chord

Cmaj9

Major 9th

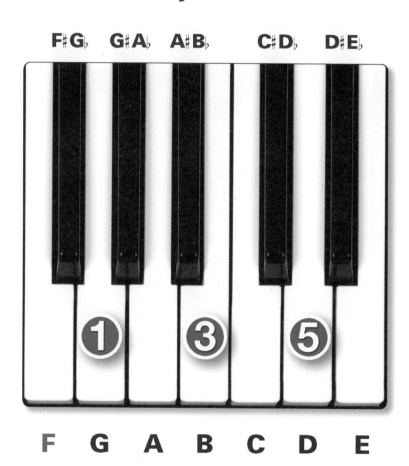

F♯G♭ G♯A♭ A♯B♭ C♯D♭ D♯E♭

1 3 5

F G A B C D E

1 = thumb 2 = index finger 3 = middle finger 4 = ring finger 5 = little finger

Chord Spelling

1st (C), 3rd (E), 5th (G), 7th (B), 9th (D)

FREE ACCESS on smartphones including iPhone & Android

Using any QR code app scan and **HEAR** the chord

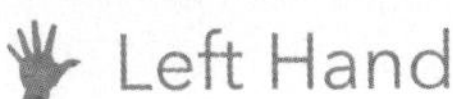

A
A♯/B♭
B
C
C♯/D♭
D
D♯/E♭
E
F
F♯/G♭
G
G♯/A♭

Cm9

Minor 9th

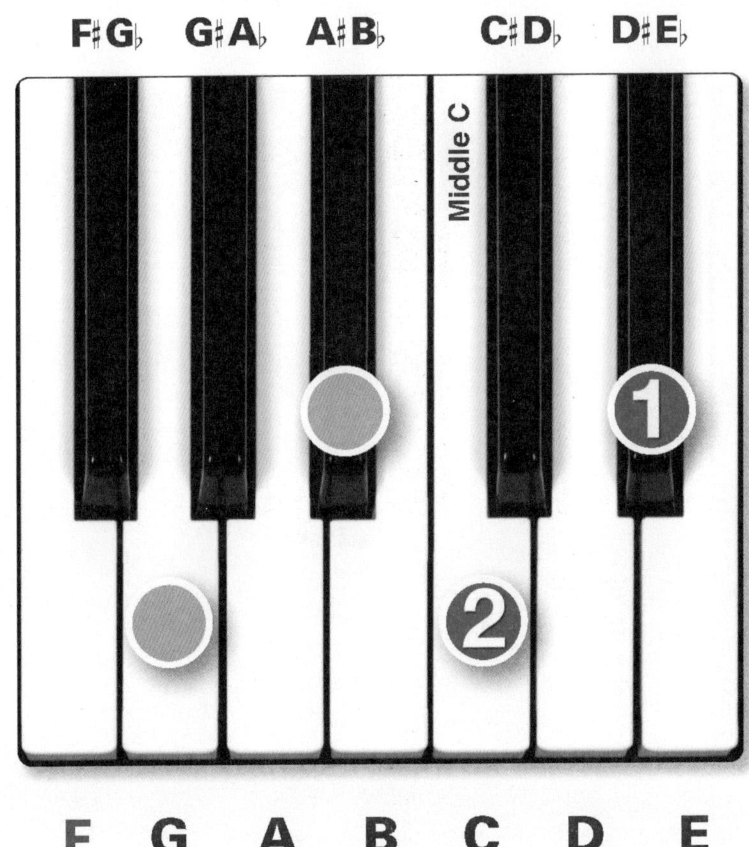

5 = little finger 4 = ring finger 3 = middle finger 2 = index finger 1 = thumb

Chord Spelling

1st (C), ♭3rd (E♭), 5th (G), ♭7th (B♭), 9th (D)

FREE ACCESS on smartphones including iPhone & Android  Using any QR code app scan and **HEAR** the chord

Cm9

Minor 9th

Right Hand 

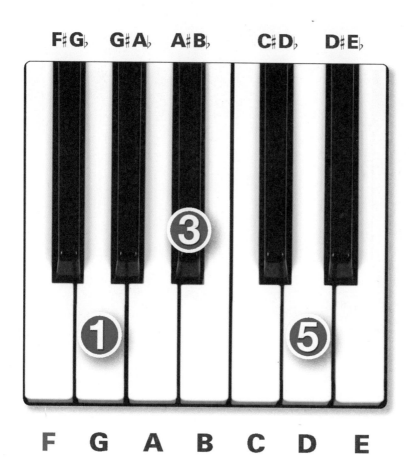

F♯G♭ G♯A♭ A♯B♭ C♯D♭ D♯E♭

3

1 5

F G A B C D E

1 = thumb 2 = index finger 3 = middle finger 4 = ring finger 5 = little finger

Chord Spelling

1st (C), ♭3rd (E♭), 5th (G), ♭7th (B♭), 9th (D)

FREE ACCESS on smartphones including iPhone & Android  Using any QR code app scan and **HEAR** the chord

C♯/D♭ Major

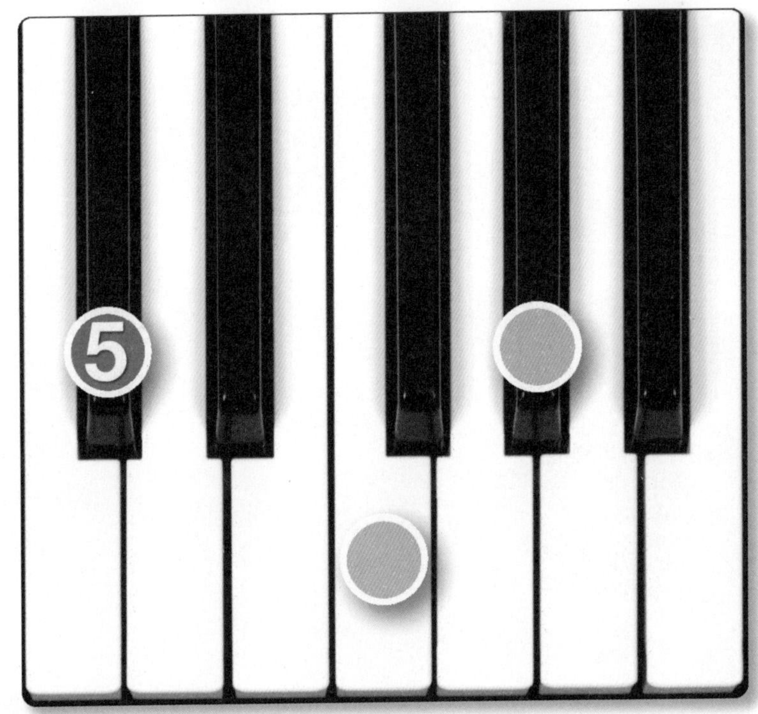

5 = little finger 4 = ring finger 3 = middle finger 2 = index finger 1 = thumb

Chord Spelling

1st (C♯), 3rd (E♯), 5th (G♯)

FREE ACCESS on smartphones including iPhone & Android

Using any QR code app scan and **HEAR** the chord

A
A♯/B♭
B
C
C♯/D♭
D
D♯/E♭
E
F
F♯/G♭
G
G♯/A♭

C♯/D♭ Major

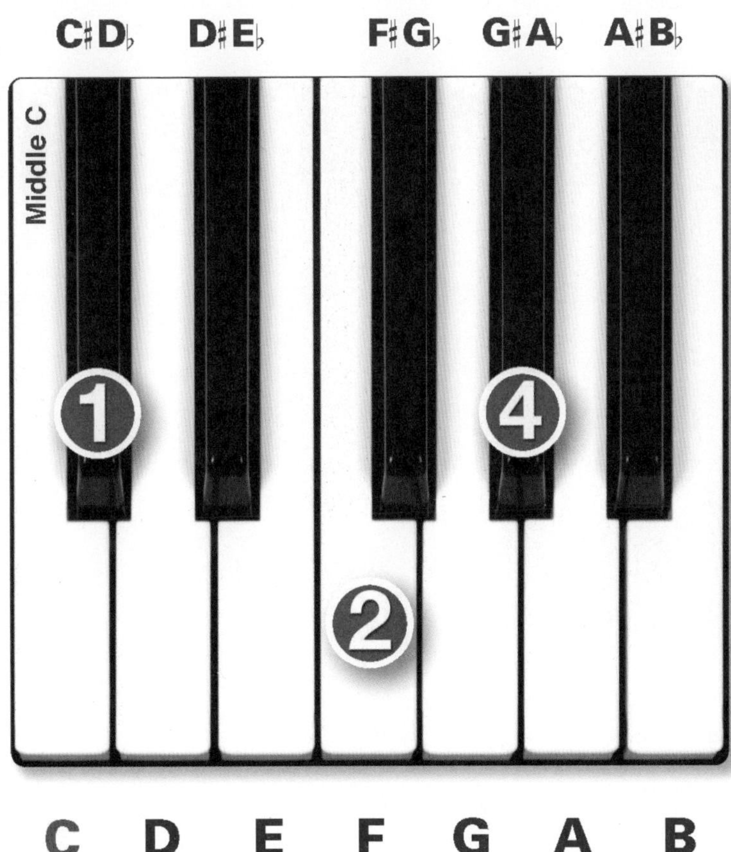

1 = thumb 2 = index finger 3 = middle finger 4 = ring finger 5 = little finger

Chord Spelling

1st (C♯), 3rd (E♯), 5th (G♯)

FREE ACCESS on smartphones including iPhone & Android

Using any QR code app scan and **HEAR** the chord

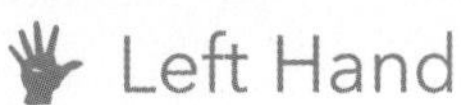

A
A♯/B♭
B
C
C♯/D♭
D
D♯/E♭
E
F
F♯/G♭
G
G♯/A♭

C♯/D♭m
Minor

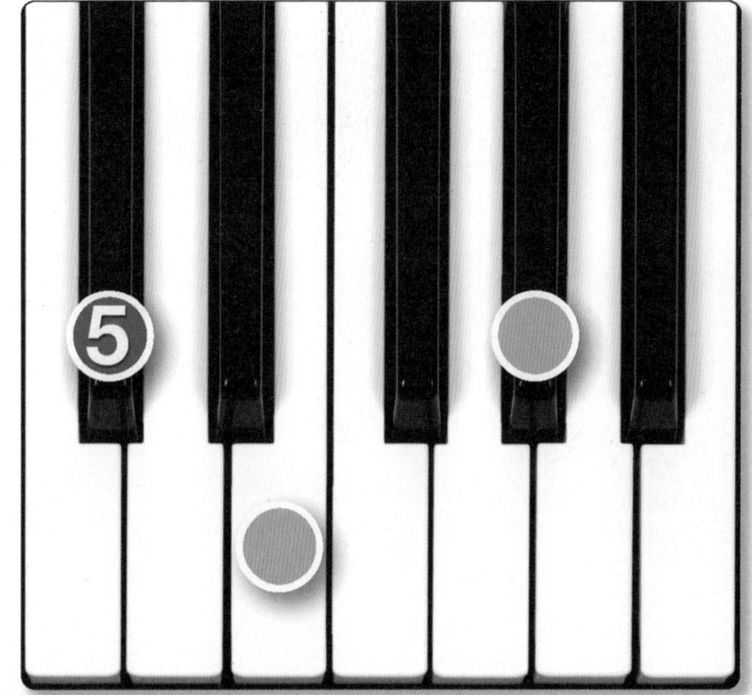

5 = little finger   4 = ring finger   3 = middle finger   2 = index finger   1 = thumb

Chord Spelling

1st (C♯), ♭3rd (E), 5th (G♯)

FREE ACCESS on smartphones including iPhone & Android  Using any QR code app scan and **HEAR** the chord

 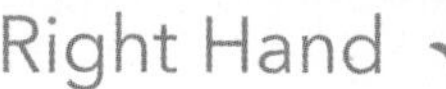 

C♯/D♭m
Minor

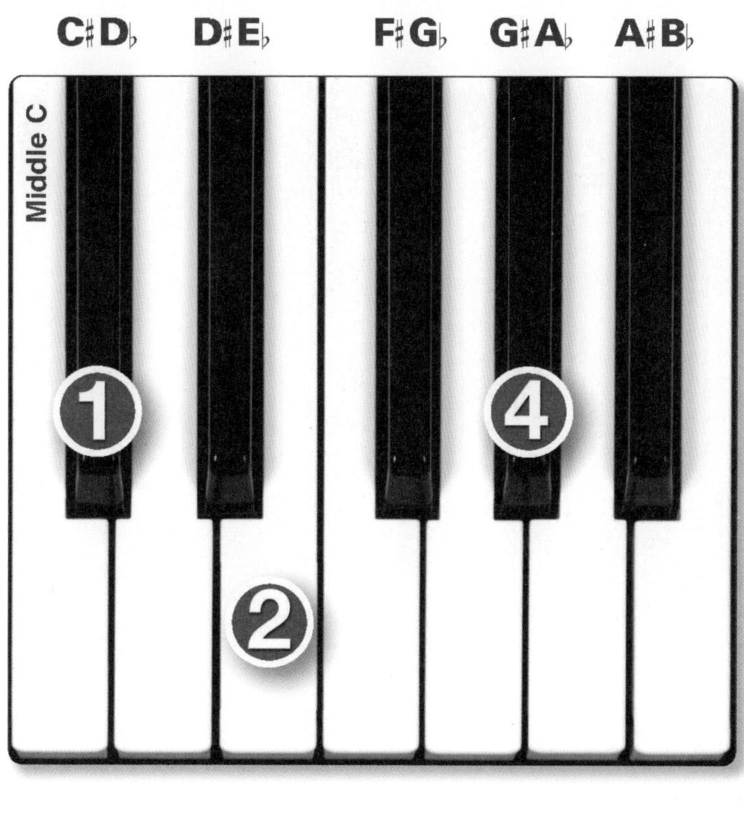

1 = thumb 2 = index finger 3 = middle finger 4 = ring finger 5 = little finger

Chord Spelling

1st (C♯), ♭3rd (E), 5th (G♯)

FREE ACCESS on smartphones including iPhone & Android  Using any QR code app scan and **HEAR** the chord

Left Hand

C♯/D♭+
Augmented Triad

C♯D♭ D♯E♭ F♯G♭ G♯A♭ A♯B♭

5

C D E F G A B

5 = little finger 4 = ring finger 3 = middle finger 2 = index finger 1 = thumb

Chord Spelling

1st (C♯), 3rd (E♯), ♯5th (Gx)

FREE ACCESS on smartphones including iPhone & Android

Using any QR code app scan and **HEAR** the chord

Right Hand 

C♯/D♭+
Augmented Triad

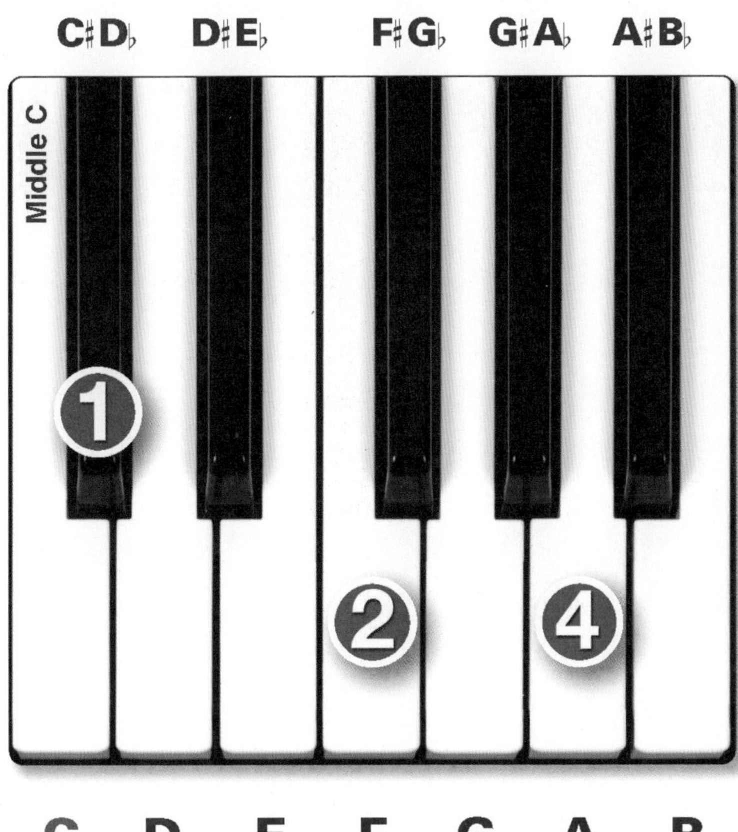

1 = thumb 2 = index finger 3 = middle finger 4 = ring finger 5 = little finger

Chord Spelling

1st (C♯), 3rd (E♯), ♯5th (Gx)

FREE ACCESS on smartphones including iPhone & Android  Using any QR code app scan and **HEAR** the chord

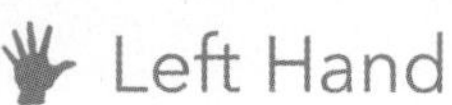

C♯/D♭°

Diminished Triad

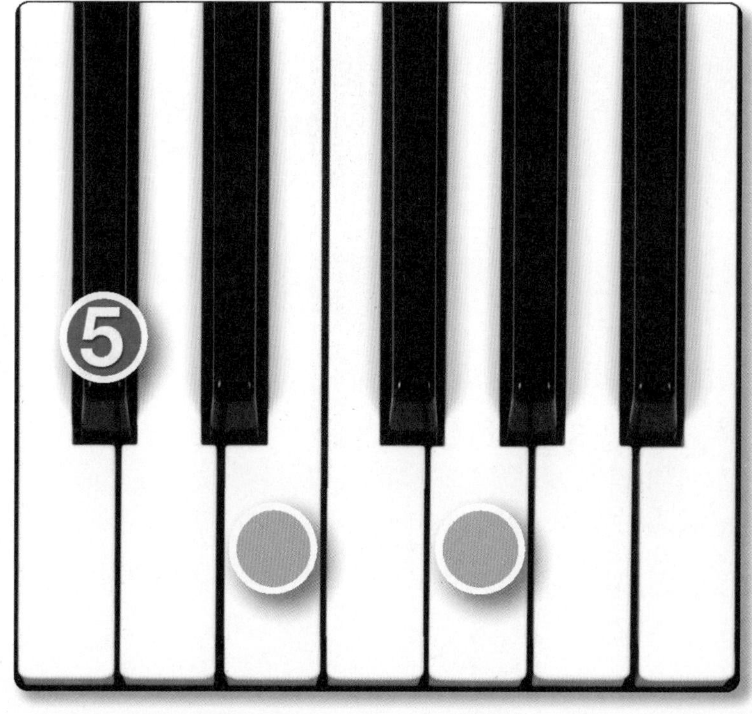

5 = little finger 4 = ring finger 3 = middle finger 2 = index finger 1 = thumb

Chord Spelling

1st (C♯), ♭3rd (E), ♭5th (G)

FREE ACCESS on smartphones including iPhone & Android

Using any QR code app scan and **HEAR** the chord

C♯/D♭°

Diminished Triad

Right Hand 

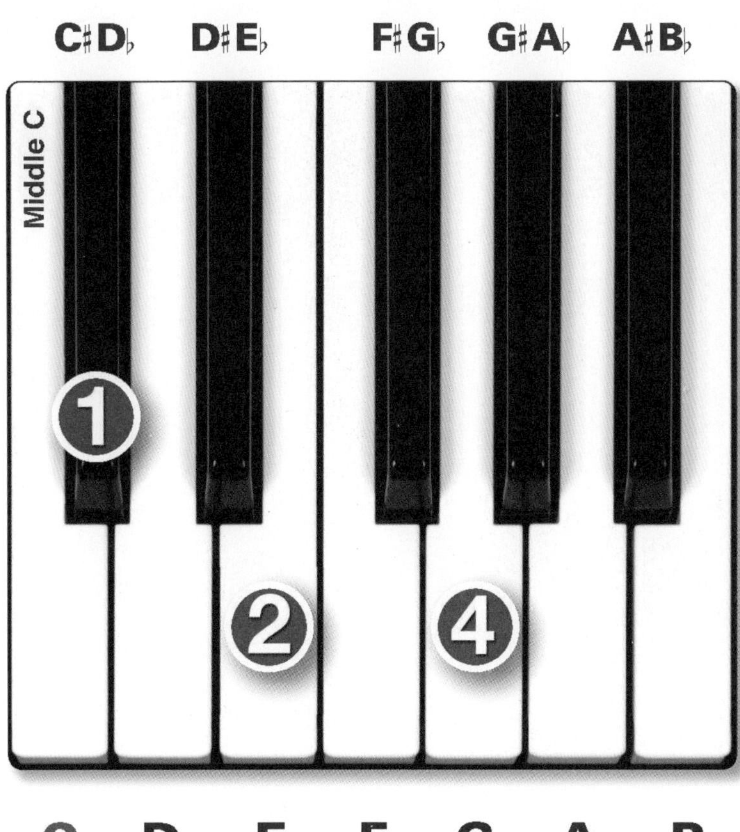

C D E F G A B

1 = thumb 2 = index finger 3 = middle finger 4 = ring finger 5 = little finger

Chord Spelling

1st (C♯), ♭3rd (E), ♭5th (G)

FREE ACCESS on smartphones including iPhone & Android  Using any QR code app scan and **HEAR** the chord

C♯/D♭6
Major 6th

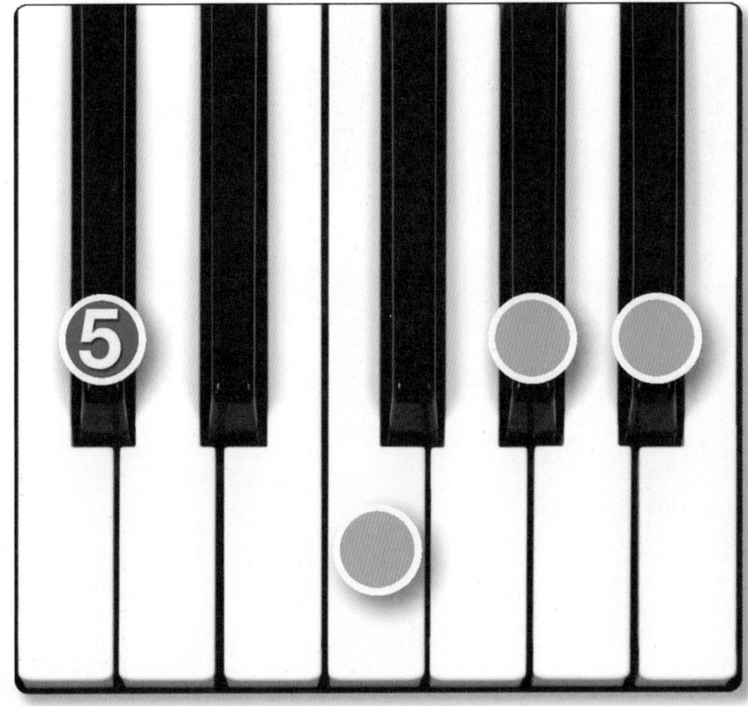

5 = little finger 4 = ring finger 3 = middle finger 2 = index finger 1 = thumb

Chord Spelling

1st (C♯), 3rd (E♯), 5th (G♯), 6th (A♯)

FREE ACCESS on smartphones including iPhone & Android  Using any QR code app scan and **HEAR** the chord

C♯/D♭6
Major 6th

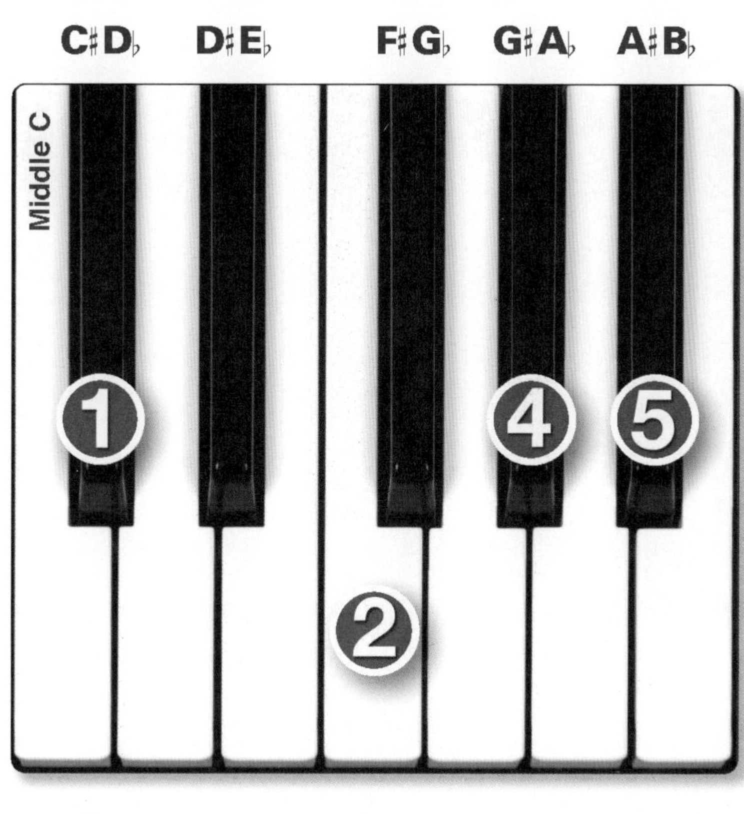

C D E F G A B

1 = thumb 2 = index finger 3 = middle finger 4 = ring finger 5 = little finger

Chord Spelling

1st (C♯), 3rd (E♯), 5th (G♯), 6th (A♯)

FREE ACCESS on smartphones including iPhone & Android  Using any QR code app scan and **HEAR** the chord

C♯/D♭m6

Minor 6th

A
A♯/B♭
B
C
C♯/D♭
D
D♯/E♭
E
F
F♯/G♭
G
G♯/A♭

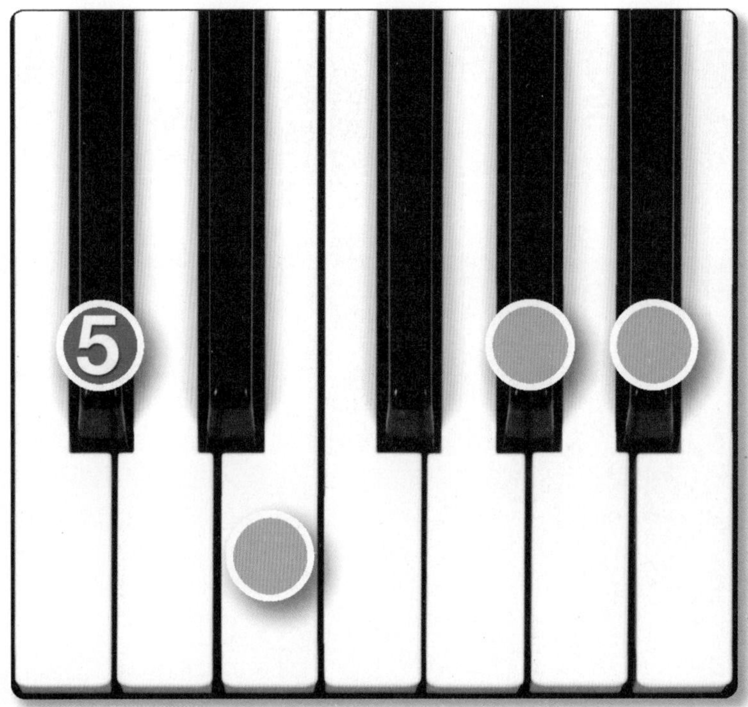

5 = little finger 4 = ring finger 3 = middle finger 2 = index finger 1 = thumb

Chord Spelling

1st (C♯), ♭3rd (E), 5th (G♯), 6th (A♯)

FREE ACCESS on smartphones including iPhone & Android

Using any QR code app scan and **HEAR** the chord

C♯/D♭m6
Minor 6th

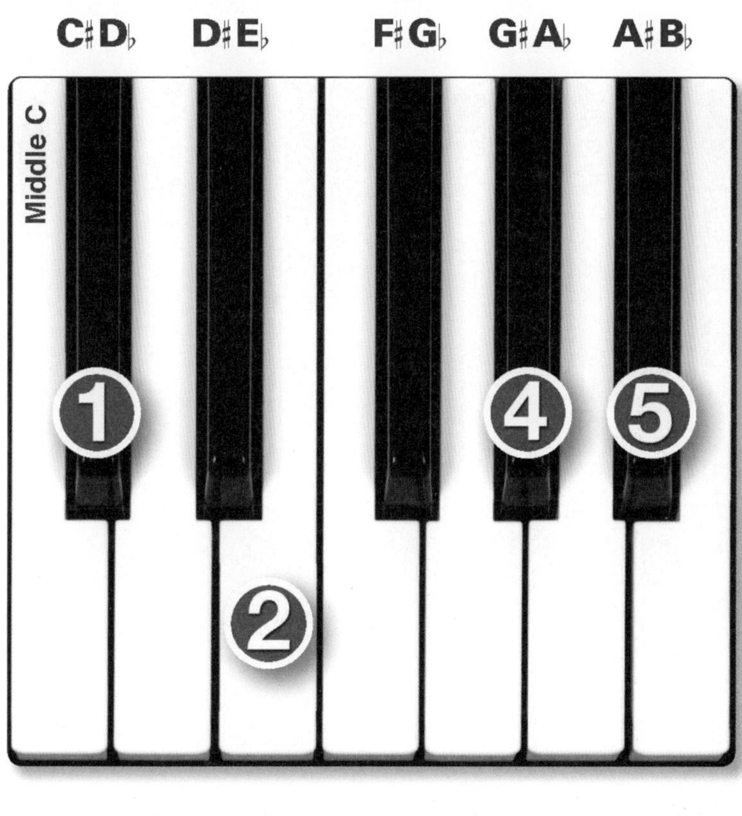

1 = thumb 2 = index finger 3 = middle finger 4 = ring finger 5 = little finger

Chord Spelling

1st (C♯), ♭3rd (E), 5th (G♯), 6th (A♯)

FREE ACCESS on smartphones including iPhone & Android

Using any QR code app scan and **HEAR** the chord

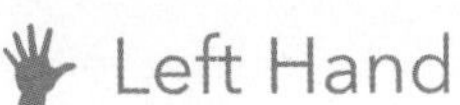

C♯/D♭maj7

Major 7th

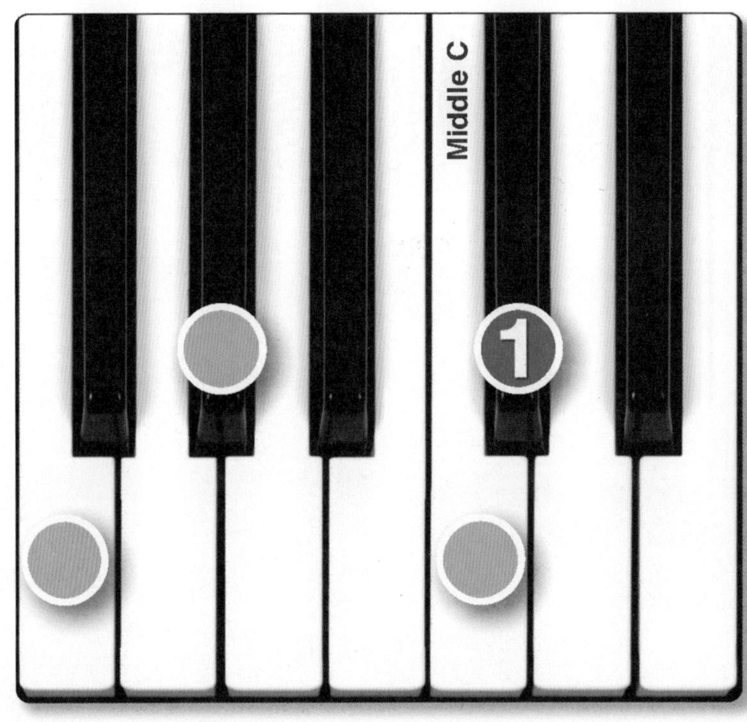

5 = little finger 4 = ring finger 3 = middle finger 2 = index finger 1 = thumb

Chord Spelling

1st (C♯), 3rd (E♯), 5th (G♯), 7th (B♯)

FREE ACCESS on smartphones including iPhone & Android

Using any QR code app scan and **HEAR** the chord

C♯/D♭maj7

Major 7th

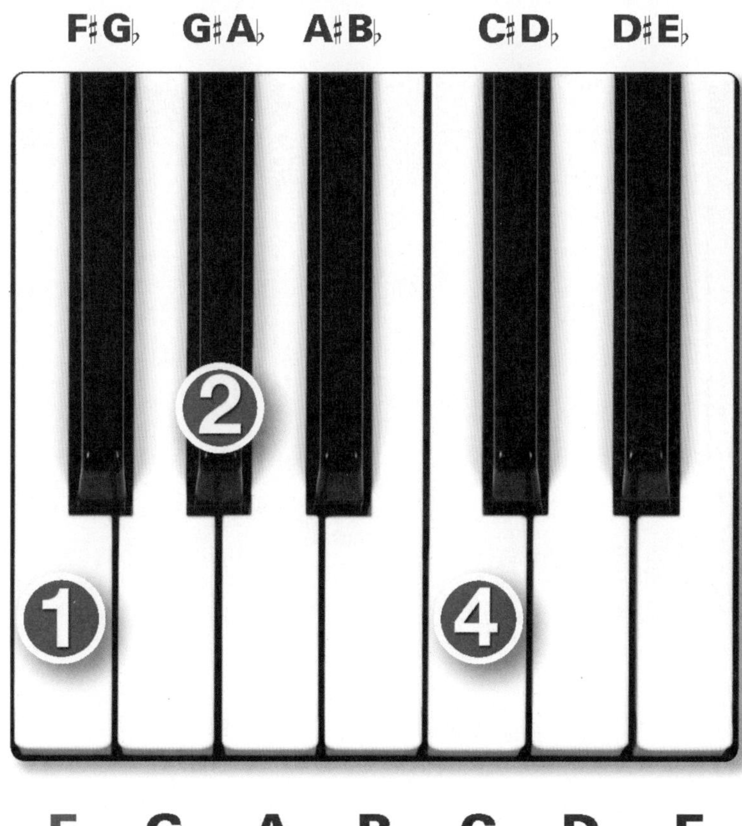

1 = thumb 2 = index finger 3 = middle finger 4 = ring finger 5 = little finger

Chord Spelling

1st (C♯), 3rd (E♯), 5th (G♯), 7th (B♯)

FREE ACCESS on smartphones including iPhone & Android

Using any QR code app scan and **HEAR** the chord

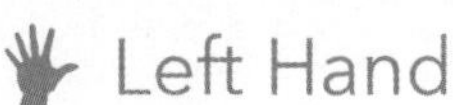

C♯/D♭m7

Minor 7th

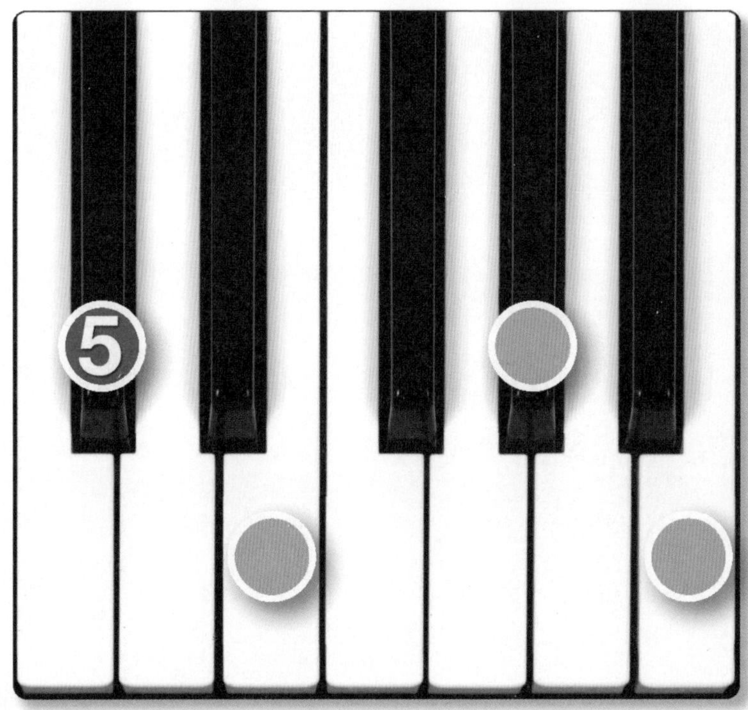

5 = little finger 4 = ring finger 3 = middle finger 2 = index finger 1 = thumb

Chord Spelling

1st (C♯), ♭3rd (E), 5th (G♯), ♭7th (B)

FREE ACCESS on smartphones including iPhone & Android  Using any QR code app scan and **HEAR** the chord

C♯/D♭m7
Minor 7th

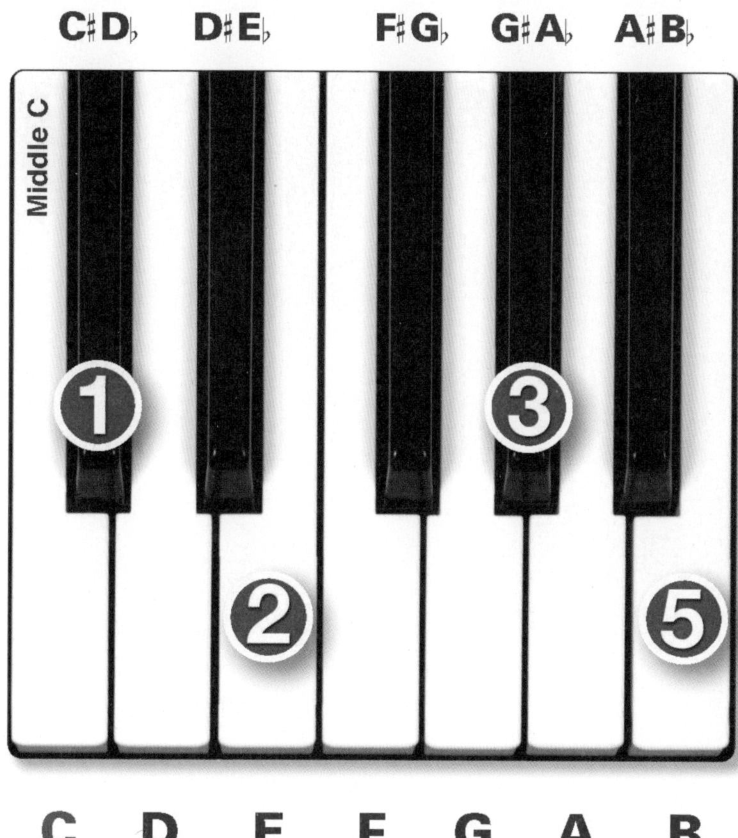

C D E F G A B

1 = thumb 2 = index finger 3 = middle finger 4 = ring finger 5 = little finger

Chord Spelling

1st (C♯), ♭3rd (E), 5th (G♯), ♭7th (B)

FREE ACCESS on smartphones including iPhone & Android  Using any QR code app scan and **HEAR** the chord

A
A♯/B♭
B
C
C♯/D♭
D
D♯/E♭
E
F
F♯/G♭
G
G♯/A♭

C♯/D♭maj9

Major 9th

F♯G♭ G♯A♭ A♯B♭ C♯D♭ D♯E♭

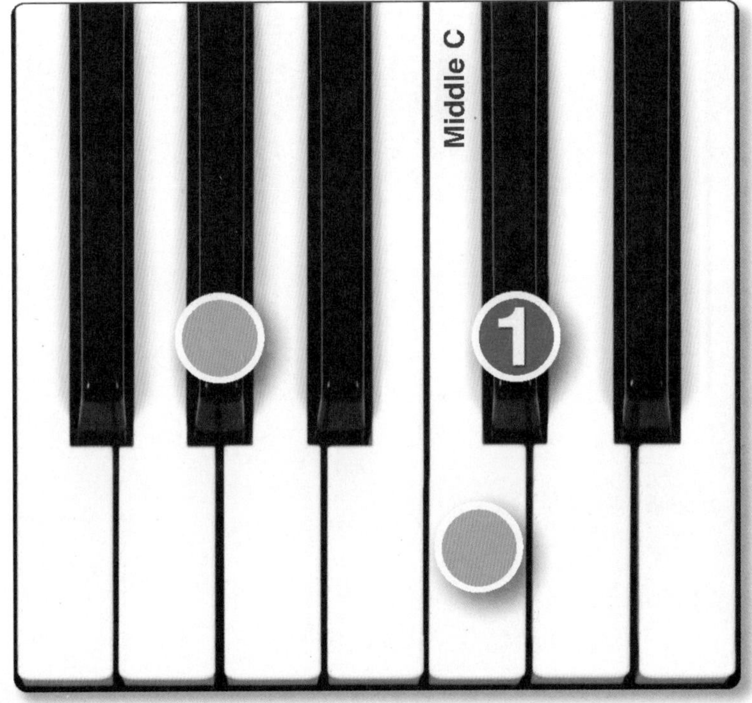

F G A B C D E

5 = little finger 4 = ring finger 3 = middle finger 2 = index finger 1 = thumb

Chord Spelling

1st (C♯), 3rd (E♯), 5th (G♯), 7th (B♯), 9th (D♯)

FREE ACCESS on smartphones including iPhone & Android  Using any QR code app scan and **HEAR** the chord

C♯/D♭maj9

Major 9th

Right Hand 

A
A♯/B♭
B
C
C♯/D♭
D
D♯/E♭
E
F
F♯/G♭
G
G♯/A♭

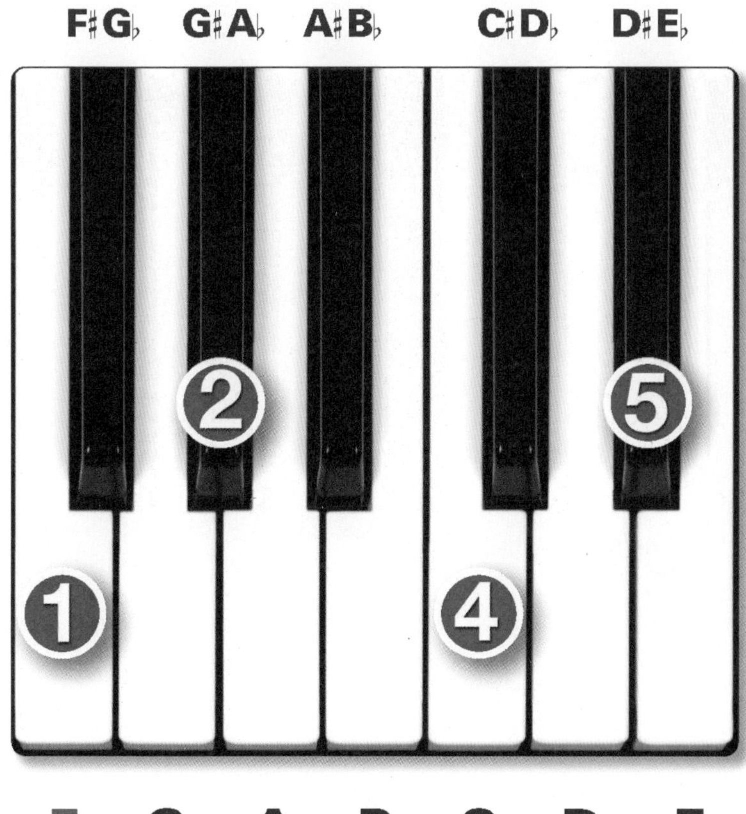

F G A B C D E

1 = thumb 2 = index finger 3 = middle finger 4 = ring finger 5 = little finger

Chord Spelling

1st (C♯), 3rd (E♯), 5th (G♯), 7th (B♯), 9th (D♯)

FREE ACCESS on smartphones including iPhone & Android  Using any QR code app scan and **HEAR** the chord

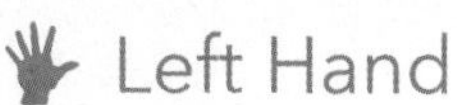

A
A♯/B♭
B
C
C♯/D♭
D
D♯/E♭
E
F
F♯/G♭
G
G♯/A♭

C♯/D♭m9

Minor 9th

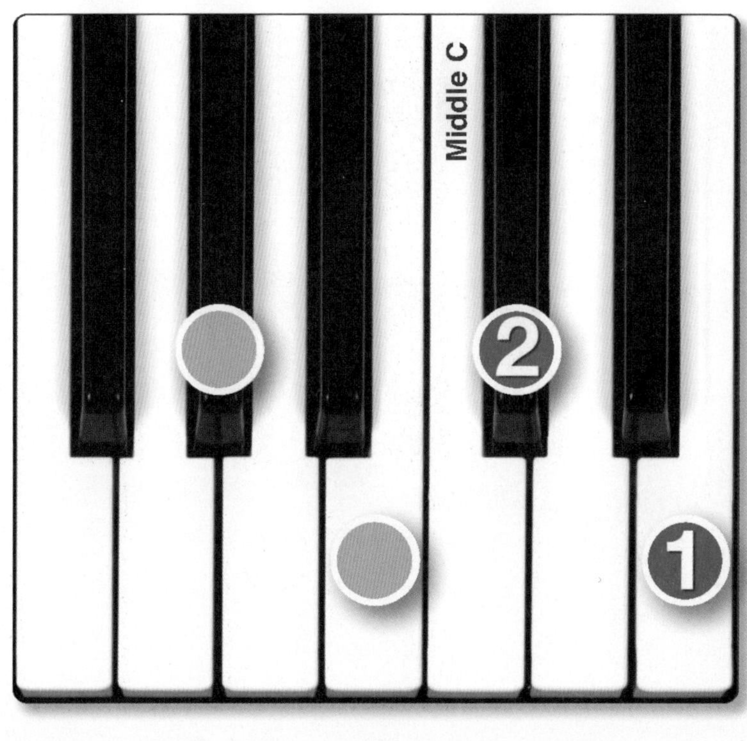

5 = little finger 4 = ring finger 3 = middle finger 2 = index finger 1 = thumb

Chord Spelling

1st (C♯), ♭3rd (E), 5th (G♯), ♭7th (B), 9th (D♯)

FREE ACCESS on smartphones including iPhone & Android

Using any QR code app scan and **HEAR** the chord

C♯/D♭m9

Minor 9th

Right Hand

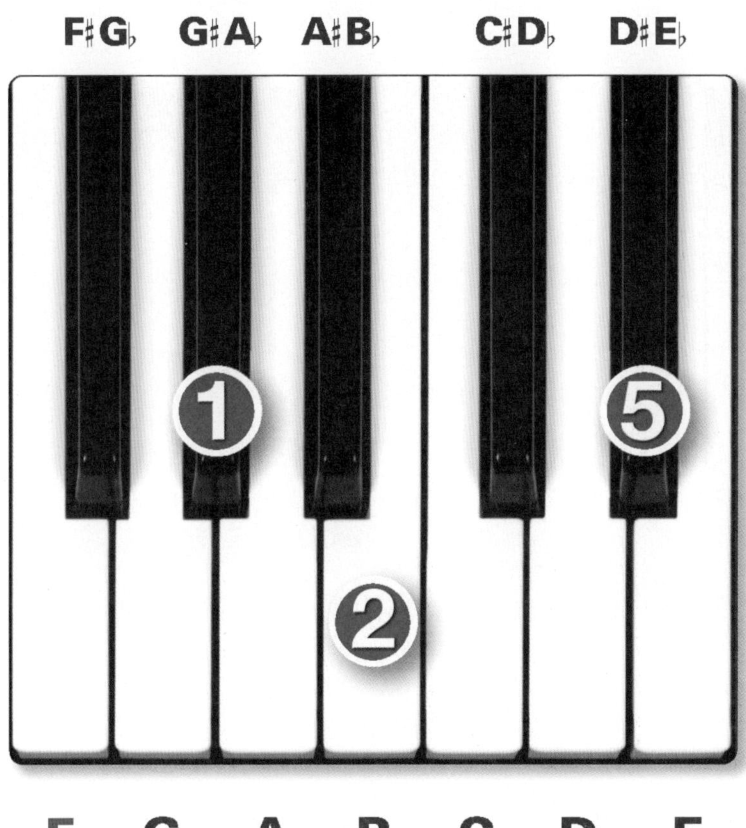

1 = thumb 2 = index finger 3 = middle finger 4 = ring finger 5 = little finger

Chord Spelling

1st (C♯), ♭3rd (E), 5th (G♯), ♭7th (B), 9th (D♯)

FREE ACCESS on smartphones including iPhone & Android

Using any QR code app scan and **HEAR** the chord

D

Major

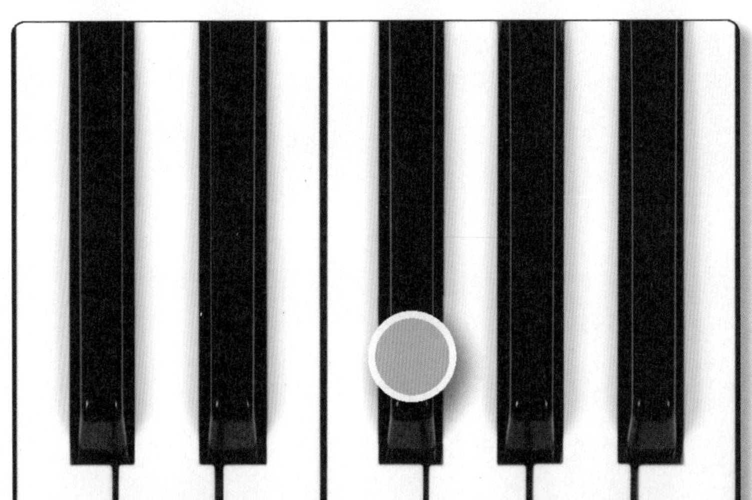

C D E F G A B

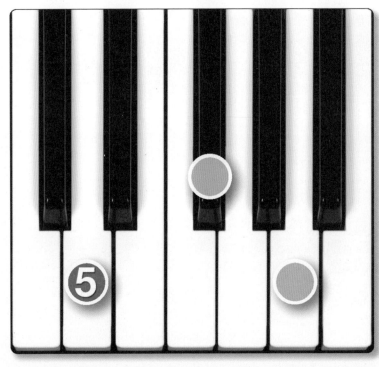

5 = little finger 4 = ring finger 3 = middle finger 2 = index finger 1 = thumb

Chord Spelling

1st (D), 3rd (F♯), 5th (A)

FREE ACCESS on smartphones including iPhone & Android  Using any QR code app scan and **HEAR** the chord

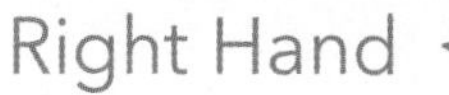

D
Major

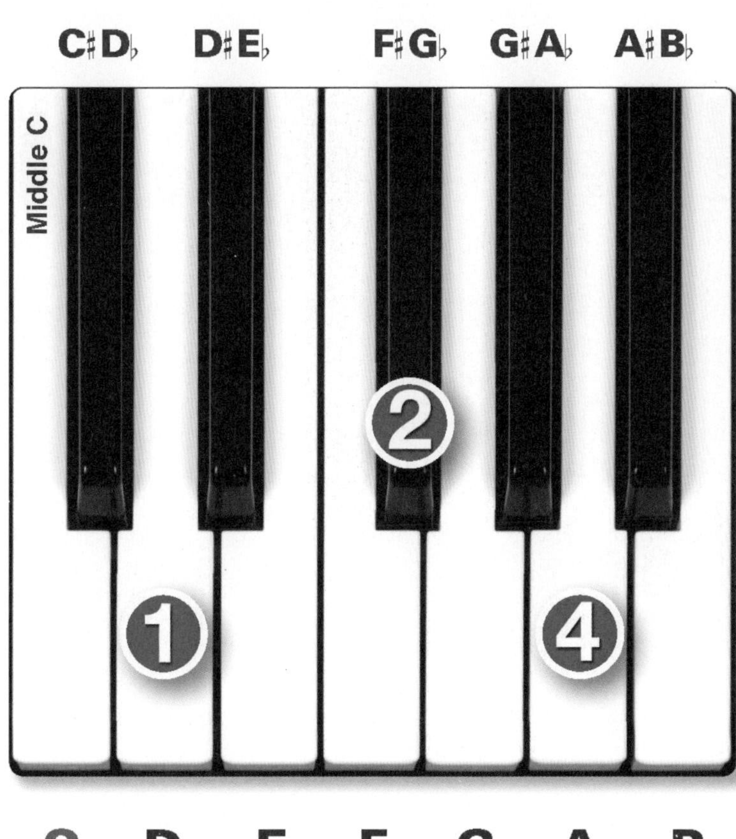

1 = thumb 2 = index finger 3 = middle finger 4 = ring finger 5 = little finger

Chord Spelling

1st (D), 3rd (F♯), 5th (A)

FREE ACCESS on smartphones including iPhone & Android

Using any QR code app scan and **HEAR** the chord

Dm

Minor

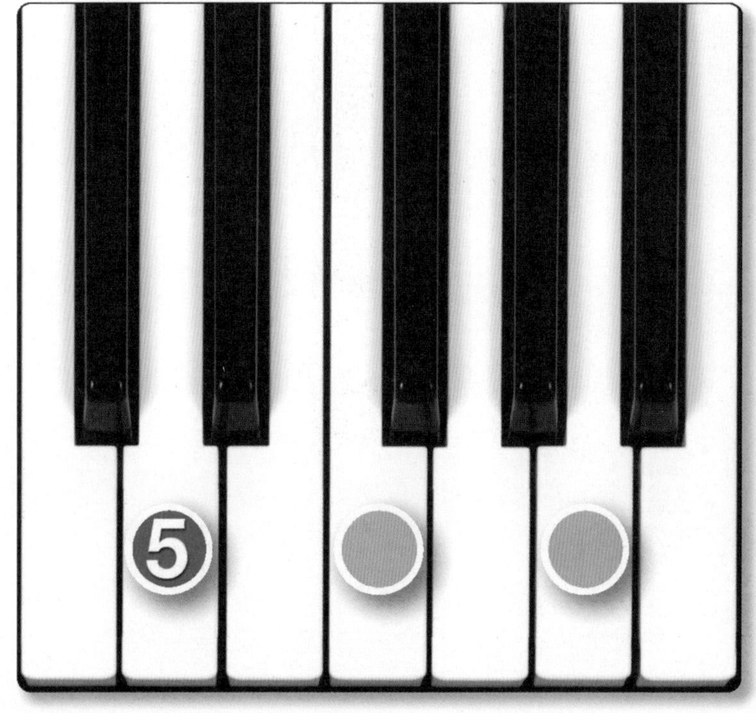

5 = little finger 4 = ring finger 3 = middle finger 2 = index finger 1 = thumb

Chord Spelling

1st (D), ♭3rd (F), 5th (A)

FREE ACCESS on smartphones including iPhone & Android

Using any QR code app scan and **HEAR** the chord

Dm
Minor

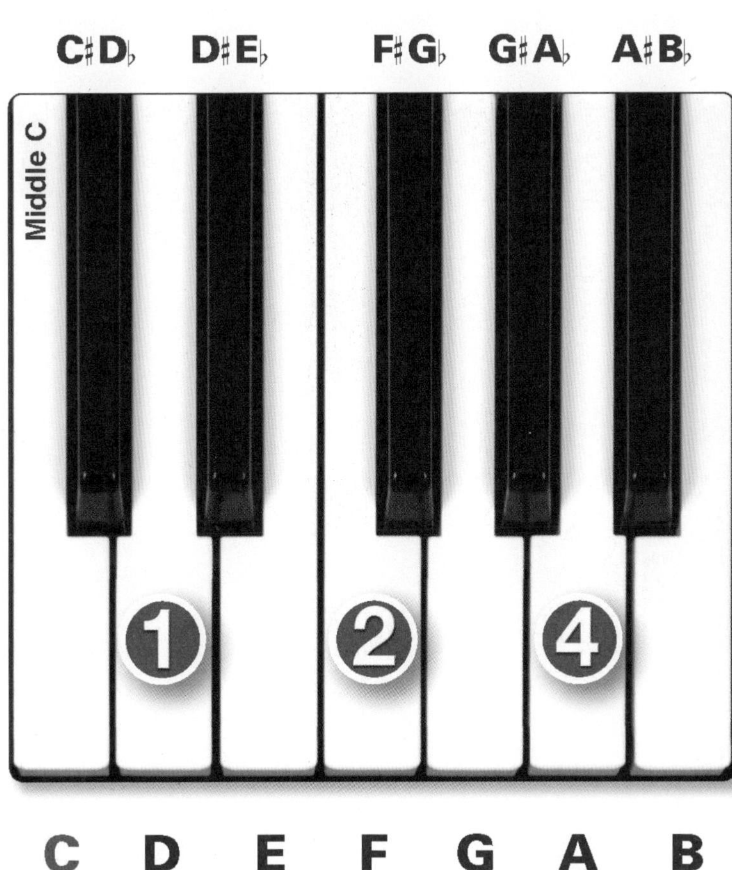

1 = thumb 2 = index finger 3 = middle finger 4 = ring finger 5 = little finger

Chord Spelling

1st (D), ♭3rd (F), 5th (A)

FREE ACCESS on smartphones including iPhone & Android

Using any QR code app scan and **HEAR** the chord

D+

Augmented Triad

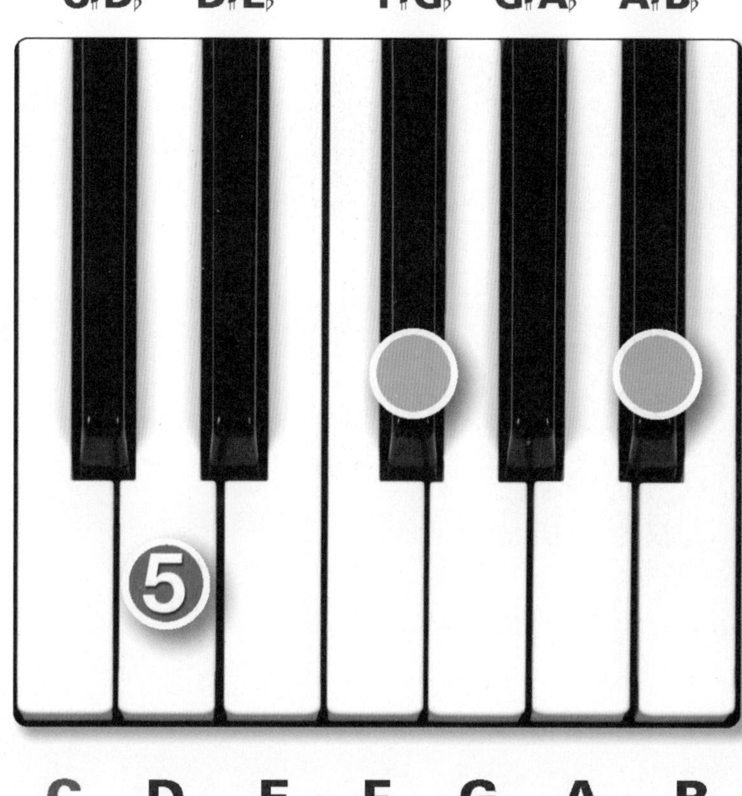

5 = little finger 4 = ring finger 3 = middle finger 2 = index finger 1 = thumb

Chord Spelling

1st (D), 3rd (F♯), ♯5th (A♯)

FREE ACCESS on smartphones including iPhone & Android

Using any QR code app scan and **HEAR** the chord

D+
Augmented Triad

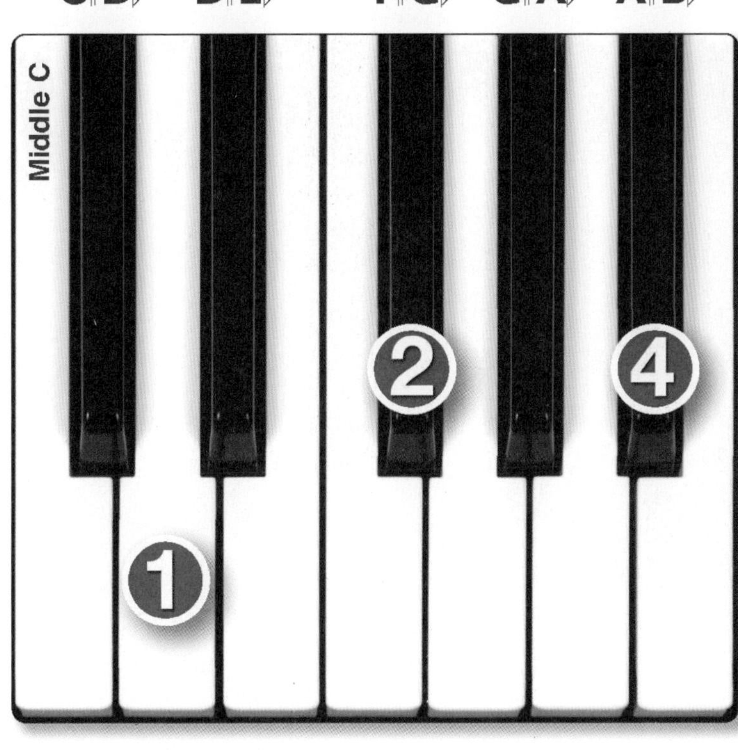

1 = thumb 2 = index finger 3 = middle finger 4 = ring finger 5 = little finger

Chord Spelling

1st (D), 3rd (F♯), ♯5th (A♯)

FREE ACCESS on smartphones including iPhone & Android

Using any QR code app scan and **HEAR** the chord

D°

Diminished Triad

5 = little finger 4 = ring finger 3 = middle finger 2 = index finger 1 = thumb

Chord Spelling

1st (D), ♭3rd (F), ♭5th (A♭)

FREE ACCESS on smartphones including iPhone & Android  Using any QR code app scan and **HEAR** the chord

D°

Diminished Triad

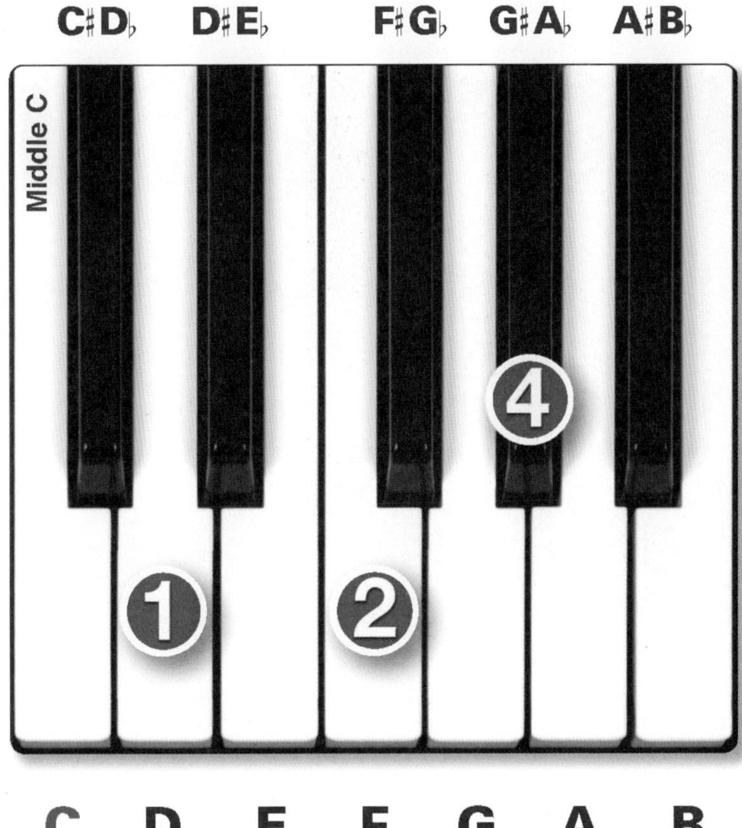

1 = thumb 2 = index finger 3 = middle finger 4 = ring finger 5 = little finger

Chord Spelling

1st (D), ♭3rd (F), ♭5th (A♭)

FREE ACCESS on smartphones including iPhone & Android

Using any QR code app scan and **HEAR** the chord

A
A♯/B♭
B
C
C♯/D♭
D
D♯/E♭
E
F
F♯/G♭
G
G♯/A♭

D6

Major 6th

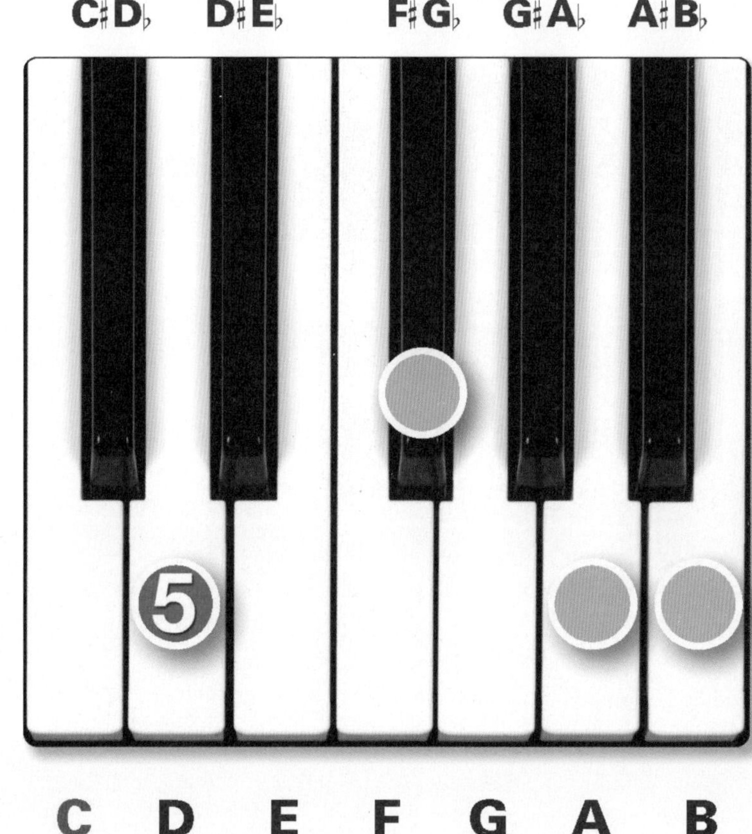

5 = little finger 4 = ring finger 3 = middle finger 2 = index finger 1 = thumb

Chord Spelling

1st (D), 3rd (F♯), 5th (A), 6th (B)

FREE ACCESS on smartphones including iPhone & Android

Using any QR code app scan and **HEAR** the chord

D6
Major 6th

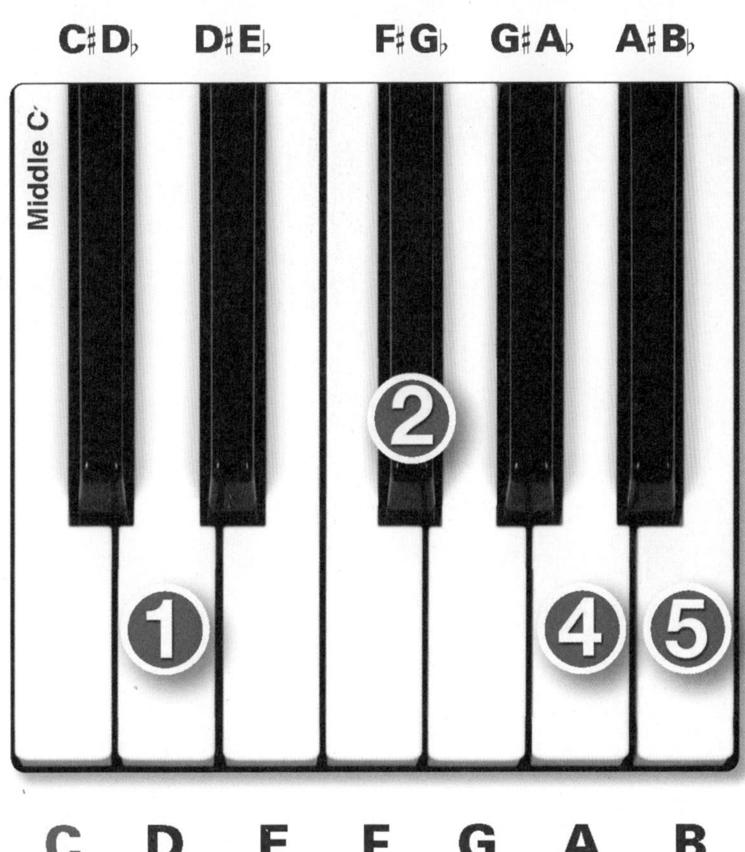

1 = thumb 2 = index finger 3 = middle finger 4 = ring finger 5 = little finger

Chord Spelling

1st (D), 3rd (F♯), 5th (A), 6th (B)

FREE ACCESS on smartphones including iPhone & Android  Using any QR code app scan and **HEAR** the chord

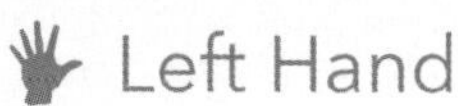

Dm6

Minor 6th

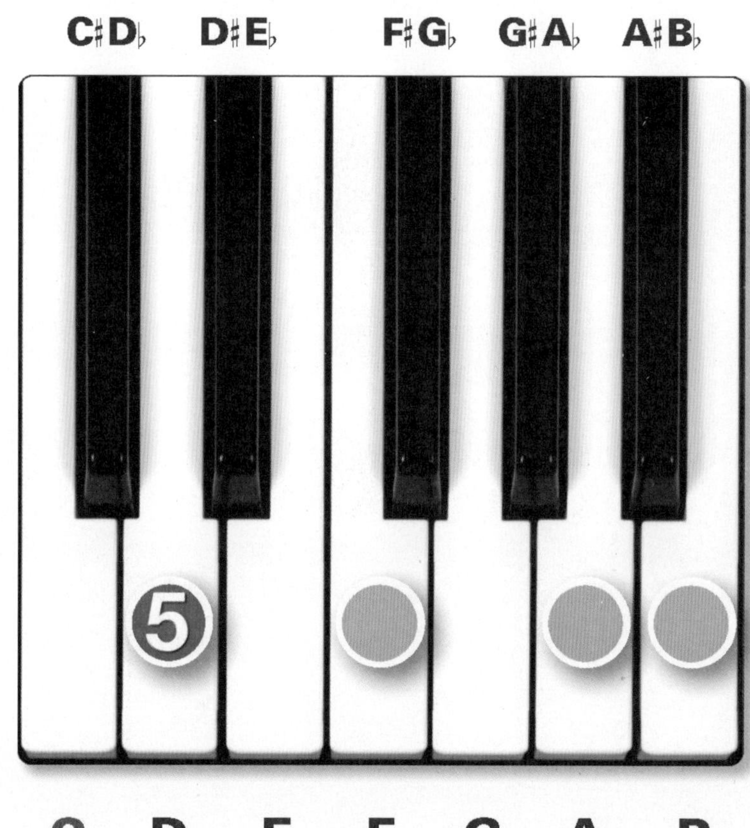

5 = little finger 4 = ring finger 3 = middle finger 2 = index finger 1 = thumb

Chord Spelling

1st (D), ♭3rd (F), 5th (A), 6th (B)

FREE ACCESS on smartphones including iPhone & Android

Using any QR code app scan and **HEAR** the chord

Dm6

Minor 6th

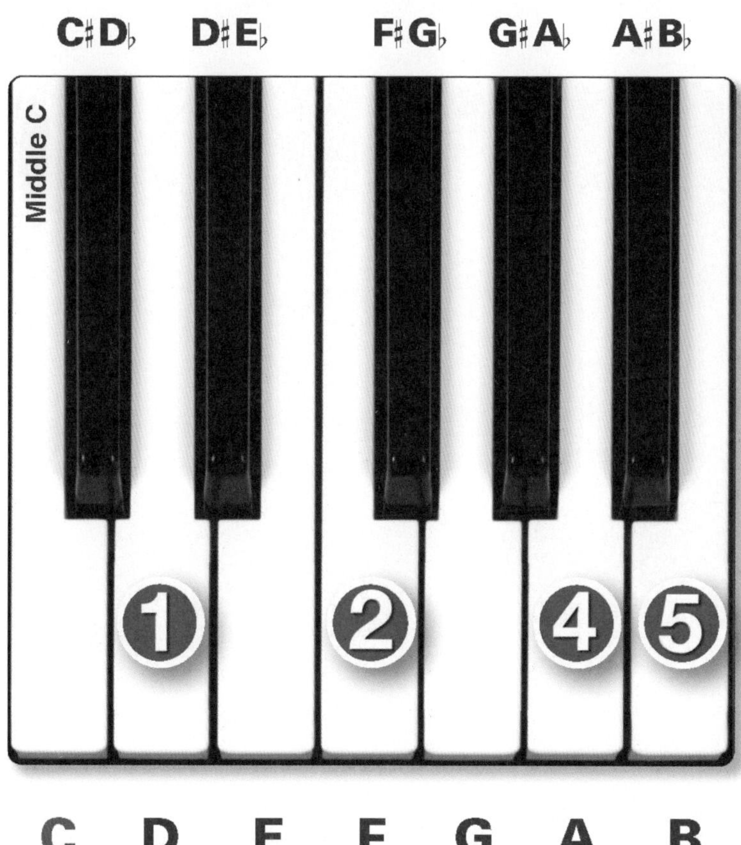

1 = thumb 2 = index finger 3 = middle finger 4 = ring finger 5 = little finger

Chord Spelling

1st (D), ♭3rd (F), 5th (A), 6th (B)

FREE ACCESS on smartphones including iPhone & Android

Using any QR code app scan and **HEAR** the chord

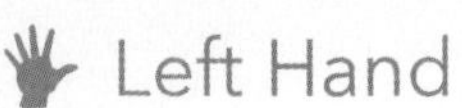

Dmaj7

Major 7th

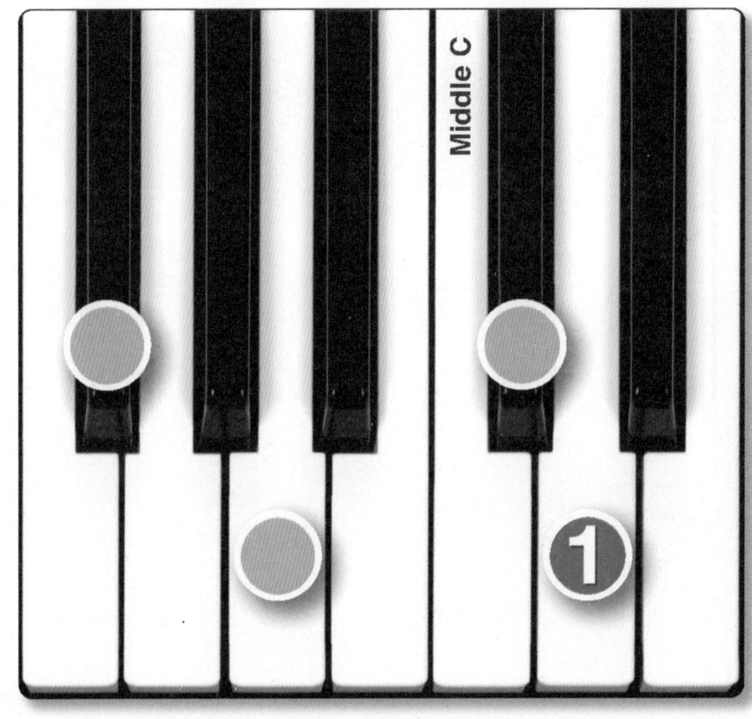

5 = little finger 4 = ring finger 3 = middle finger 2 = index finger 1 = thumb

Chord Spelling

1st (D), 3rd (F♯), 5th (A), 7th (C♯)

FREE ACCESS on smartphones including iPhone & Android

Using any QR code app scan and **HEAR** the chord

Dmaj7
Major 7th

Right Hand

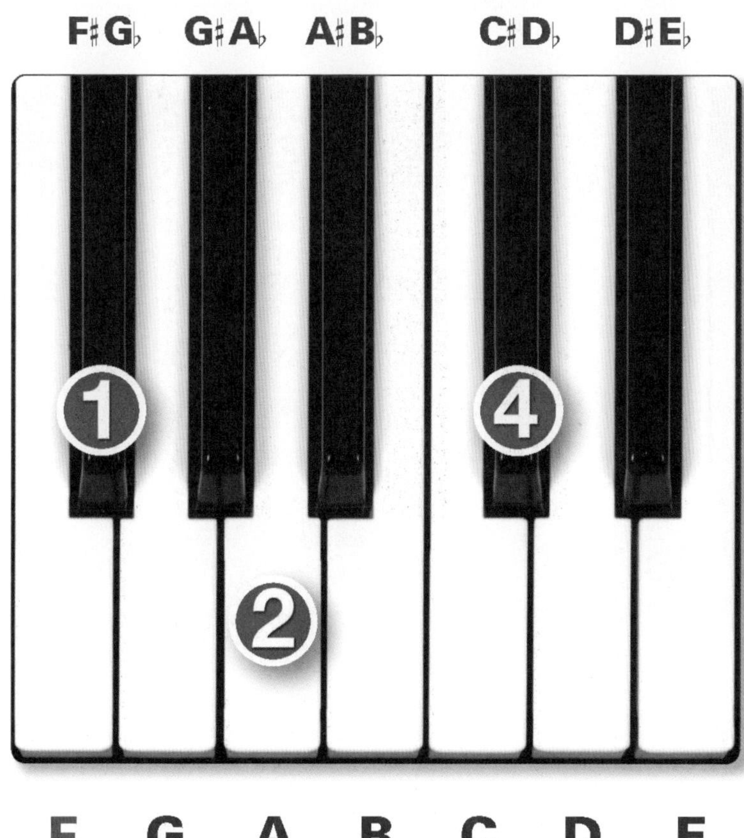

1 = thumb 2 = index finger 3 = middle finger 4 = ring finger 5 = little finger

Chord Spelling

1st (D), 3rd (F♯), 5th (A), 7th (C♯)

FREE ACCESS on smartphones including iPhone & Android  Using any QR code app scan and **HEAR** the chord

A
A♯/B♭
B
C
C♯/D♭
D
D♯/E♭
E
F
F♯/G♭
G
G♯/A♭

Dm7

Minor 7th

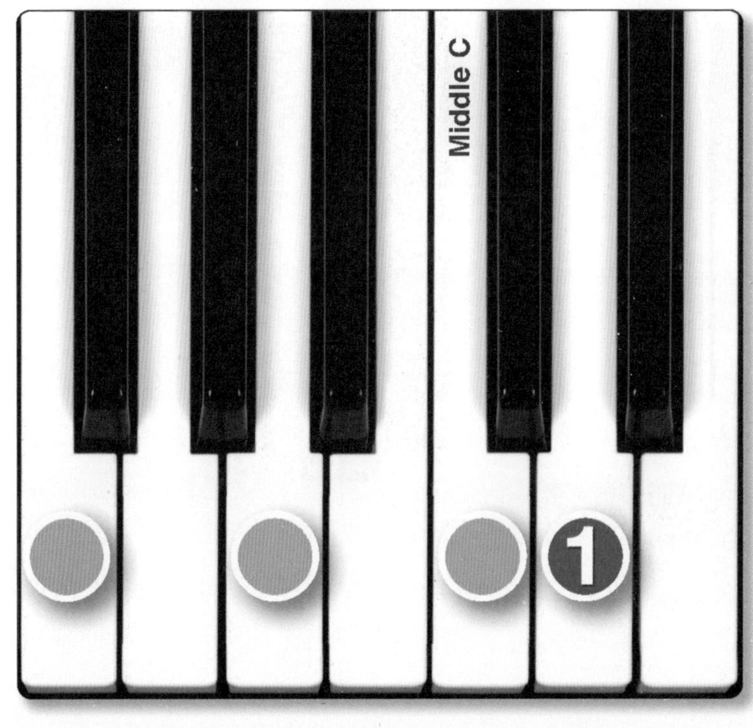

5 = little finger 4 = ring finger 3 = middle finger 2 = index finger 1 = thumb

Chord Spelling

1st (D), ♭3rd (F), 5th (A), ♭7th (C)

FREE ACCESS on smartphones including iPhone & Android

Using any QR code app scan and **HEAR** the chord

Dm7

Minor 7th

F♯G♭ G♯A♭ A♯B♭ C♯D♭ D♯E♭

1 2 4

F G A B C D E

1 = thumb 2 = index finger 3 = middle finger 4 = ring finger 5 = little finger

Chord Spelling

1st (D), ♭3rd (F), 5th (A), ♭7th (C)

FREE ACCESS on smartphones including iPhone & Android  Using any QR code app scan and **HEAR** the chord

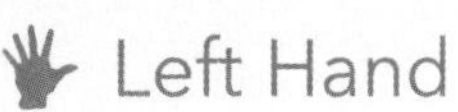
Left Hand

Dmaj9

Major 9th

F♯G♭ G♯A♭ A♯B♭ C♯D♭ D♯E♭

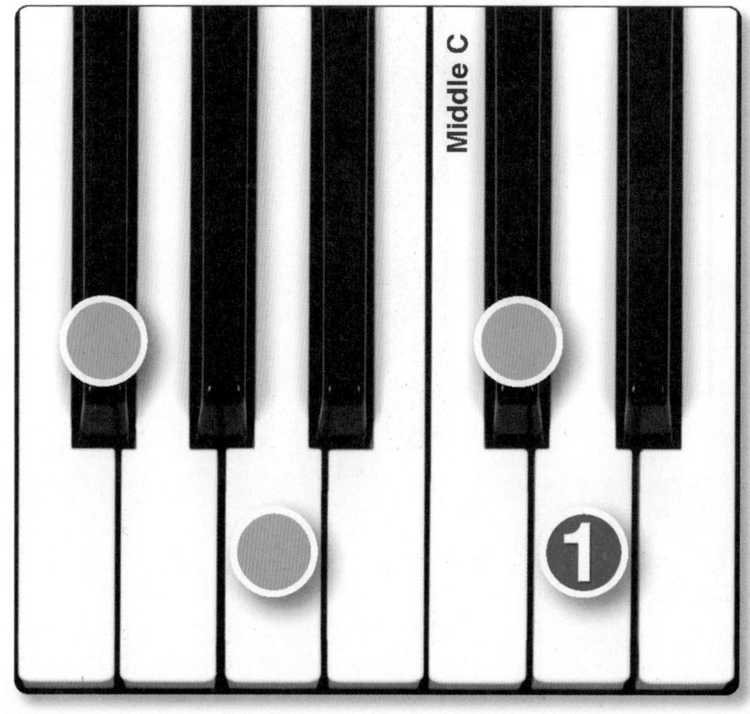

F G A B C D E

5 = little finger 4 = ring finger 3 = middle finger 2 = index finger 1 = thumb

Chord Spelling

1st (D), 3rd (F♯), 5th (A), 7th (C♯), 9th (E)

FREE ACCESS on smartphones including iPhone & Android

Using any QR code app scan and **HEAR** the chord

Dmaj9

Major 9th

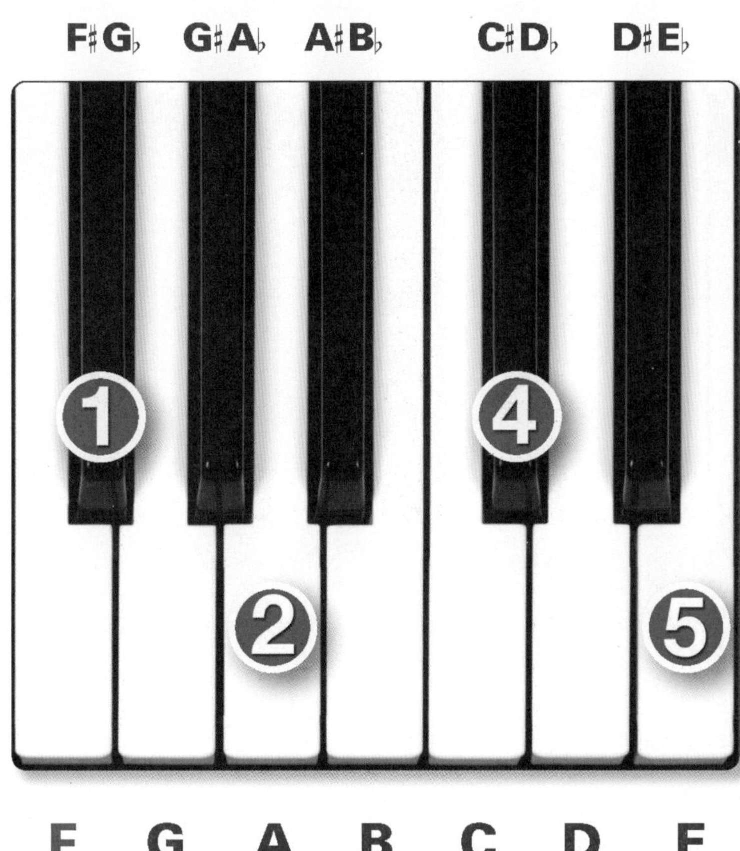

1 = thumb 2 = index finger 3 = middle finger 4 = ring finger 5 = little finger

Chord Spelling

1st (D), 3rd (F♯), 5th (A), 7th (C♯), 9th (E)

FREE ACCESS on smartphones including iPhone & Android  Using any QR code app scan and **HEAR** the chord

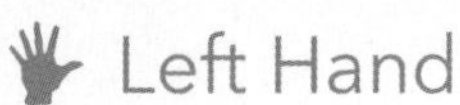

A
A♯/B♭
B
C
C♯/D♭
D
D♯/E♭
E
F
F♯/G♭
G
G♯/A♭

Dm9

Minor 9th

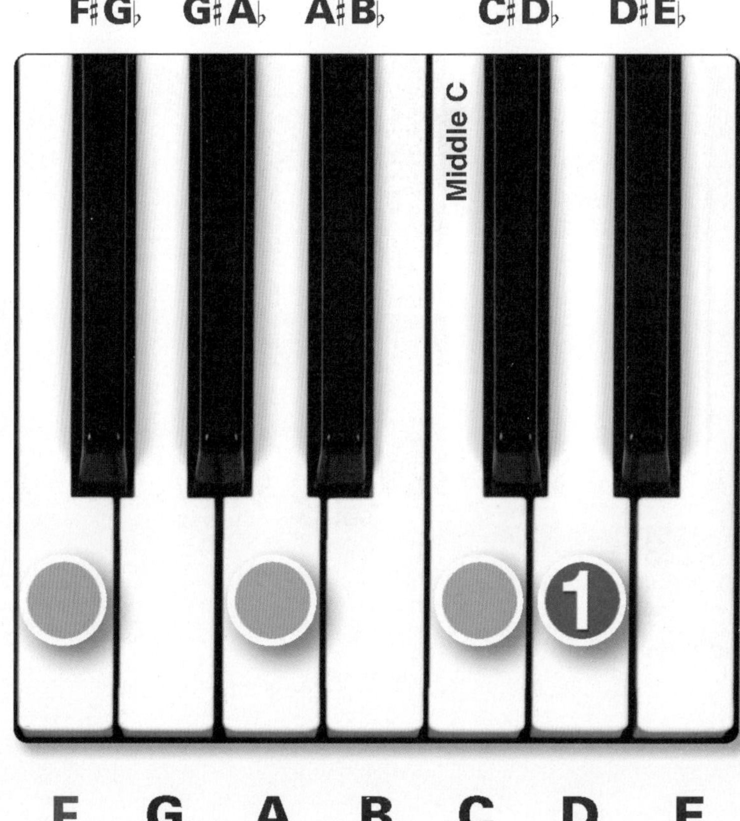

5 = little finger 4 = ring finger 3 = middle finger 2 = index finger 1 = thumb

Chord Spelling

1st (D), 3rd (F), 5th (A), ♭7th (C), 9th (E)

FREE ACCESS on smartphones including iPhone & Android

Using any QR code app scan and **HEAR** the chord

Dm9

Minor 9th

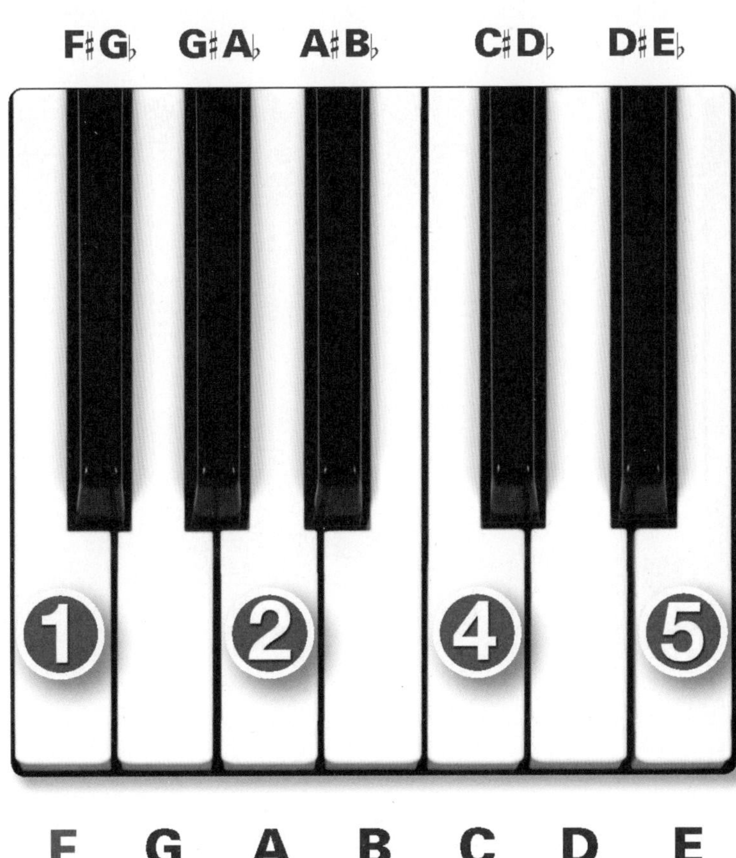

1 = thumb 2 = index finger 3 = middle finger 4 = ring finger 5 = little finger

Chord Spelling

1st (D), 3rd (F), 5th (A), ♭7th (C), 9th (E)

FREE ACCESS on smartphones including iPhone & Android

Using any QR code app scan and **HEAR** the chord

A
A♯/B♭
B
C
C♯/D♭
D
D♯/E♭
E
F
F♯/G♭
G
G♯/A♭

C♯D♭ D♯E♭ F♯G♭ G♯A♭ A♯B♭

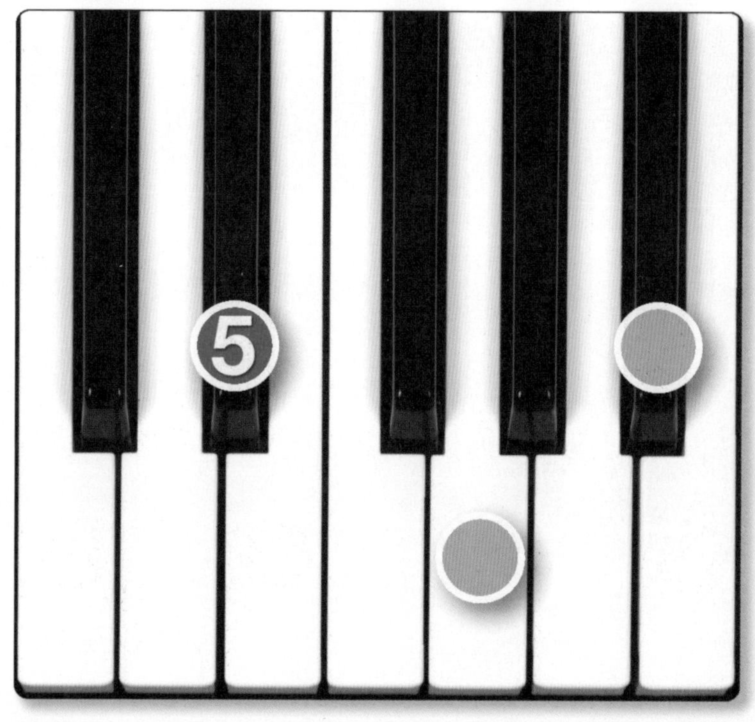

C D E F G A B

5 = little finger 4 = ring finger 3 = middle finger 2 = index finger 1 = thumb

Chord Spelling

1st (E♭), 3rd (G), 5th (B♭)

FREE ACCESS on smartphones including iPhone & Android

Using any QR code app scan and **HEAR** the chord

D♯/E♭
Major

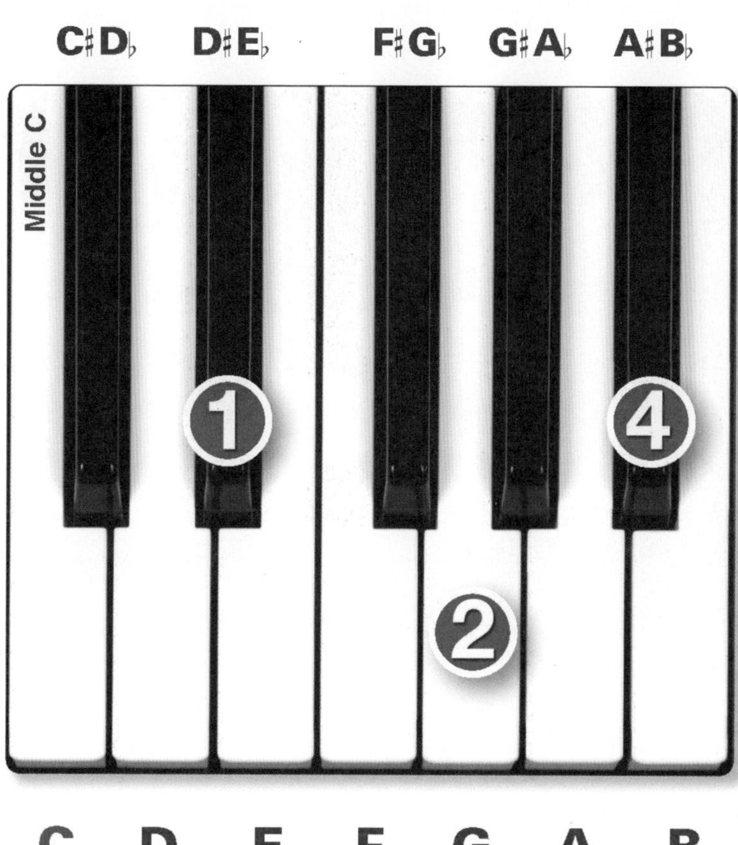

1 = thumb   2 = index finger   3 = middle finger   4 = ring finger   5 = little finger

Chord Spelling

1st (E♭), 3rd (G), 5th (B♭)

FREE ACCESS on smartphones including iPhone & Android  Using any QR code app scan and **HEAR** the chord

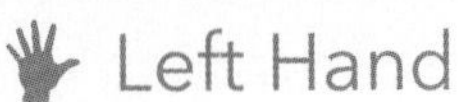

D♯/E♭m
Minor

C♯D♭ D♯E♭ F♯G♭ G♯A♭ A♯B♭

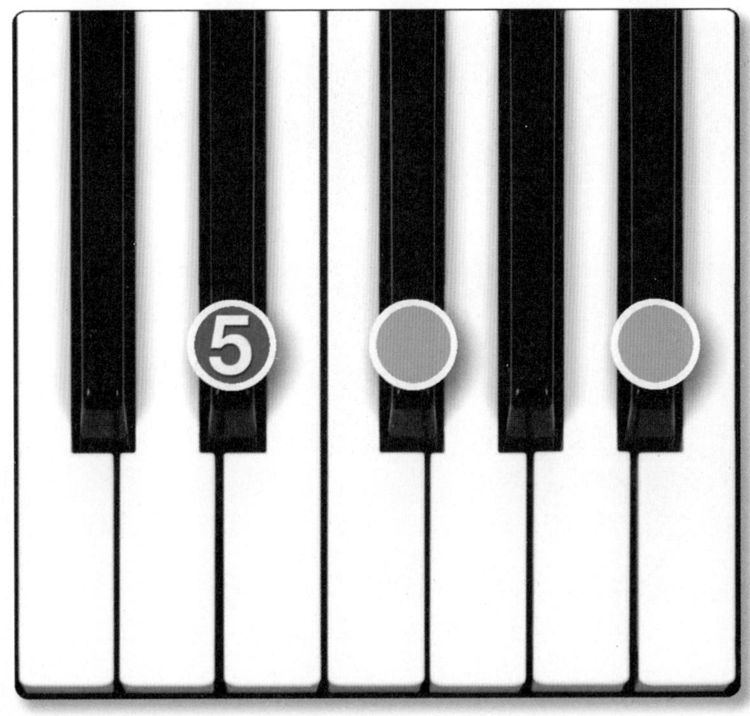

C D E F G A B

5 = little finger 4 = ring finger 3 = middle finger 2 = index finger 1 = thumb

Chord Spelling

1st (E♭), ♭3rd (G♭), 5th (B♭)

FREE ACCESS on smartphones including iPhone & Android

Using any QR code app scan and **HEAR** the chord

D♯/E♭m
Minor

Right Hand

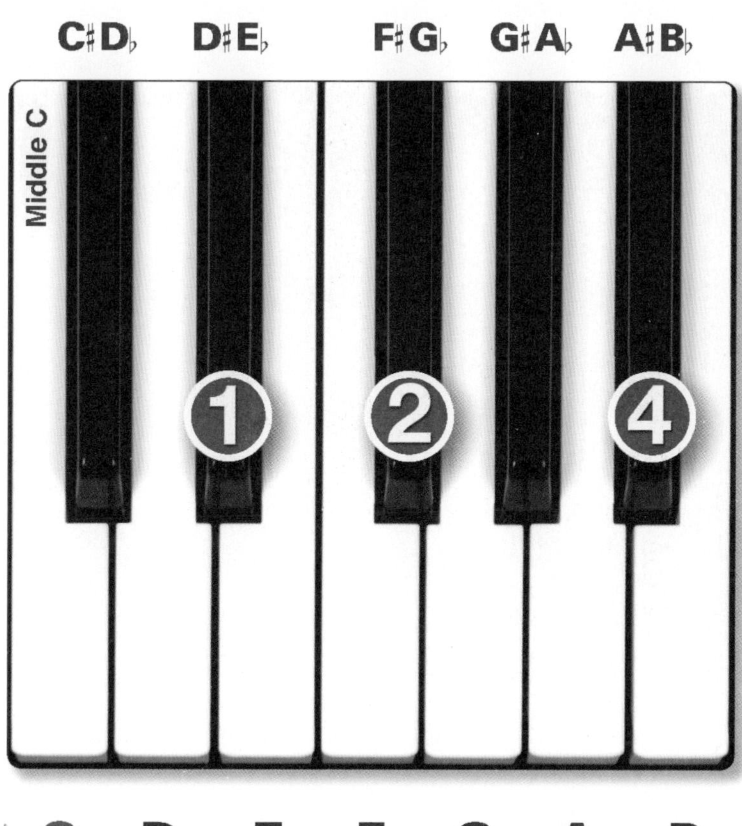

C D E F G A B

1 = thumb 2 = index finger 3 = middle finger 4 = ring finger 5 = little finger

Chord Spelling

1st (E♭), ♭3rd (G♭), 5th (B♭)

FREE ACCESS on smartphones including iPhone & Android

Using any QR code app scan and **HEAR** the chord

D♯/E♭+
Augmented Triad

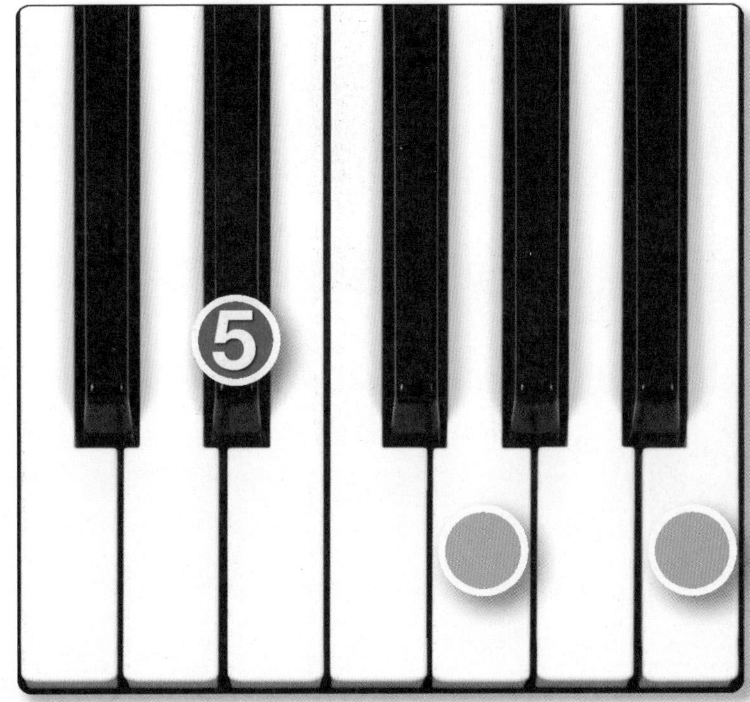

5 = little finger 4 = ring finger 3 = middle finger 2 = index finger 1 = thumb

Chord Spelling

1st (E♭), 3rd (G), ♯5th (B)

FREE ACCESS on smartphones including iPhone & Android

Using any QR code app scan and **HEAR** the chord

Right Hand 

D♯/E♭+
Augmented Triad

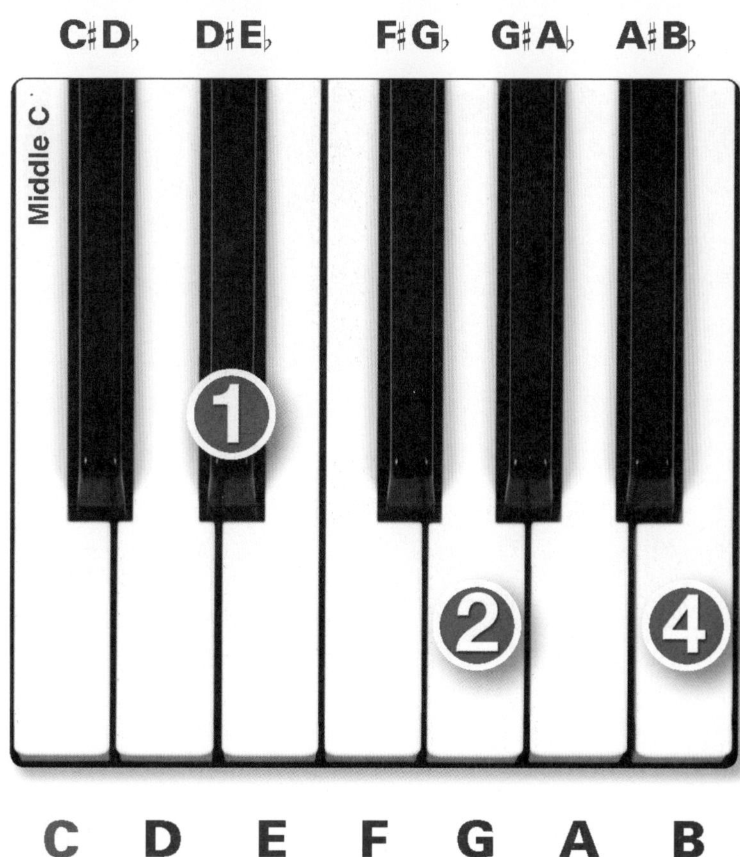

1 = thumb 2 = index finger 3 = middle finger 4 = ring finger 5 = little finger

Chord Spelling

1st (E♭), 3rd (G), ♯5th (B)

FREE ACCESS on smartphones including iPhone & Android  Using any QR code app scan and **HEAR** the chord

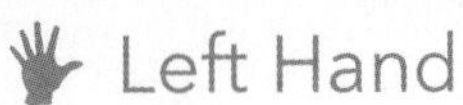

A
A♯/B♭
B
C
C♯/D♭
D
D♯/E♭
E
F
F♯/G♭
G
G♯/A♭

D♯/E♭°

Diminished Triad

5 = little finger   4 = ring finger   3 = middle finger   2 = index finger   1 = thumb

Chord Spelling

1st (E♭), ♭3rd (G♭), ♭5th (B𝄫)

FREE ACCESS on smartphones including iPhone & Android

Using any QR code app scan and **HEAR** the chord

D♯/E♭°
Diminished Triad

Right Hand 

A
A♯/B♭
B
C
C♯/D♭
D
D♯/E♭
E
F
F♯/G♭
G
G♯/A♭

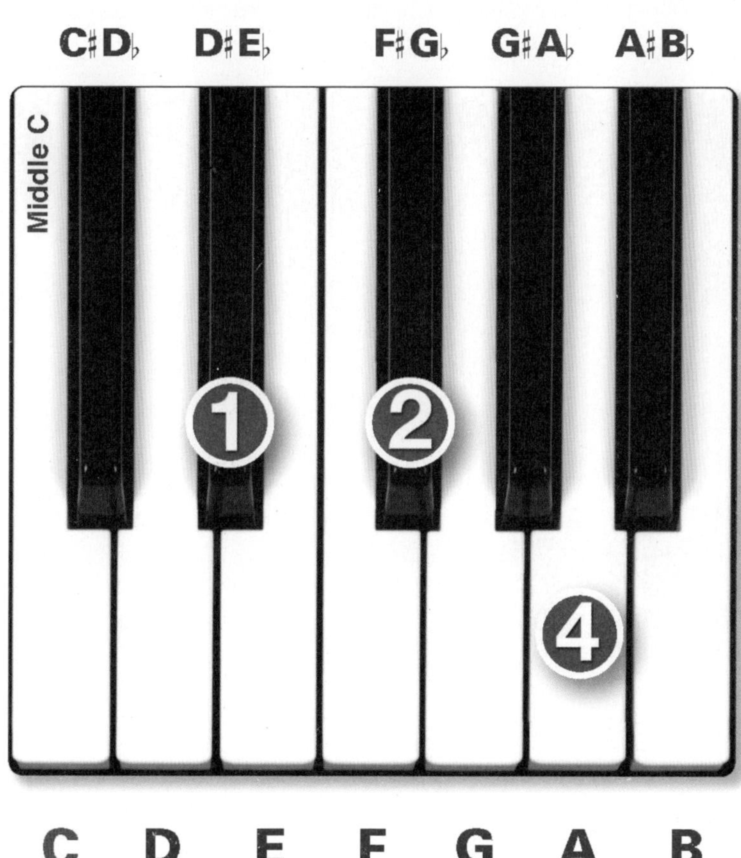

1 = thumb 2 = index finger 3 = middle finger 4 = ring finger 5 = little finger

Chord Spelling

1st (E♭), ♭3rd (G♭), ♭5th (B♭♭)

FREE ACCESS on smartphones including iPhone & Android  Using any QR code app scan and **HEAR** the chord

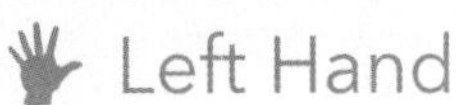

D♯/E♭6
Major 6th

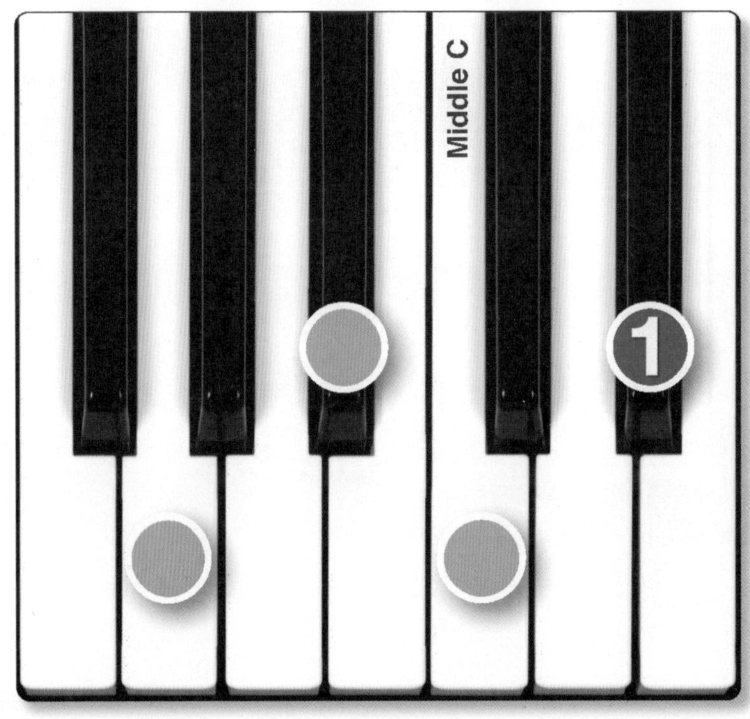

5 = little finger 4 = ring finger 3 = middle finger 2 = index finger 1 = thumb

Chord Spelling

1st (E♭), 3rd (G), 5th (B♭), 6th (C)

FREE ACCESS on smartphones including iPhone & Android  Using any QR code app scan and **HEAR** the chord

D♯/E♭6
Major 6th

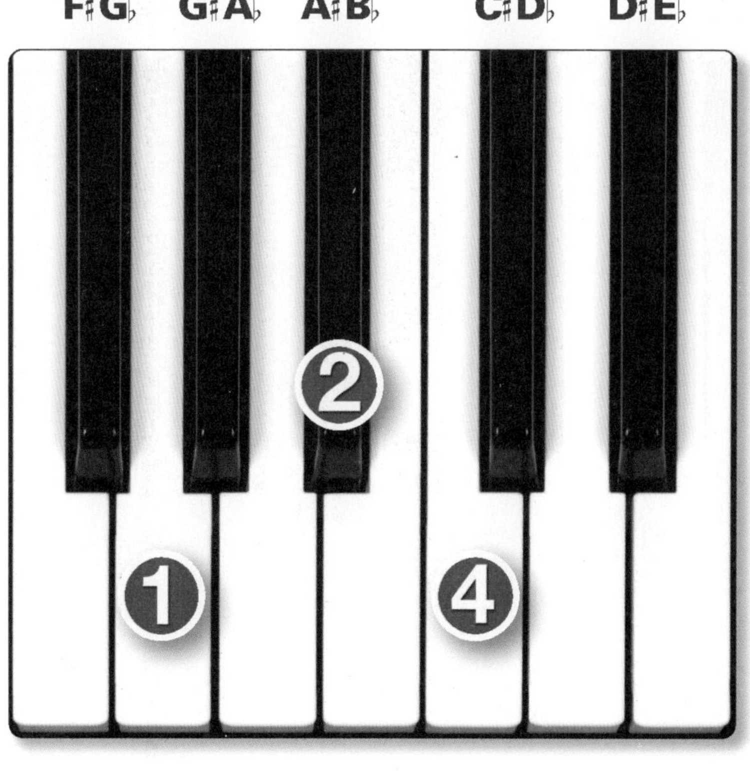

1 = thumb 2 = index finger 3 = middle finger 4 = ring finger 5 = little finger

Chord Spelling

1st (E♭), 3rd (G), 5th (B♭), 6th (C)

FREE ACCESS on smartphones including iPhone & Android  Using any QR code app scan and **HEAR** the chord

D♯/E♭m6

Minor 6th

F G A B C D E

5 = little finger 4 = ring finger 3 = middle finger 2 = index finger 1 = thumb

Chord Spelling

1st (E♭), ♭3rd (G♭), 5th (B♭), 6th (C)

FREE ACCESS on smartphones including iPhone & Android

Using any QR code app scan and **HEAR** the chord

D♯/E♭m6
Minor 6th

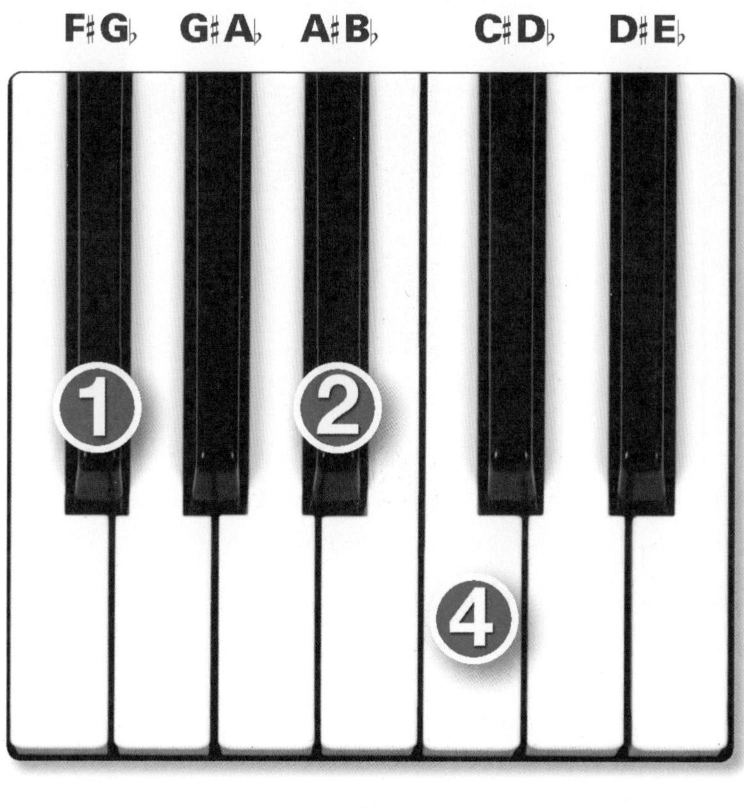

1 = thumb 2 = index finger 3 = middle finger 4 = ring finger 5 = little finger

Chord Spelling

1st (E♭), ♭3rd (G♭), 5th (B♭), 6th (C)

FREE ACCESS on smartphones including iPhone & Android

Using any QR code app scan and **HEAR** the chord

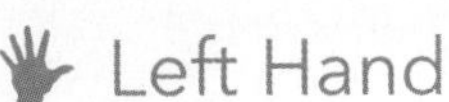

D♯/E♭maj7
Major 7th

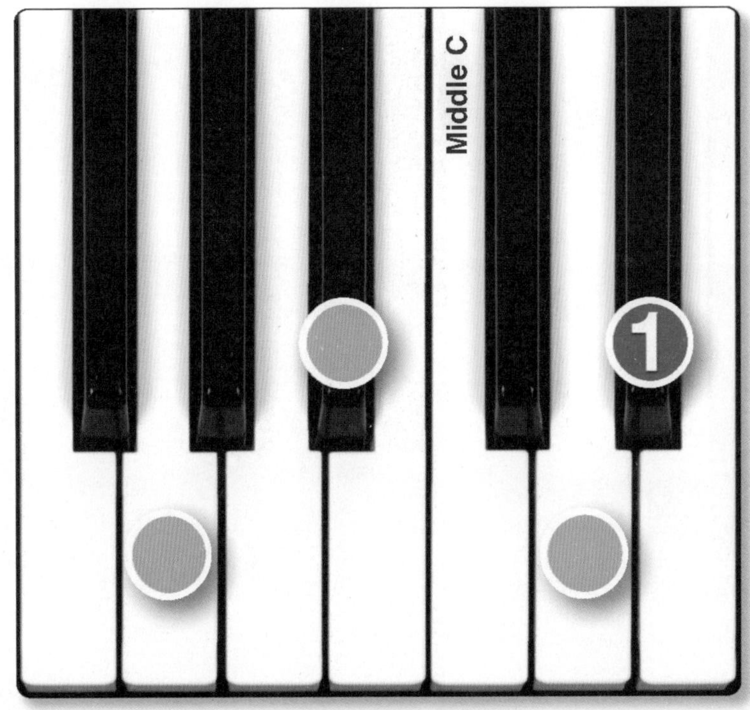

5 = little finger 4 = ring finger 3 = middle finger 2 = index finger 1 = thumb

Chord Spelling

1st (E♭), 3rd (G), 5th (B♭), 7th (D)

FREE ACCESS on smartphones including iPhone & Android  Using any QR code app scan and **HEAR** the chord

D♯/E♭maj7
Major 7th

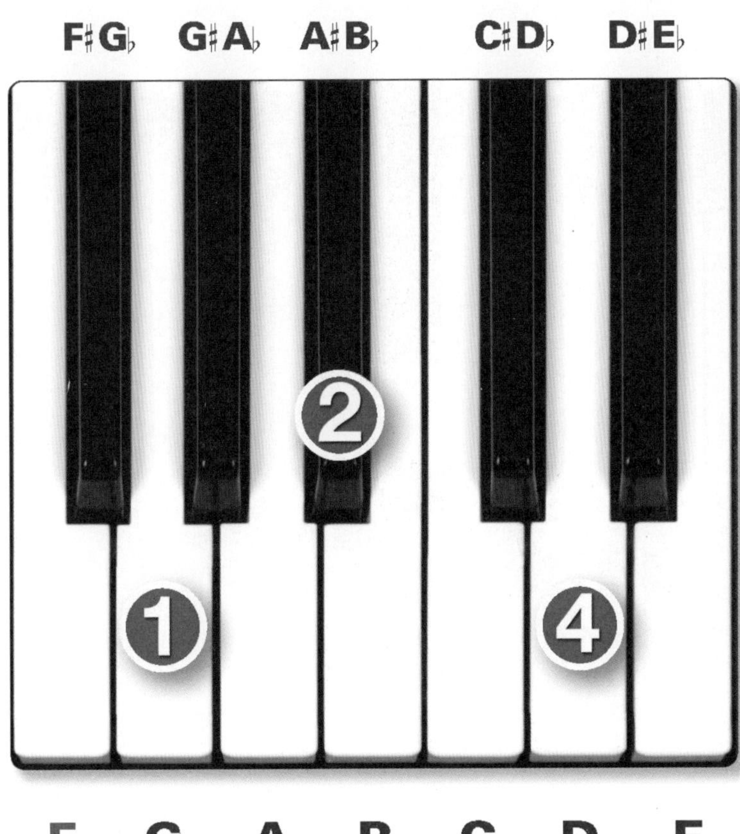

1 = thumb 2 = index finger 3 = middle finger 4 = ring finger 5 = little finger

Chord Spelling

1st (E♭), 3rd (G), 5th (B♭), 7th (D)

FREE ACCESS on smartphones including iPhone & Android

Using any QR code app scan and **HEAR** the chord

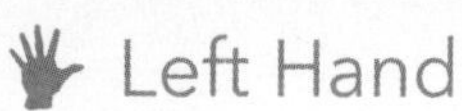

D♯/E♭m7

Minor 7th

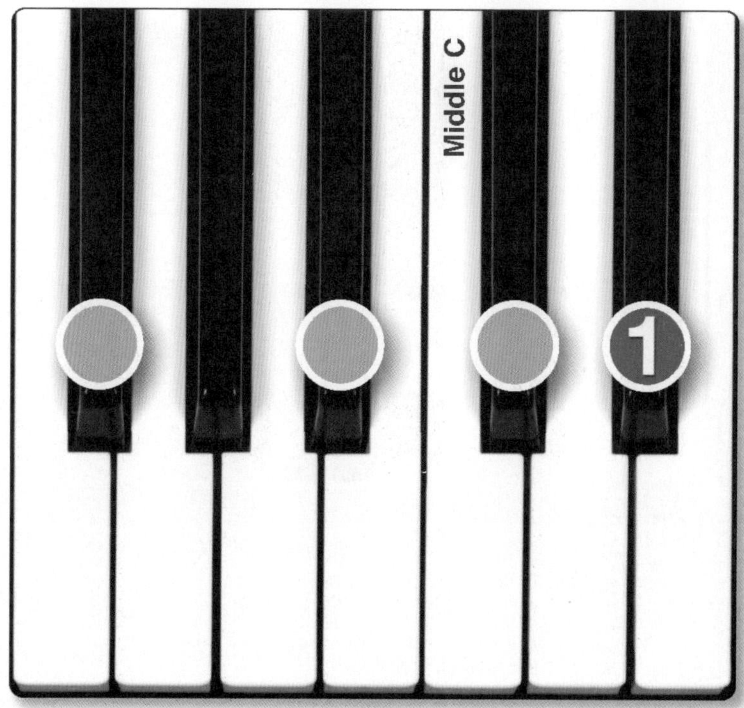

5 = little finger 4 = ring finger 3 = middle finger 2 = index finger 1 = thumb

Chord Spelling

1st (E♭), ♭3rd (G♭), 5th (B♭), ♭7th (D♭)

FREE ACCESS on smartphones including iPhone & Android

Using any QR code app scan and **HEAR** the chord

D♯/E♭m7
Minor 7th

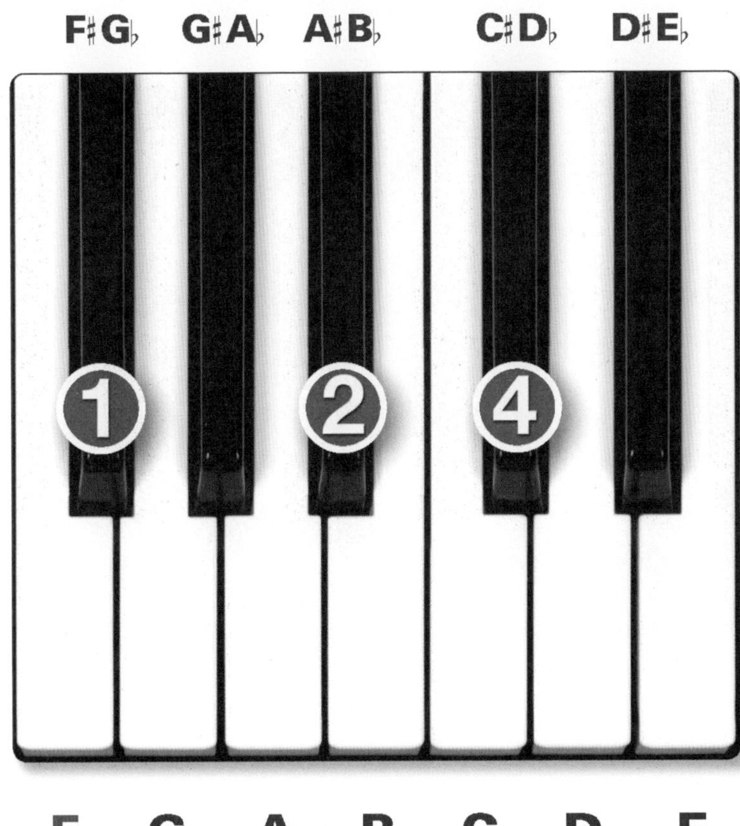

F G A B C D E

1 = thumb 2 = index finger 3 = middle finger 4 = ring finger 5 = little finger

Chord Spelling

1st (E♭), ♭3rd (G♭), 5th (B♭), ♭7th (D♭)

FREE ACCESS on smartphones including iPhone & Android  Using any QR code app scan and **HEAR** the chord

A
A♯/B♭
B
C
C♯/D♭
D
D♯/E♭
E
F
F♯/G♭
G
G♯/A♭

D♯/E♭maj9

Major 9th

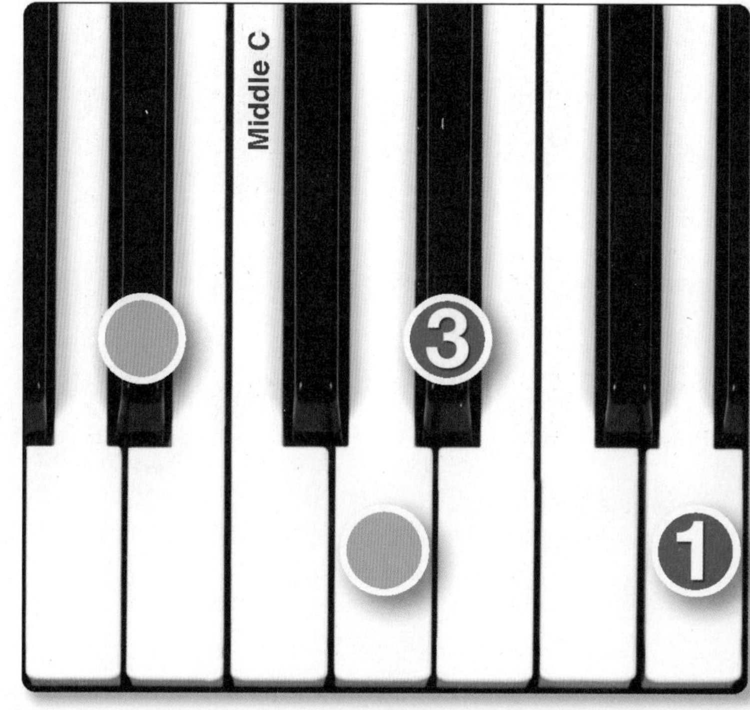

5 = little finger 4 = ring finger 3 = middle finger 2 = index finger 1 = thumb

Chord Spelling

1st (E♭), 3rd (G), 5th (B♭), 7th (D), 9th (F)

FREE ACCESS on smartphones including iPhone & Android

Using any QR code app scan and **HEAR** the chord

D♯/E♭maj9

Major 9th

Right Hand

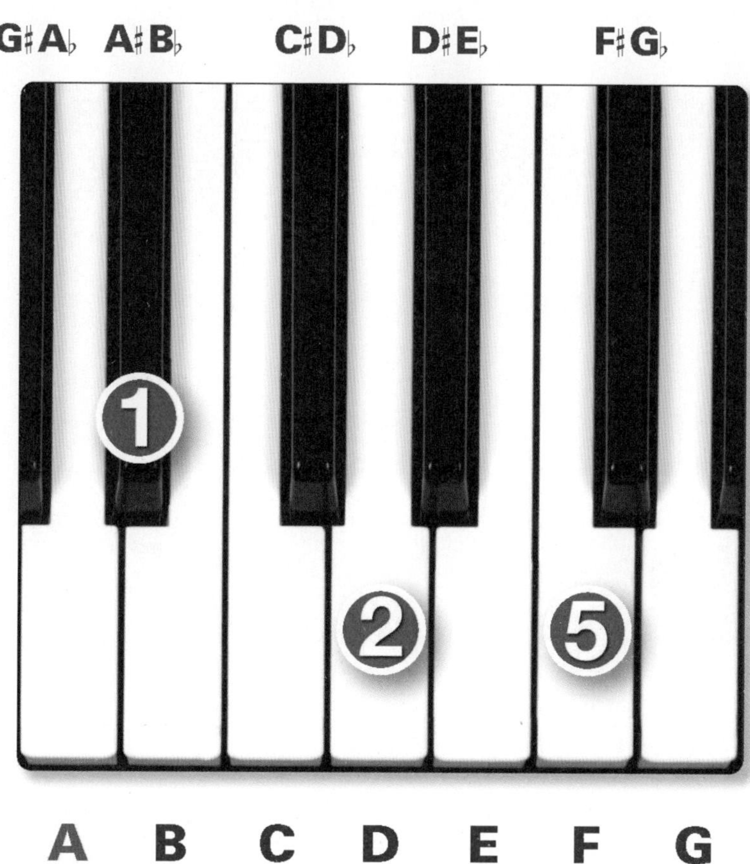

1 = thumb 2 = index finger 3 = middle finger 4 = ring finger 5 = little finger

Chord Spelling

1st (E♭), 3rd (G), 5th (B♭), 7th (D), 9th (F)

FREE ACCESS on smartphones including iPhone & Android

Using any QR code app scan and **HEAR** the chord

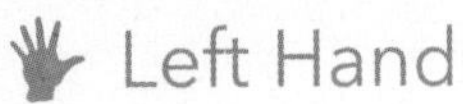

D♯/E♭m9

Minor 9th

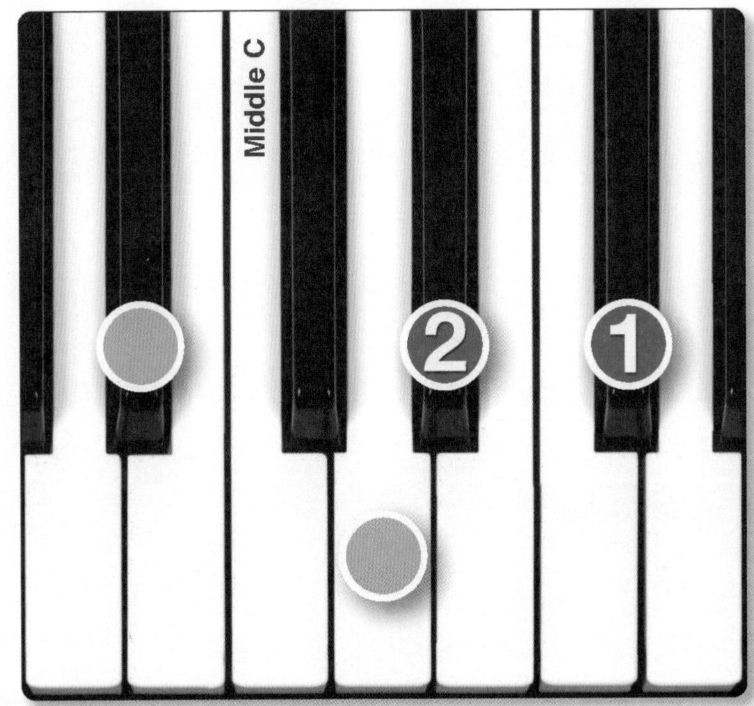

5 = little finger 4 = ring finger 3 = middle finger 2 = index finger 1 = thumb

Chord Spelling

1st (E♭), ♭3rd (G♭), 5th (B♭), ♭7th (D♭), 9th (F)

FREE ACCESS on smartphones including iPhone & Android

Using any QR code app scan and **HEAR** the chord

D♯/E♭m9
Minor 9th

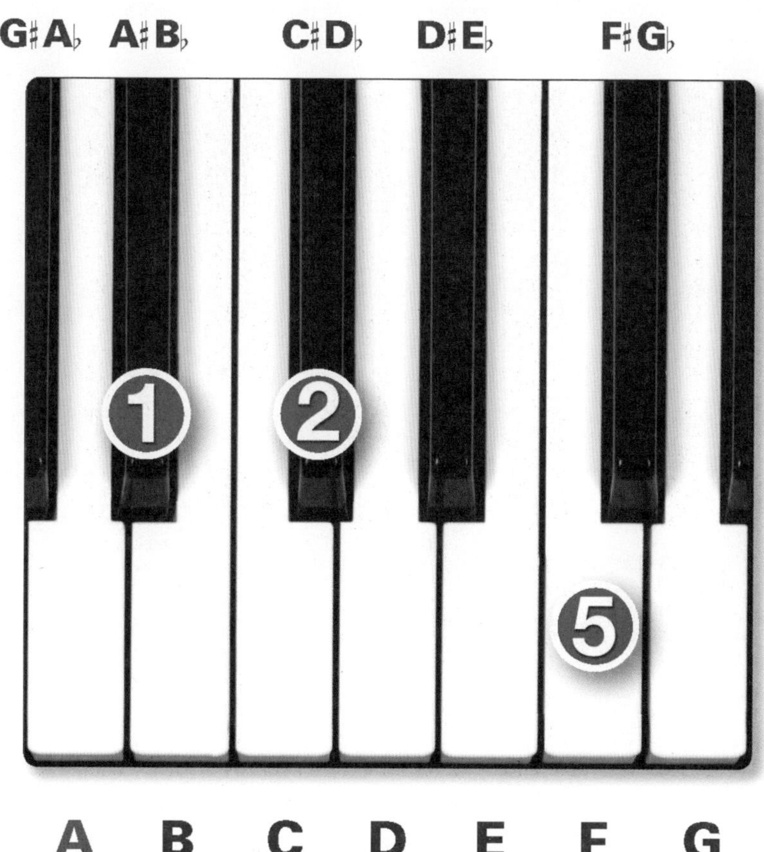

1 = thumb 2 = index finger 3 = middle finger 4 = ring finger 5 = little finger

Chord Spelling

1st (E♭), ♭3rd (G♭), 5th (B♭), ♭7th (D♭), 9th (F)

FREE ACCESS on smartphones including iPhone & Android

Using any QR code app scan and **HEAR** the chord

E
Major

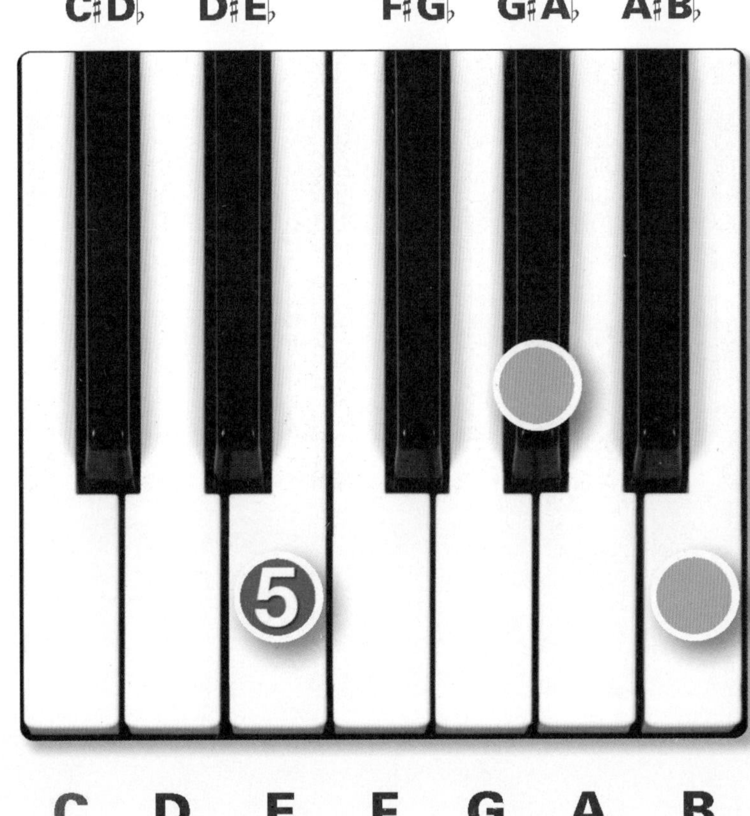

5 = little finger 4 = ring finger 3 = middle finger 2 = index finger 1 = thumb

Chord Spelling

1st (E), 3rd (G♯), 5th (B)

FREE ACCESS on smartphones including iPhone & Android  Using any QR code app scan and **HEAR** the chord

E
Major

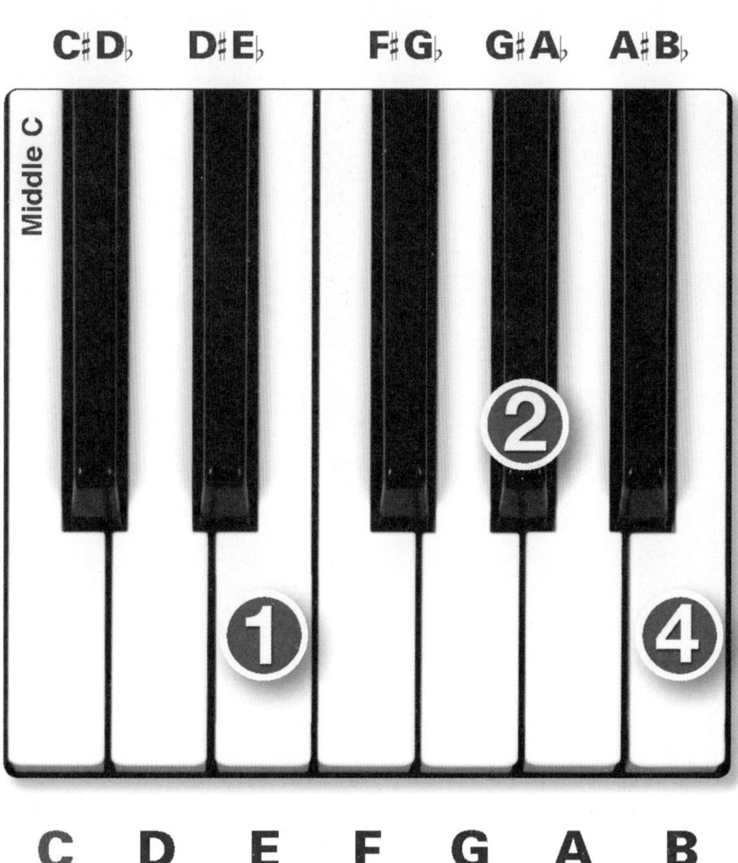

1 = thumb 2 = index finger 3 = middle finger 4 = ring finger 5 = little finger

Chord Spelling

1st (E), 3rd (G♯), 5th (B)

FREE ACCESS on smartphones including iPhone & Android

Using any QR code app scan and **HEAR** the chord

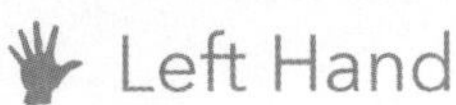

A
A♯/B♭
B
C
C♯/D♭
D
D♯/E♭
E
F
F♯/G♭
G
G♯/A♭

Em

Minor

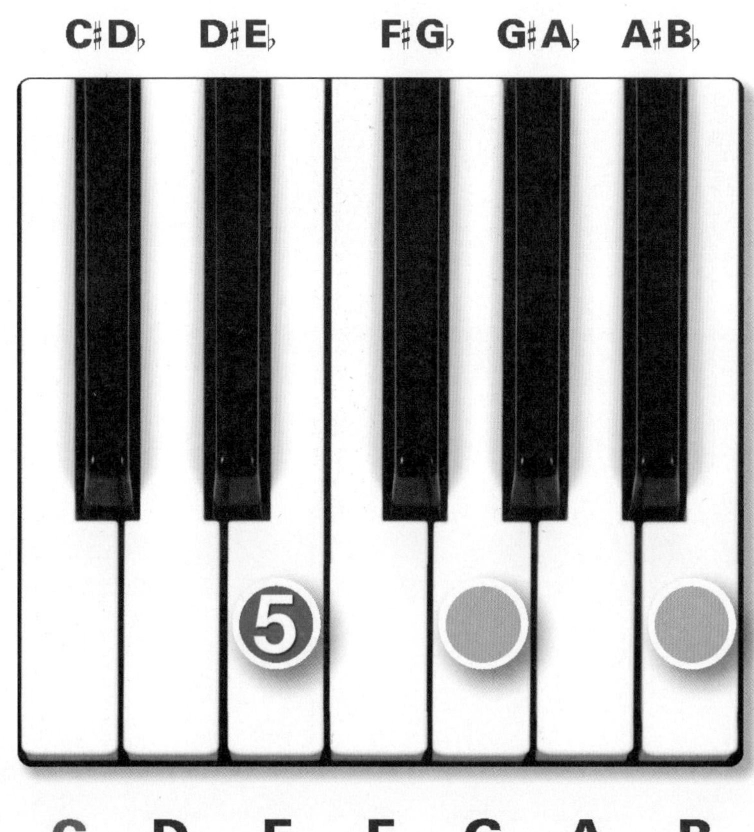

5 = little finger   4 = ring finger   3 = middle finger   2 = index finger   1 = thumb

Chord Spelling

1st (E), ♭3rd (G), 5th (B)

FREE ACCESS on smartphones including iPhone & Android

Using any QR code app scan and **HEAR** the chord

Em

Minor

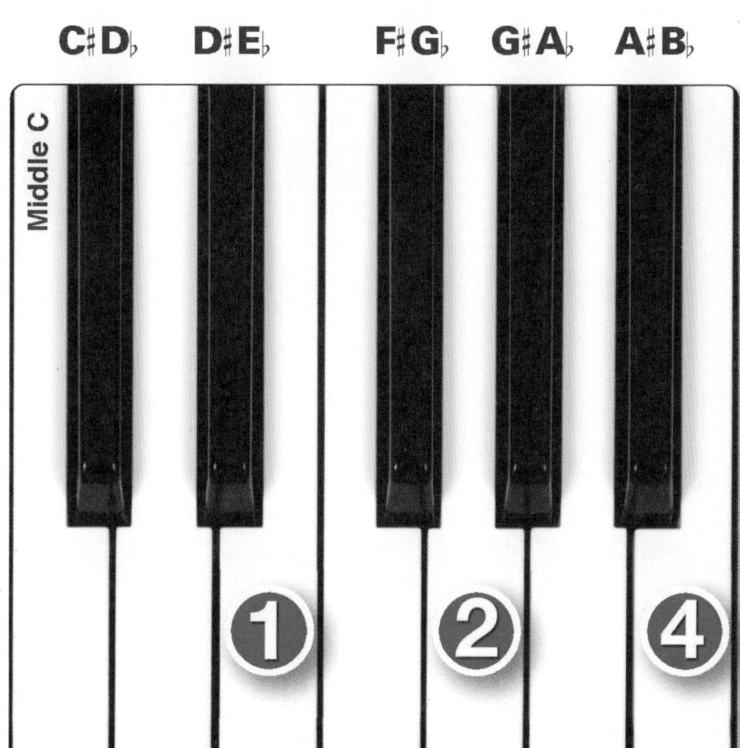

C D E F G A B

1 = thumb 2 = index finger 3 = middle finger 4 = ring finger 5 = little finger

Chord Spelling

1st (E), ♭3rd (G), 5th (B)

A
A♯/B♭
B
C
C♯/D♭
D
D♯/E♭
E
F
F♯/G♭
G
G♯/A♭

E+

Augmented Triad

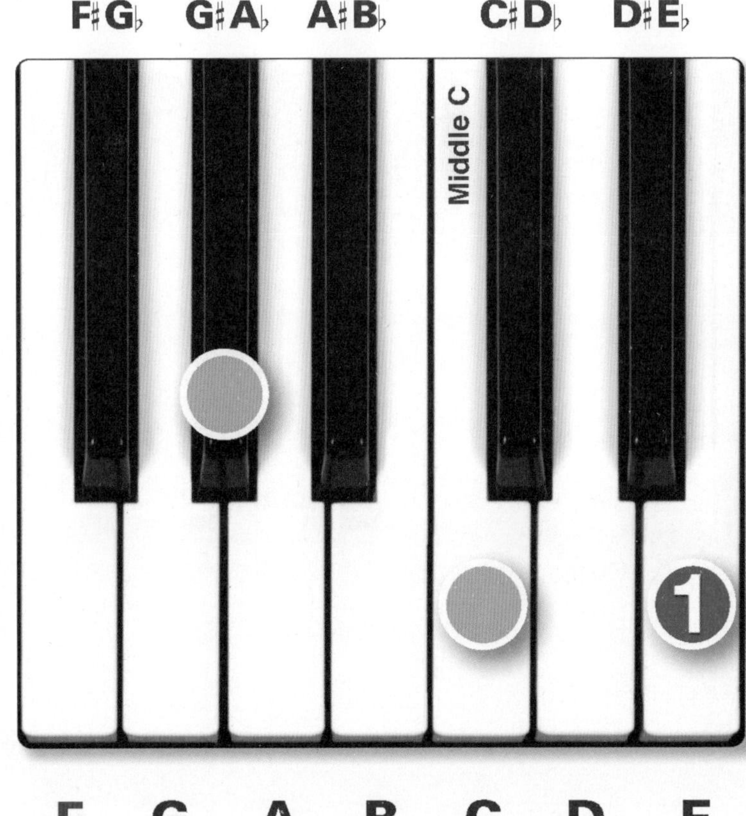

5 = little finger 4 = ring finger 3 = middle finger 2 = index finger 1 = thumb

Chord Spelling

1st (E), 3rd (G♯), ♯5th (B♯)

FREE ACCESS on smartphones including iPhone & Android

Using any QR code app scan and **HEAR** the chord

E+

Augmented Triad

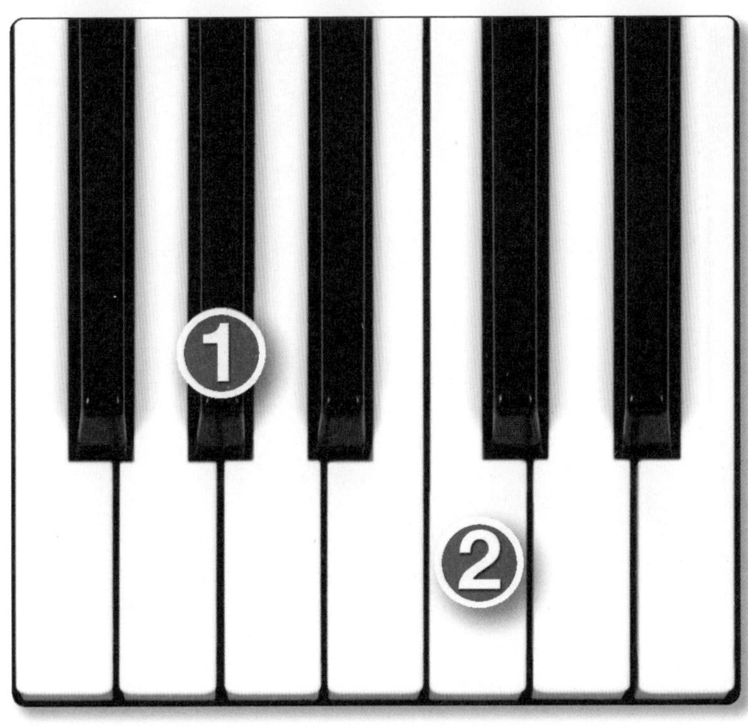

1 = thumb 2 = index finger 3 = middle finger 4 = ring finger 5 = little finger

Chord Spelling

1st (E), 3rd (G♯), ♯5th (B♯)

FREE ACCESS on smartphones including iPhone & Android

Using any QR code app scan and **HEAR** the chord

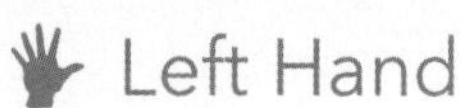

E°

Diminished Triad

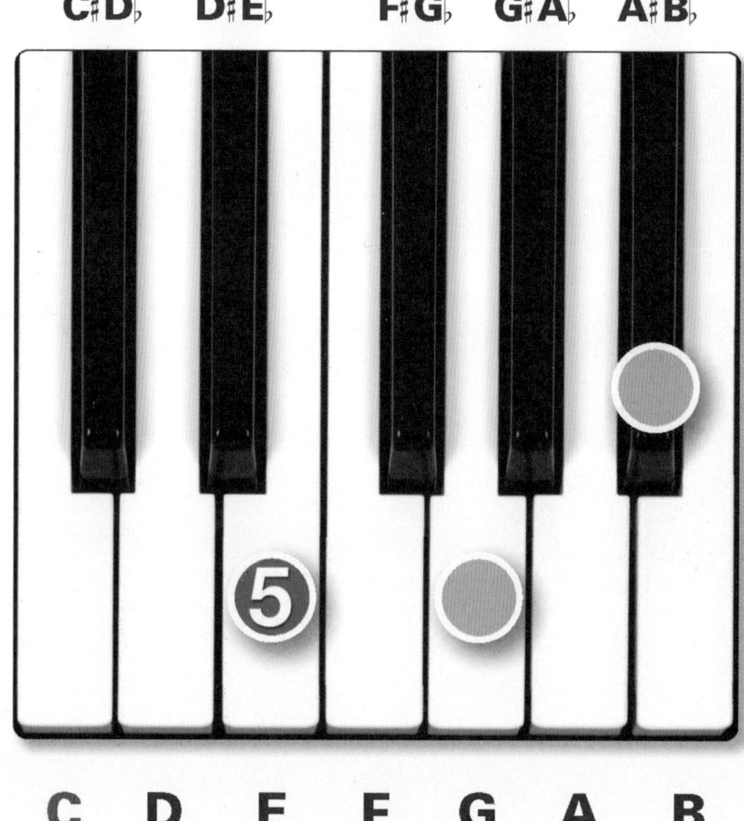

5 = little finger   4 = ring finger   3 = middle finger   2 = index finger   1 = thumb

Chord Spelling

1st (E), ♭3rd (G), ♭5th (B♭)

FREE ACCESS on smartphones including iPhone & Android

Using any QR code app scan and **HEAR** the chord

E°

Diminished Triad

C♯D♭ D♯E♭ F♯G♭ G♯A♭ A♯B♭

1 2

C D E F G A B

1 = thumb 2 = index finger 3 = middle finger 4 = ring finger 5 = little finger

Chord Spelling

1st (E), ♭3rd (G), ♭5th (B♭)

FREE ACCESS on smartphones including iPhone & Android

Using any QR code app scan and **HEAR** the chord

E6

Major 6th

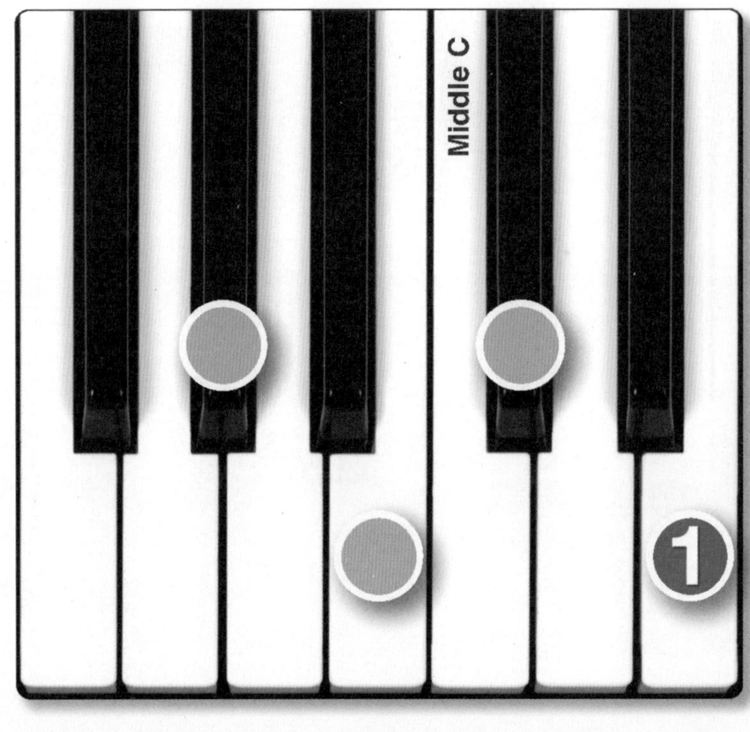

5 = little finger 4 = ring finger 3 = middle finger 2 = index finger 1 = thumb

Chord Spelling

1st (E), 3rd (G♯), 5th (B), 6th (C♯)

FREE ACCESS on smartphones including iPhone & Android

Using any QR code app scan and **HEAR** the chord

E6

Major 6th

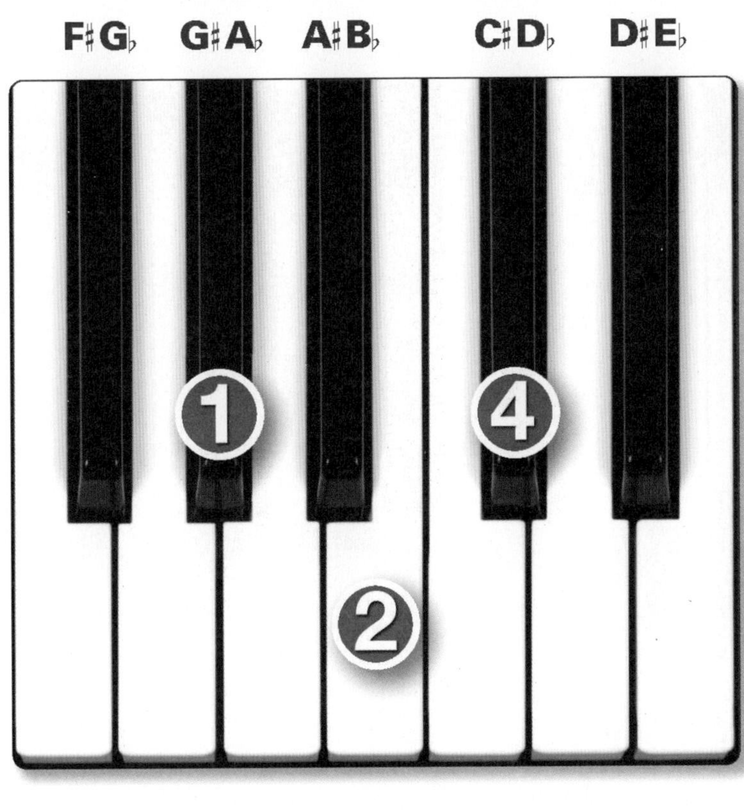

1 = thumb 2 = index finger 3 = middle finger 4 = ring finger 5 = little finger

Chord Spelling

1st (E), 3rd (G♯), 5th (B), 6th (C♯)

FREE ACCESS on smartphones including iPhone & Android  Using any QR code app scan and **HEAR** the chord

Em6

Minor 6th

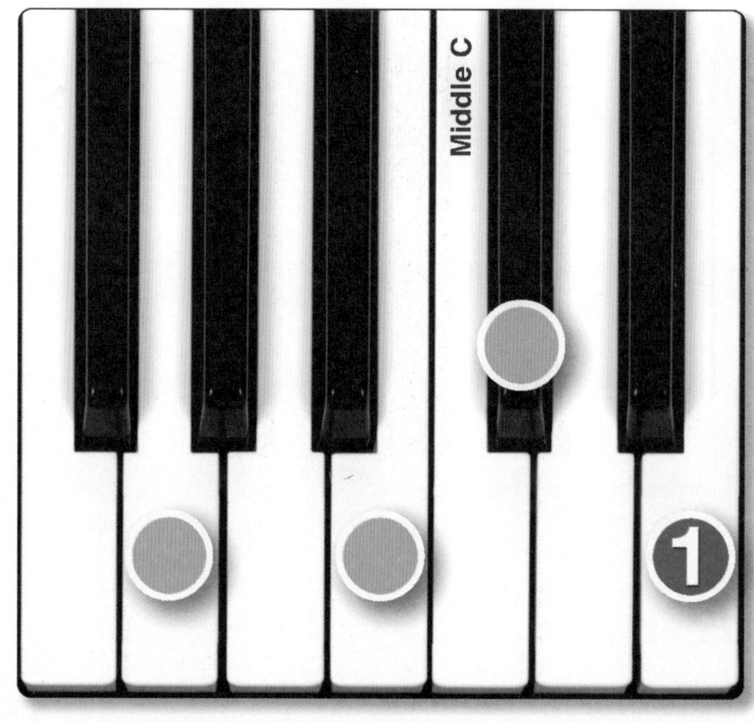

5 = little finger 4 = ring finger 3 = middle finger 2 = index finger 1 = thumb

Chord Spelling

1st (E), ♭3rd (G), 5th (B), 6th (C♯)

FREE ACCESS on smartphones including iPhone & Android

Using any QR code app scan and **HEAR** the chord

Right Hand 

Em6

Minor 6th

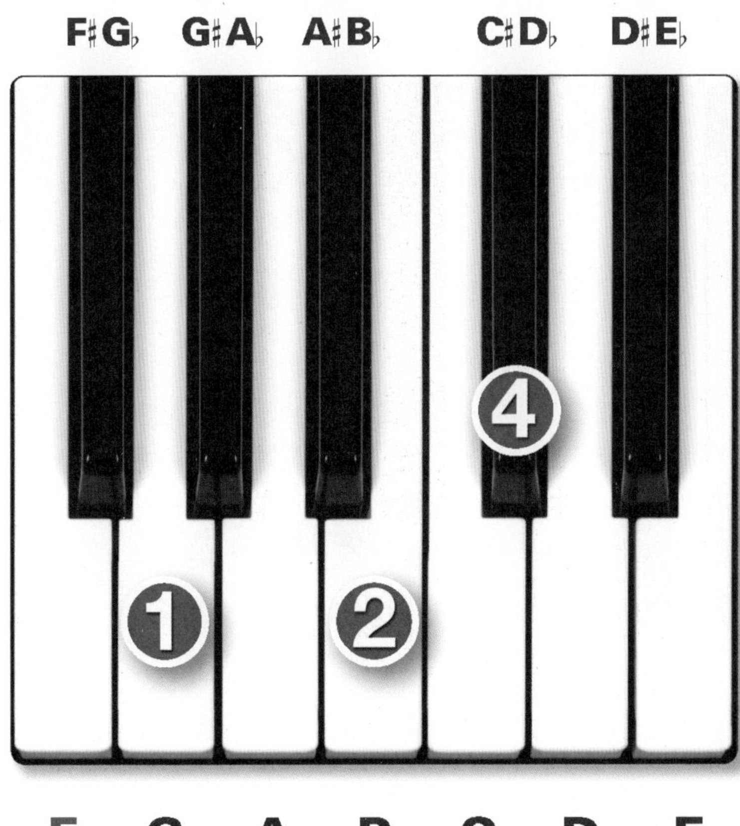

1 = thumb 2 = index finger 3 = middle finger 4 = ring finger 5 = little finger

Chord Spelling

1st (E), ♭3rd (G), 5th (B), 6th (C♯)

FREE ACCESS on smartphones including iPhone & Android

Using any QR code app scan and **HEAR** the chord

A

A♯/B♭

B

C

C♯/D♭

D

D♯/E♭

E

F

F♯/G♭

G

G♯/A♭

Emaj7

Major 7th

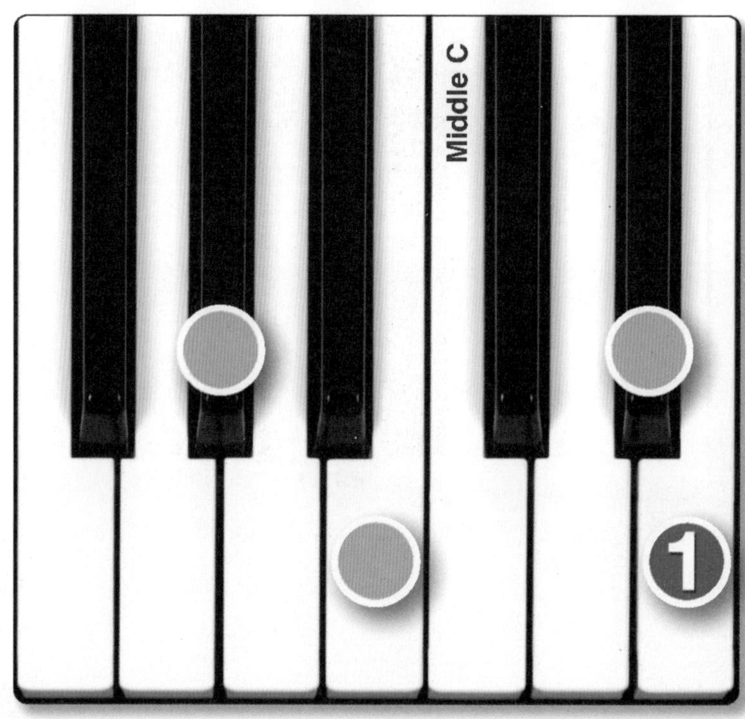

5 = little finger 4 = ring finger 3 = middle finger 2 = index finger 1 = thumb

Chord Spelling

1st (E), 3rd (G♯), 5th (B), 7th (D♯)

FREE ACCESS on smartphones including iPhone & Android

Using any QR code app scan and **HEAR** the chord

Emaj7
Major 7th

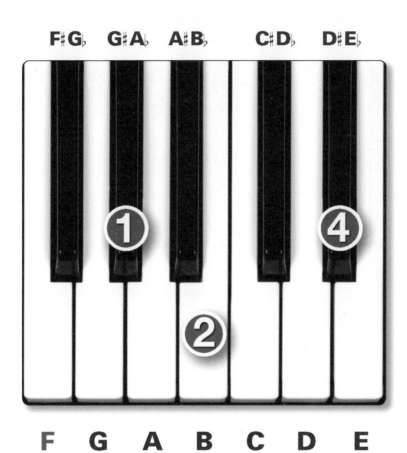

F♯G♭ G♯A♭ A♯B♭ C♯D♭ D♯E♭

1 4

2

F G A B C D E

1 = thumb 2 = index finger 3 = middle finger 4 = ring finger 5 = little finger

Chord Spelling

1st (E), 3rd (G♯), 5th (B), 7th (D♯)

FREE ACCESS on smartphones including iPhone & Android  Using any QR code app scan and **HEAR** the chord

Em7

Minor 7th

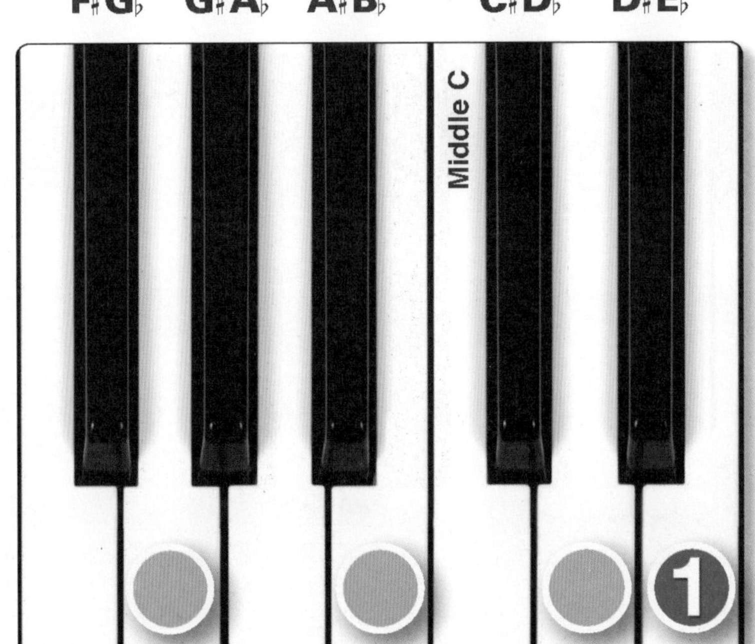

5 = little finger 4 = ring finger 3 = middle finger 2 = index finger 1 = thumb

Chord Spelling

1st (E), ♭3rd (G), 5th (B), ♭7th (D)

FREE ACCESS on smartphones including iPhone & Android

Using any QR code app scan and **HEAR** the chord

Em7

Minor 7th

Right Hand

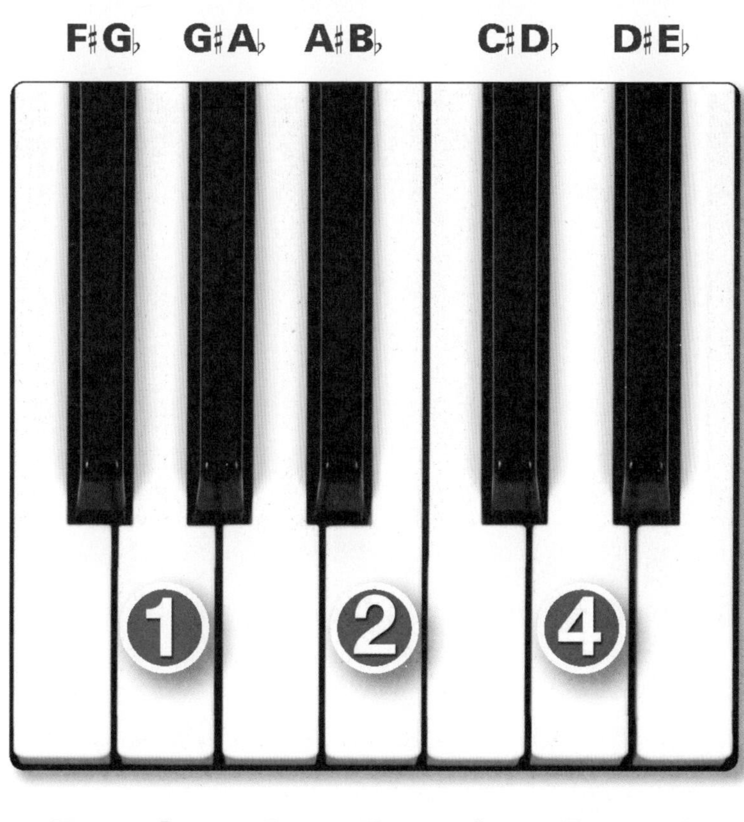

1 = thumb 2 = index finger 3 = middle finger 4 = ring finger 5 = little finger

Chord Spelling

1st (E), ♭3rd (G), 5th (B), ♭7th (D)

FREE ACCESS on smartphones including iPhone & Android

Using any QR code app scan and **HEAR** the chord

A
A♯/B♭
B
C
C♯/D♭
D
D♯/E♭
E
F
F♯/G♭
G
G♯/A♭

Emaj9
Major 9th

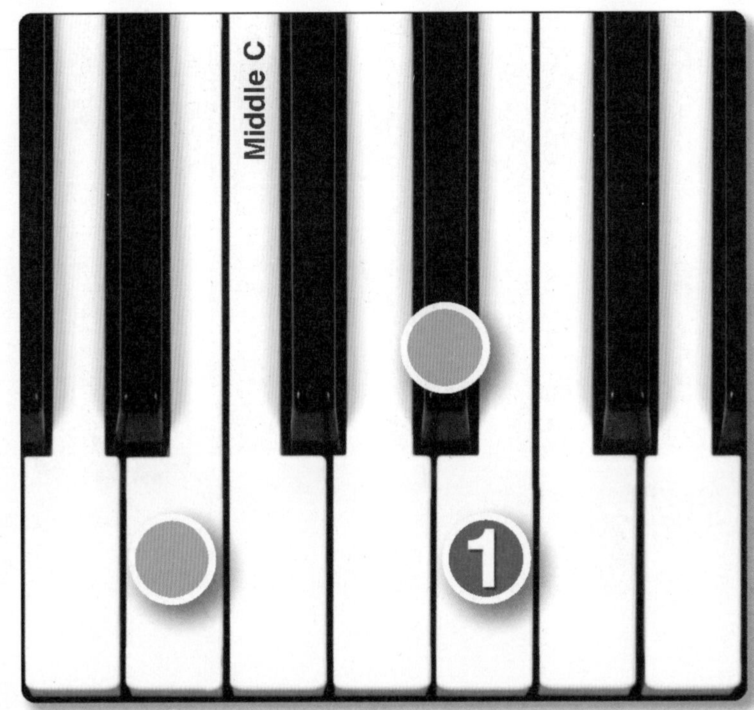

5 = little finger 4 = ring finger 3 = middle finger 2 = index finger 1 = thumb

Chord Spelling

1st (E), 3rd (G♯), 5th (B), 7th (D♯), 9th (F♯)

FREE ACCESS on smartphones including iPhone & Android

Using any QR code app scan and **HEAR** the chord

Emaj9

Major 9th

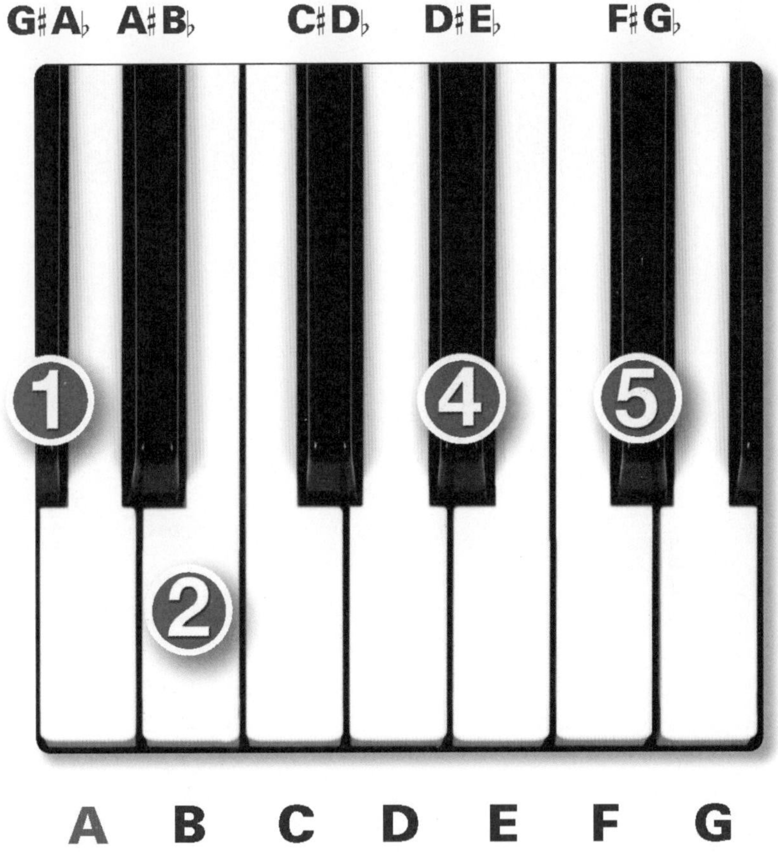

G♯A♭ A♯B♭ C♯D♭ D♯E♭ F♯G♭

A B C D E F G

1 = thumb 2 = index finger 3 = middle finger 4 = ring finger 5 = little finger

Chord Spelling

1st (E), 3rd (G♯), 5th (B), 7th (D♯), 9th (F♯)

FREE ACCESS on smartphones including iPhone & Android

Using any QR code app scan and **HEAR** the chord

A
A♯/B♭
B
C
C♯/D♭
D
D♯/E♭
E
F
F♯/G♭
G
G♯/A♭

Em9

Minor 9th

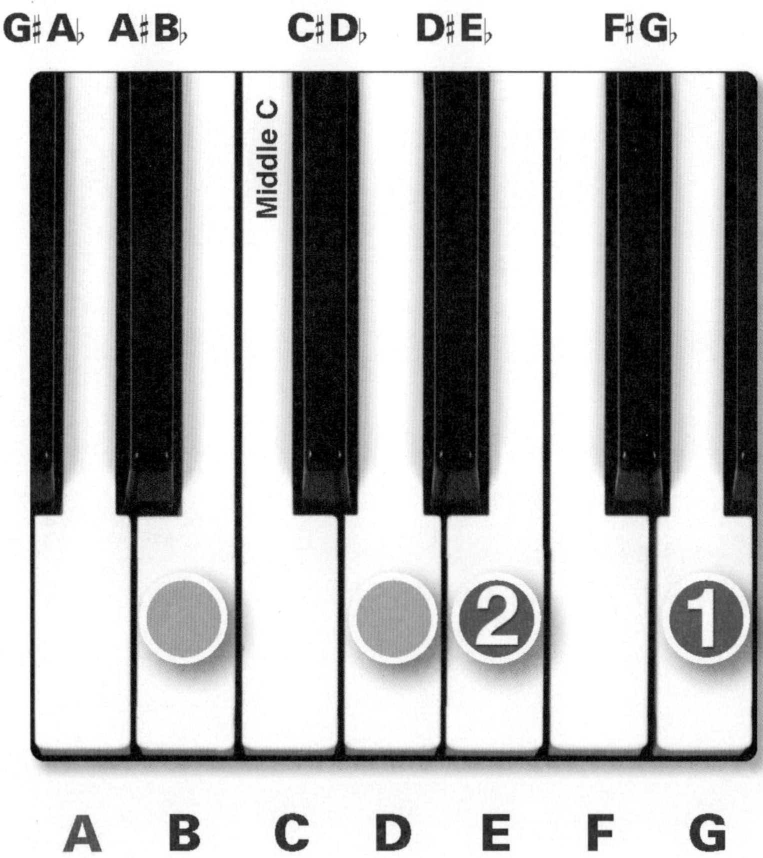

5 = little finger 4 = ring finger 3 = middle finger 2 = index finger 1 = thumb

Chord Spelling

1st (E), ♭3rd (G), 5th (B), ♭7th (D), 9th (F♯)

FREE ACCESS on smartphones including iPhone & Android  Using any QR code app scan and **HEAR** the chord

Em9

Minor 9th

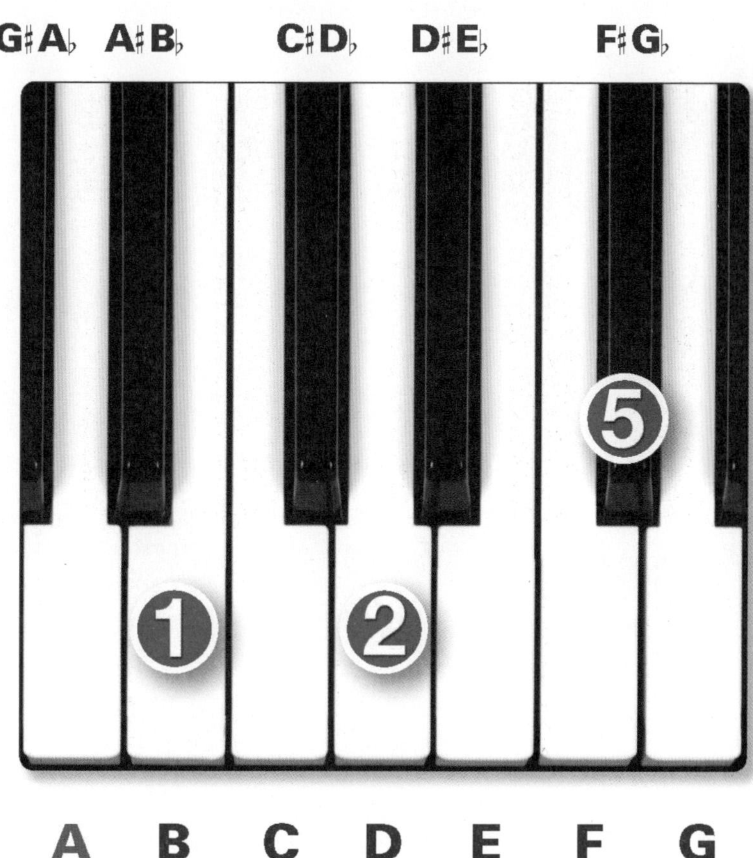

1 = thumb 2 = index finger 3 = middle finger 4 = ring finger 5 = little finger

Chord Spelling

1st (E), ♭3rd (G), 5th (B), ♭7th (D), 9th (F♯)

FREE ACCESS on smartphones including iPhone & Android  Using any QR code app scan and **HEAR** the chord

F
Major

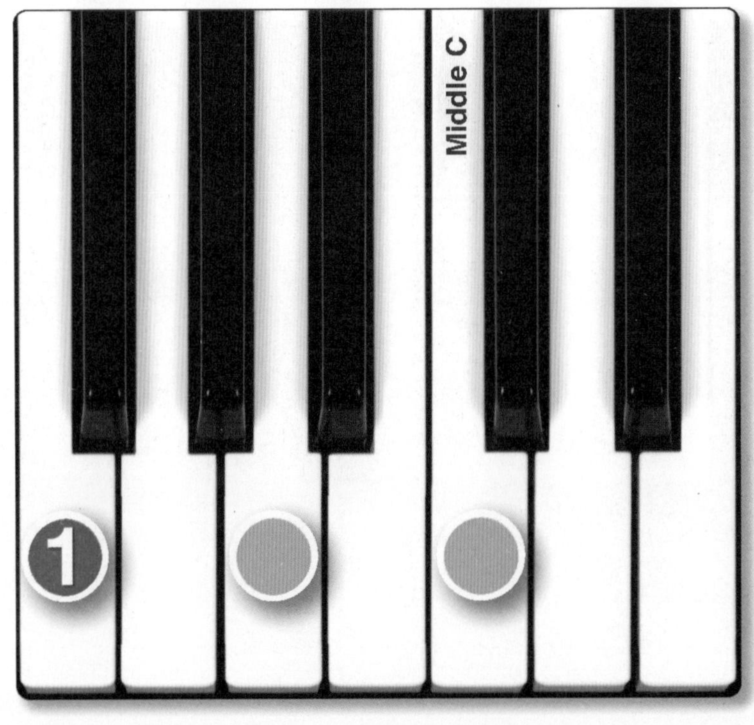

5 = little finger 4 = ring finger 3 = middle finger 2 = index finger 1 = thumb

Chord Spelling

1st (F), 3rd (A), 5th (C)

FREE ACCESS on smartphones including iPhone & Android

Using any QR code app scan and **HEAR** the chord

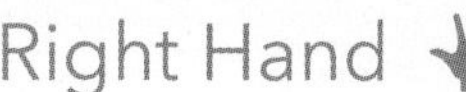

F
Major

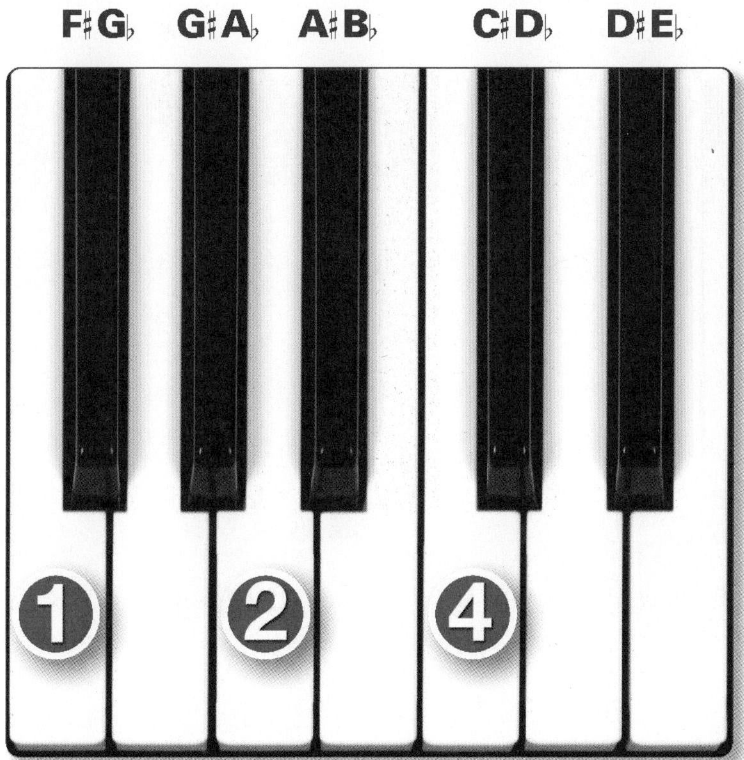

1 = thumb 2 = index finger 3 = middle finger 4 = ring finger 5 = little finger

Chord Spelling

1st (F), 3rd (A), 5th (C)

FREE ACCESS on smartphones including iPhone & Android

Using any QR code app scan and **HEAR** the chord

Fm

Minor

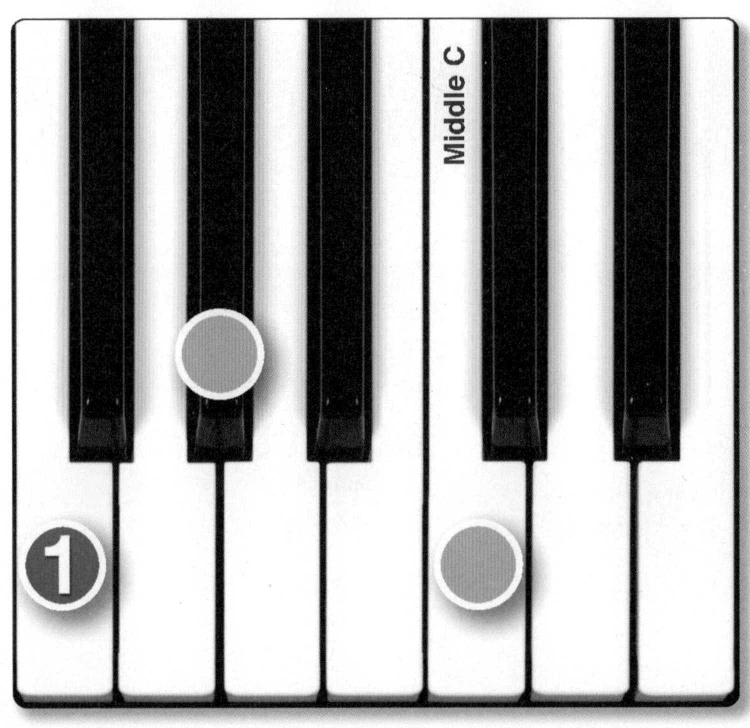

5 = little finger 4 = ring finger 3 = middle finger 2 = index finger 1 = thumb

Chord Spelling

1st (F), ♭3rd (A♭), 5th (C)

FREE ACCESS on smartphones including iPhone & Android

Using any QR code app scan and **HEAR** the chord

Fm
Minor

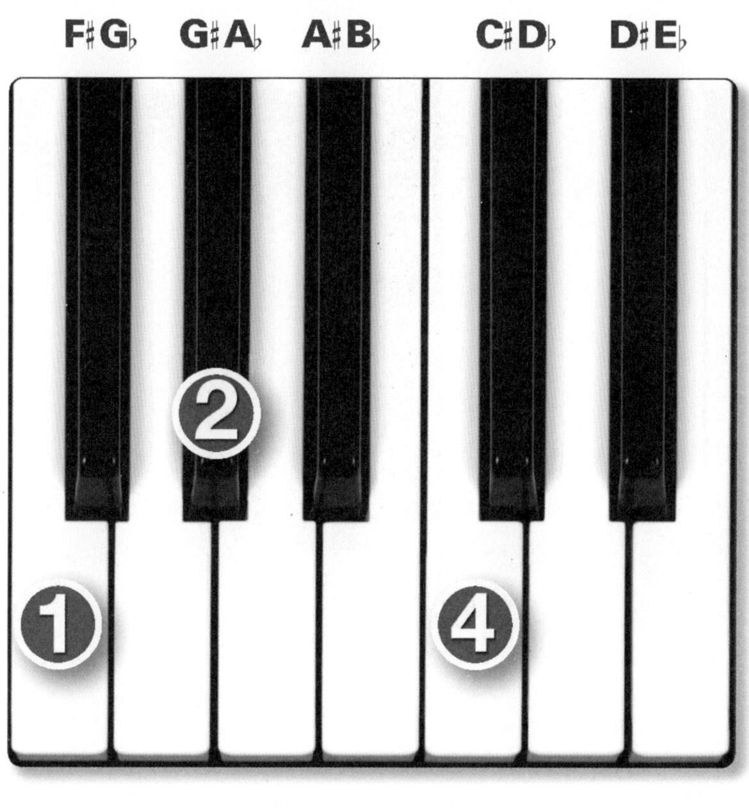

1 = thumb 2 = index finger 3 = middle finger 4 = ring finger 5 = little finger

Chord Spelling

1st (F), ♭3rd (A♭), 5th (C)

FREE ACCESS on smartphones including iPhone & Android

Using any QR code app scan and **HEAR** the chord

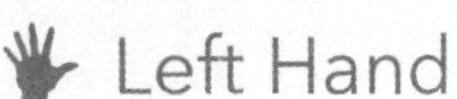

F+
Augmented Triad

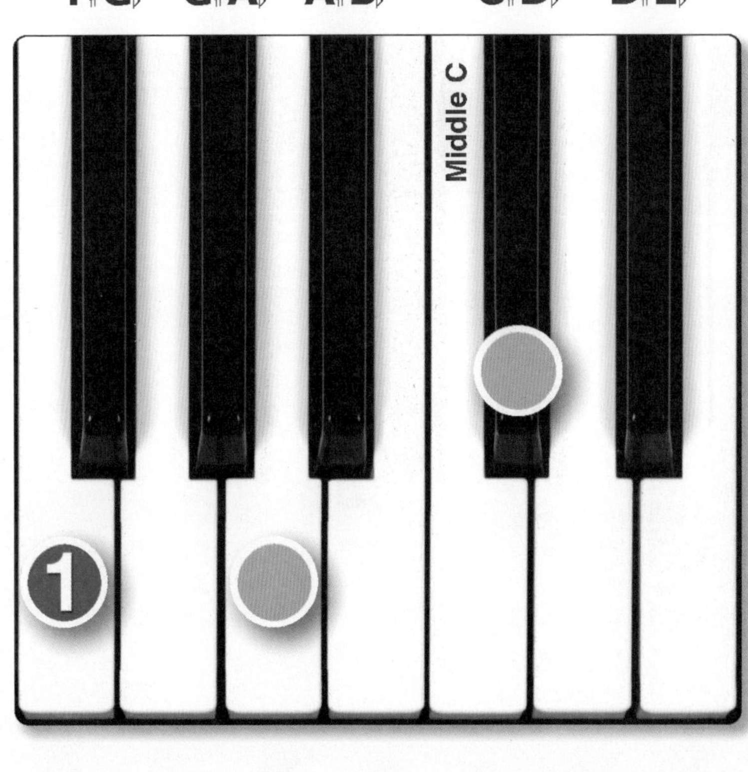

5 = little finger   4 = ring finger   3 = middle finger   2 = index finger   1 = thumb

Chord Spelling

1st (F), 3rd (A), ♯5th (C♯)

FREE ACCESS on smartphones including iPhone & Android  Using any QR code app scan and **HEAR** the chord

F+

Augmented Triad

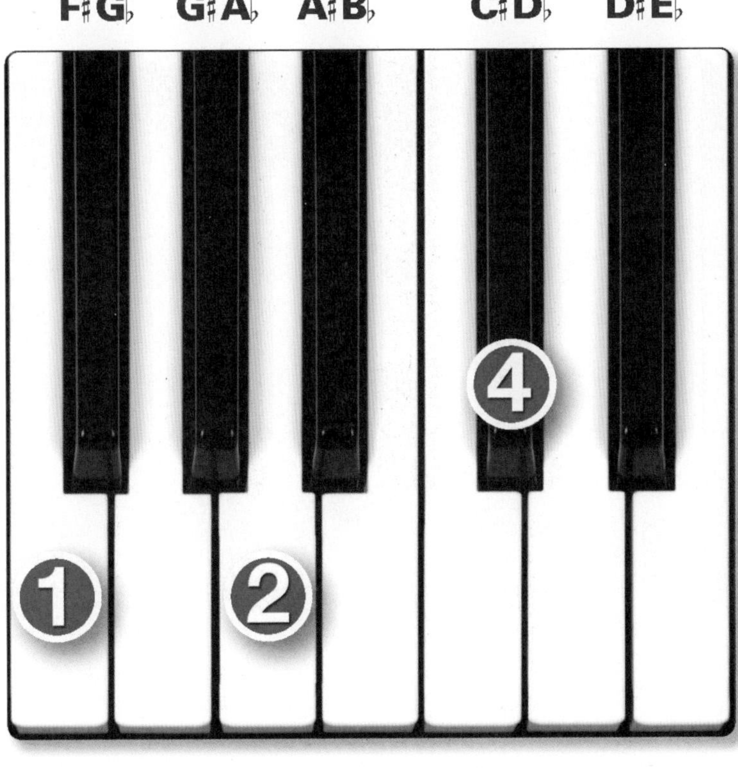

1 = thumb 2 = index finger 3 = middle finger 4 = ring finger 5 = little finger

Chord Spelling

1st (F), 3rd (A), ♯5th (C♯)

FREE ACCESS on smartphones including iPhone & Android

Using any QR code app scan and **HEAR** the chord

F°

Diminished Triad

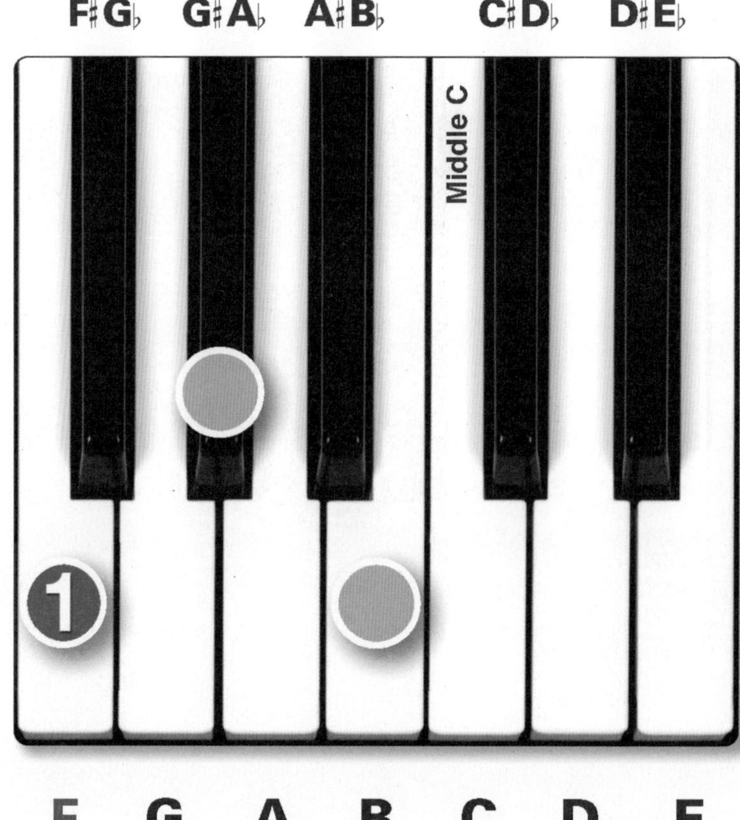

F G A B C D E

5 = little finger 4 = ring finger 3 = middle finger 2 = index finger 1 = thumb

Chord Spelling

1st (F), ♭3rd (A♭), ♭5th (C♭)

FREE ACCESS on smartphones including iPhone & Android

Using any QR code app scan and **HEAR** the chord

F°

Diminished Triad

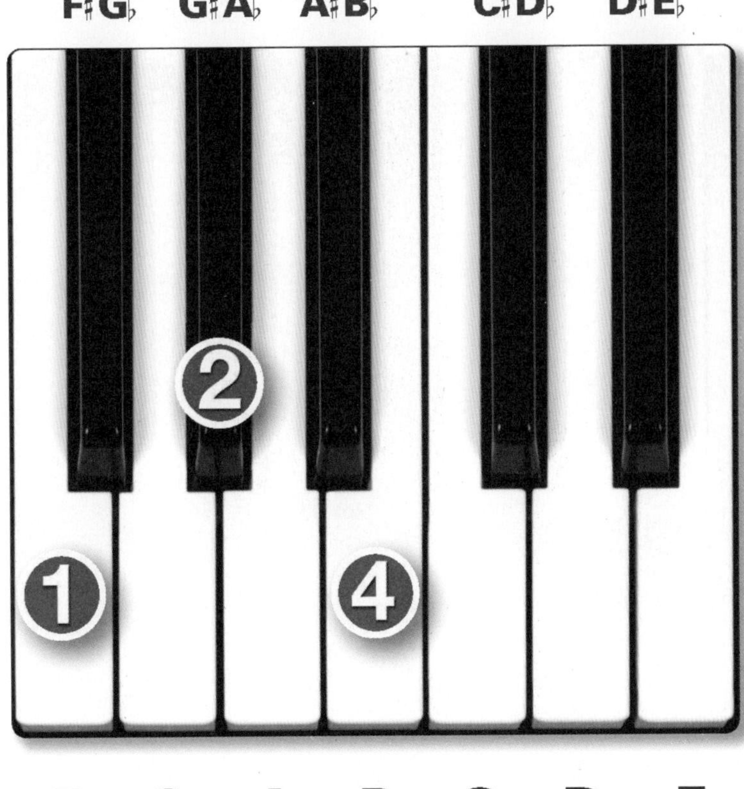

1 = thumb 2 = index finger 3 = middle finger 4 = ring finger 5 = little finger

Chord Spelling

1st (F), ♭3rd (A♭), ♭5th (C♭)

FREE ACCESS on smartphones including iPhone & Android  Using any QR code app scan and **HEAR** the chord

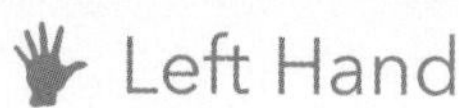

F6

Major 6th

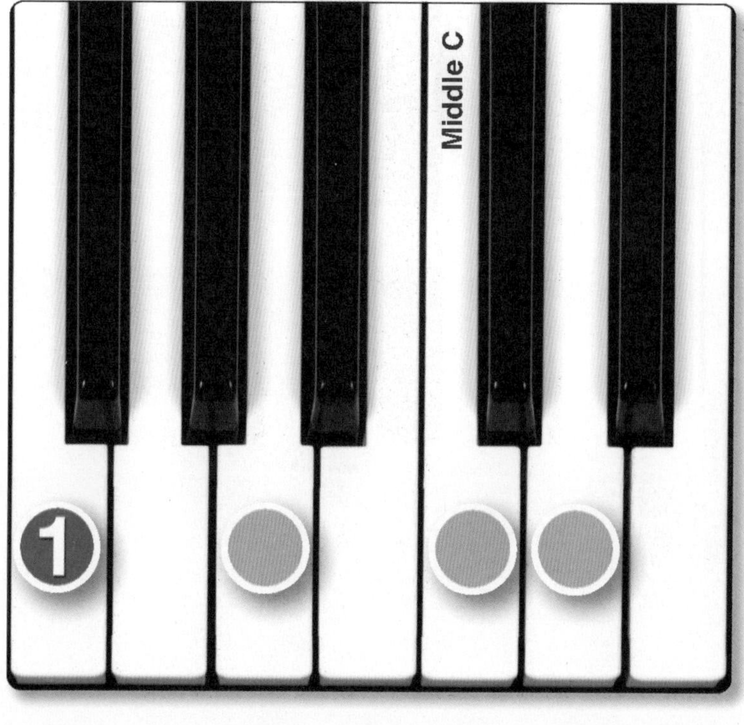

5 = little finger 4 = ring finger 3 = middle finger 2 = index finger 1 = thumb

Chord Spelling

1st (F), 3rd (A), 5th (C), 6th (D)

FREE ACCESS on smartphones including iPhone & Android

Using any QR code app scan and **HEAR** the chord

F6

Major 6th

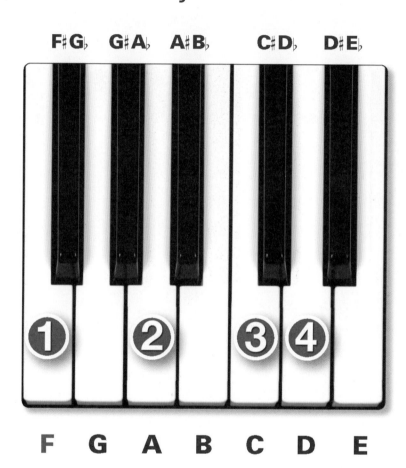

F♯G♭ G♯A♭ A♯B♭ C♯D♭ D♯E♭

1 2 3 4

F G A B C D E

1 = thumb 2 = index finger 3 = middle finger 4 = ring finger 5 = little finger

Chord Spelling

1st (F), 3rd (A), 5th (C), 6th (D)

FREE ACCESS on smartphones including iPhone & Android

Using any QR code app scan and **HEAR** the chord

Fm6

Minor 6th

F♯G♭ G♯A♭ A♯B♭ C♯D♭ D♯E♭

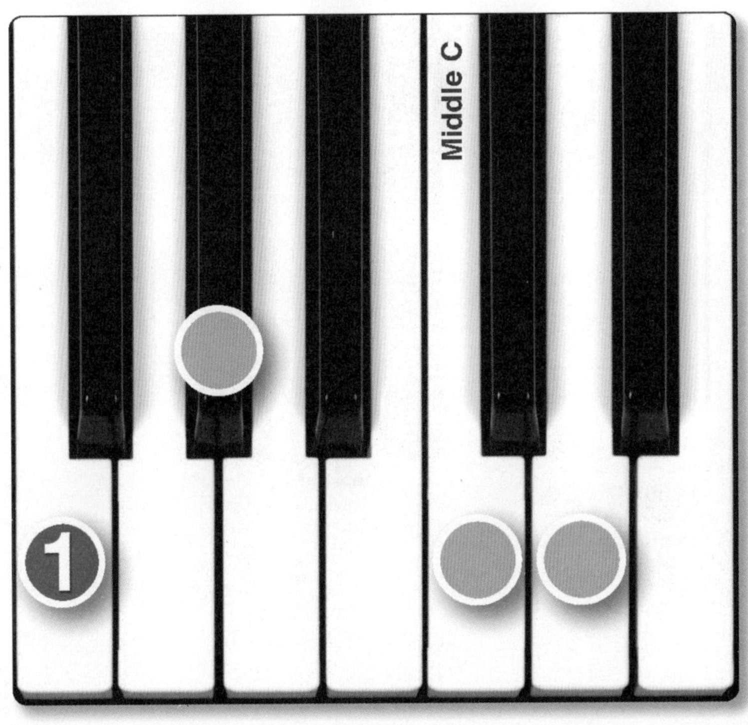

F G A B C D E

5 = little finger 4 = ring finger 3 = middle finger 2 = index finger 1 = thumb

Chord Spelling

1st (F), ♭3rd (A♭), 5th (C), 6th (D)

FREE ACCESS on smartphones including iPhone & Android

Using any QR code app scan and **HEAR** the chord

Fm6

Minor 6th

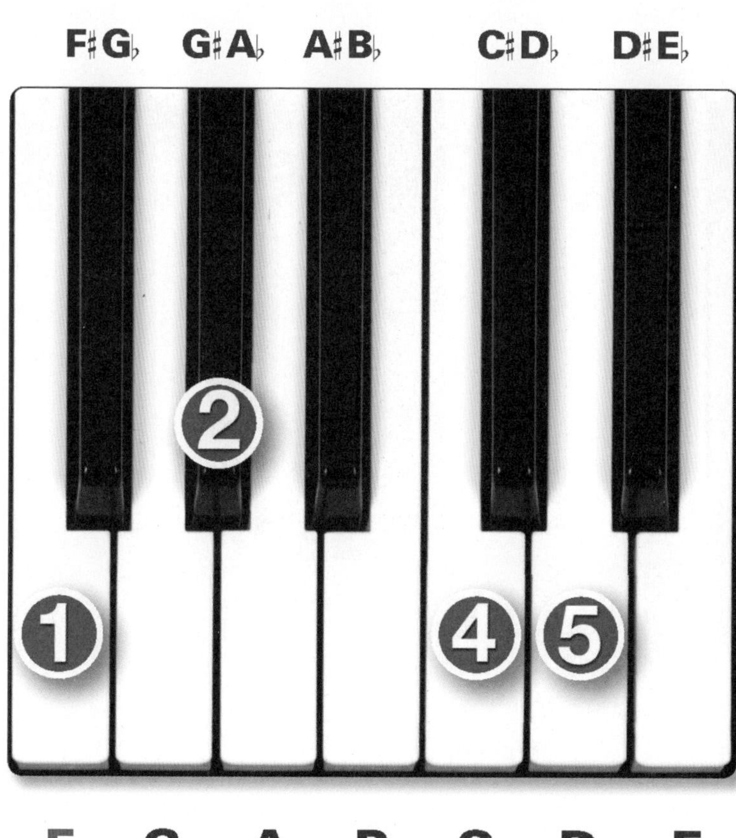

1 = thumb 2 = index finger 3 = middle finger 4 = ring finger 5 = little finger

Chord Spelling

1st (F), ♭3rd (A♭), 5th (C), 6th (D)

FREE ACCESS on smartphones including iPhone & Android

Using any QR code app scan and **HEAR** the chord

Fmaj7

Major 7th

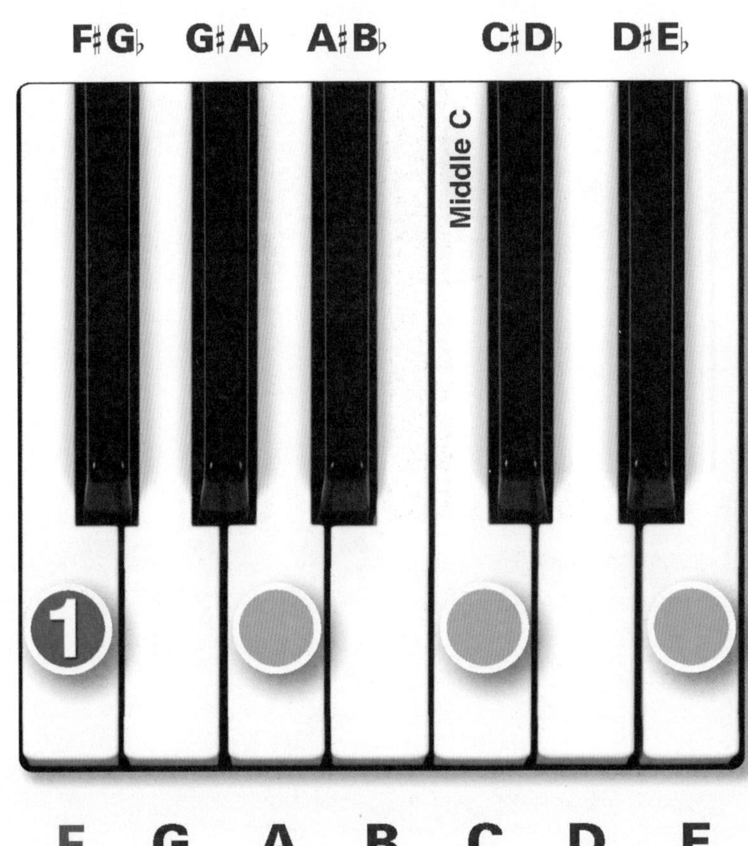

5 = little finger   4 = ring finger   3 = middle finger   2 = index finger   1 = thumb

Chord Spelling

1st (F), 3rd (A), 5th (C), 7th (E)

FREE ACCESS on smartphones including iPhone & Android

Using any QR code app scan and **HEAR** the chord

Fmaj7

Major 7th

Right Hand 

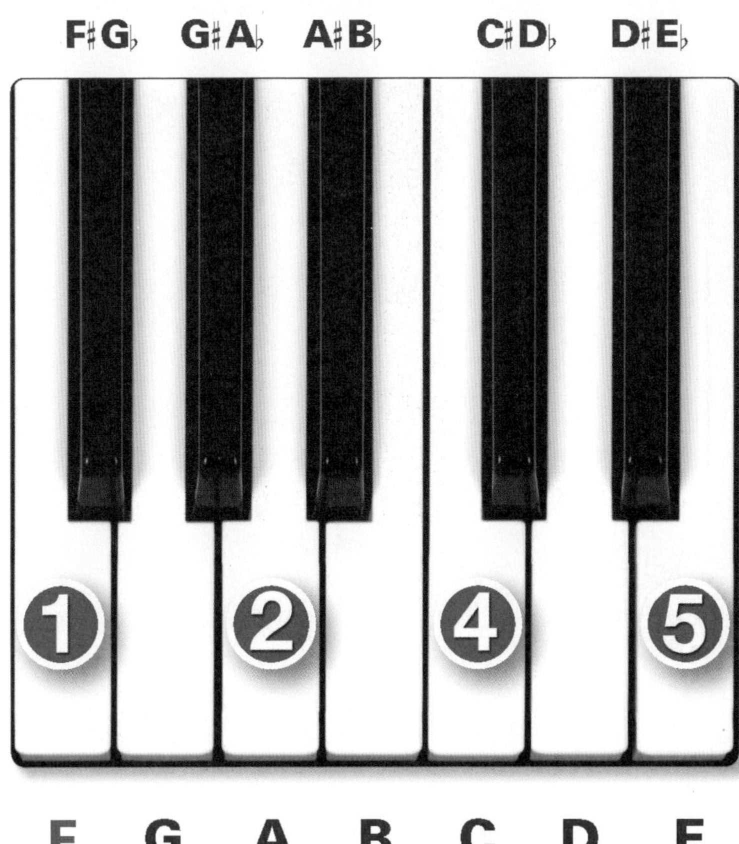

1 = thumb 2 = index finger 3 = middle finger 4 = ring finger 5 = little finger

Chord Spelling

1st (F), 3rd (A), 5th (C), 7th (E)

FREE ACCESS on smartphones including iPhone & Android  Using any QR code app scan and **HEAR** the chord

Fm7

Minor 7th

A
A♯/B♭
B
C
C♯/D♭
D
D♯/E♭
E
F
F♯/G♭
G
G♯/A♭

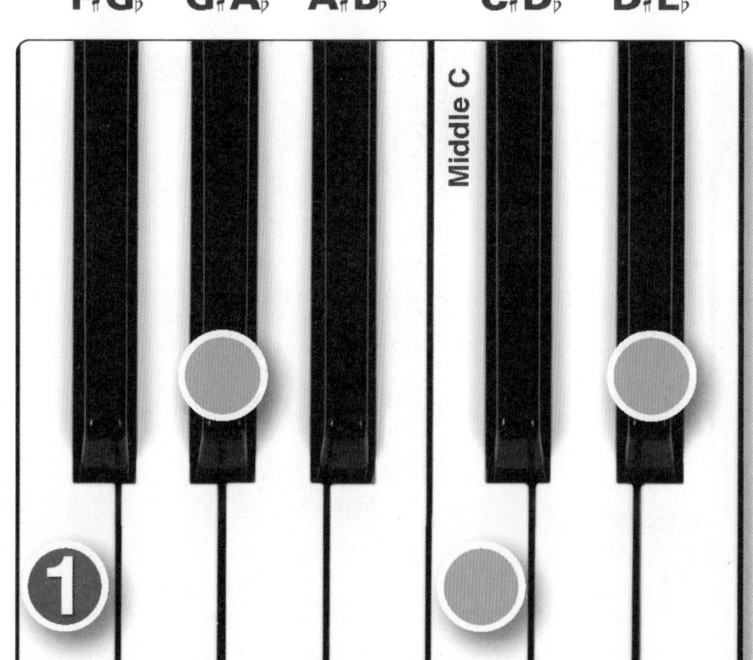

5 = little finger 4 = ring finger 3 = middle finger 2 = index finger 1 = thumb

Chord Spelling

1st (F), ♭3rd (A♭), 5th (C), ♭7th (E♭)

FREE ACCESS on smartphones including iPhone & Android  Using any QR code app scan and **HEAR** the chord

Fm7

Minor 7th

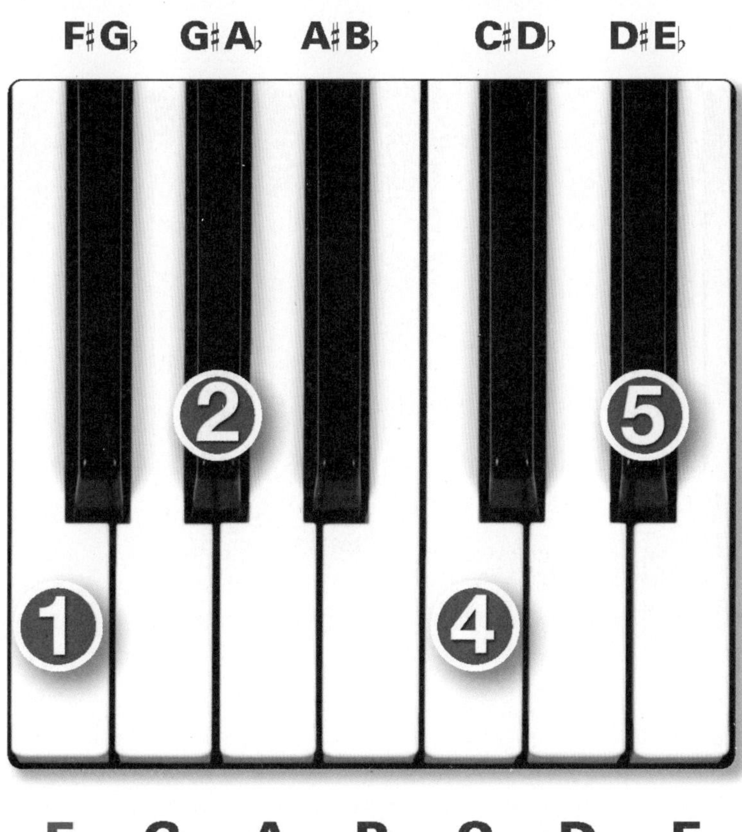

1 = thumb 2 = index finger 3 = middle finger 4 = ring finger 5 = little finger

Chord Spelling

1st (F), ♭3rd (A♭), 5th (C), ♭7th (E♭)

FREE ACCESS on smartphones including iPhone & Android

Using any QR code app scan and **HEAR** the chord

Fmaj9

Major 9th

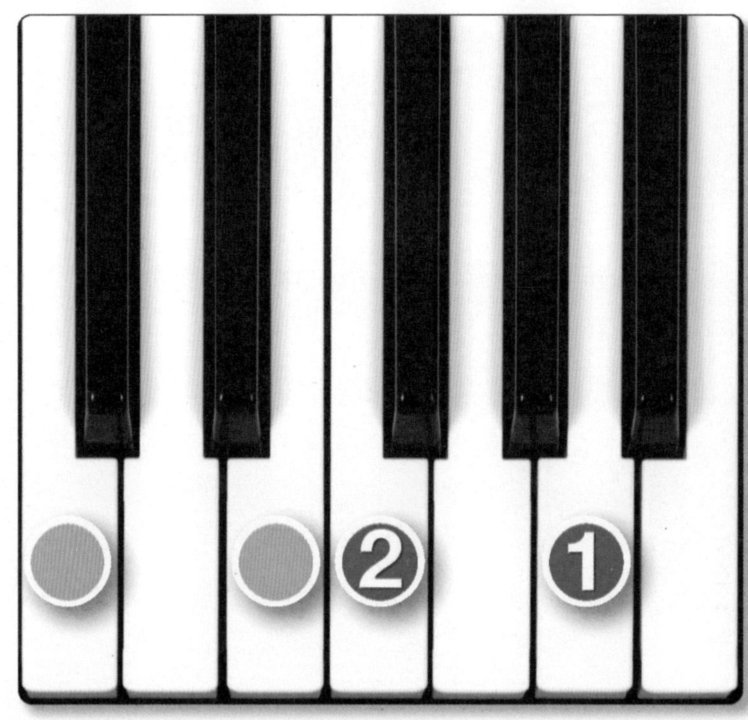

5 = little finger 4 = ring finger 3 = middle finger 2 = index finger 1 = thumb

Chord Spelling

1st (F), 3rd (A), 5th (C), 7th (E), 9th (G)

FREE ACCESS on smartphones including iPhone & Android

Using any QR code app scan and **HEAR** the chord

Fmaj9
Major 9th

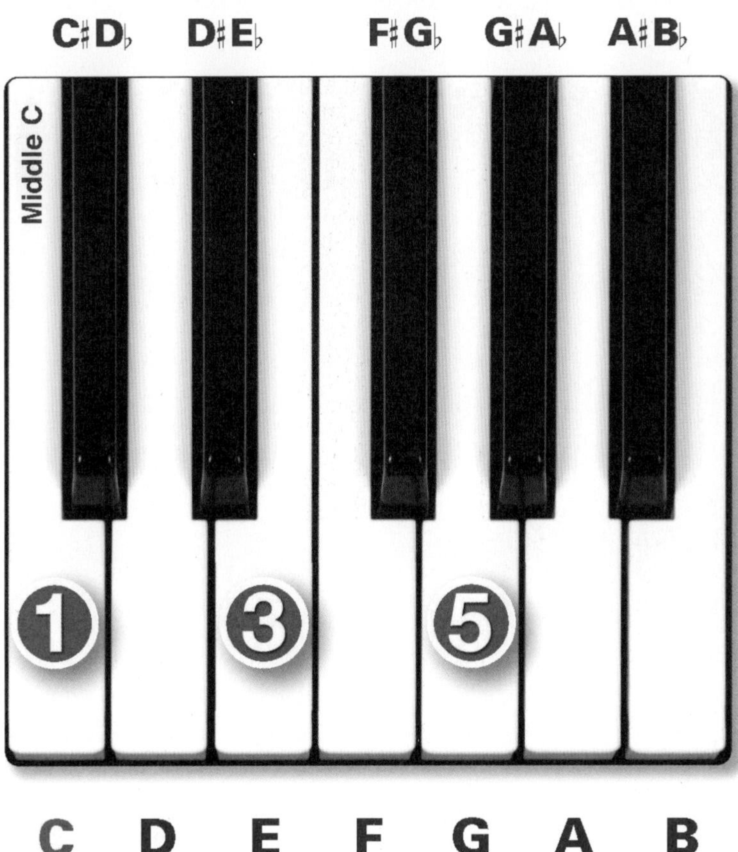

1 = thumb 2 = index finger 3 = middle finger 4 = ring finger 5 = little finger

Chord Spelling

1st (F), 3rd (A), 5th (C), 7th (E), 9th (G)

FREE ACCESS on smartphones including iPhone & Android  Using any QR code app scan and **HEAR** the chord

Fm9

Minor 9th

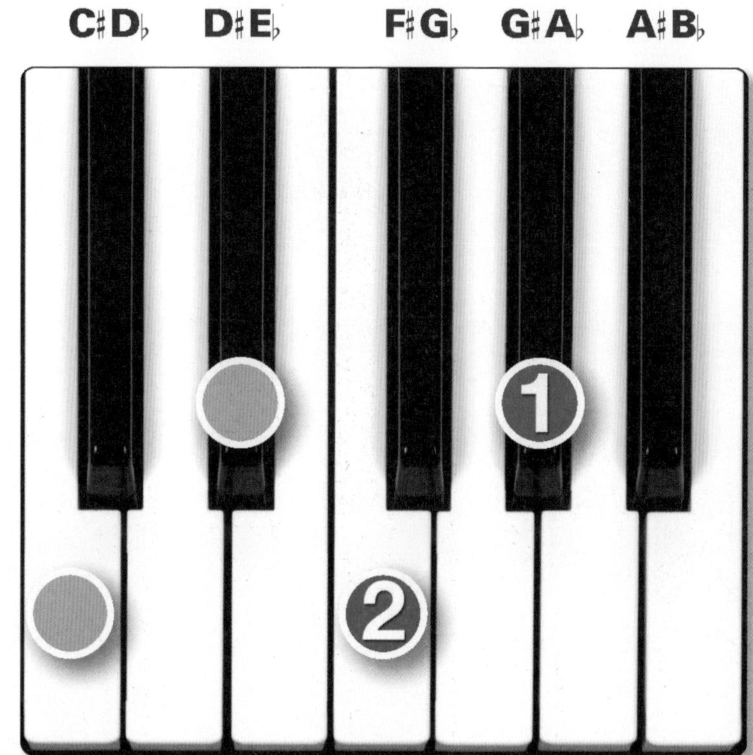

5 = little finger 4 = ring finger 3 = middle finger 2 = index finger 1 = thumb

Chord Spelling

1st (F), ♭3rd (A♭), 5th (C), ♭7th (E♭), 9th (G)

FREE ACCESS on smartphones including iPhone & Android

Using any QR code app scan and **HEAR** the chord

Right Hand 

Fm9

Minor 9th

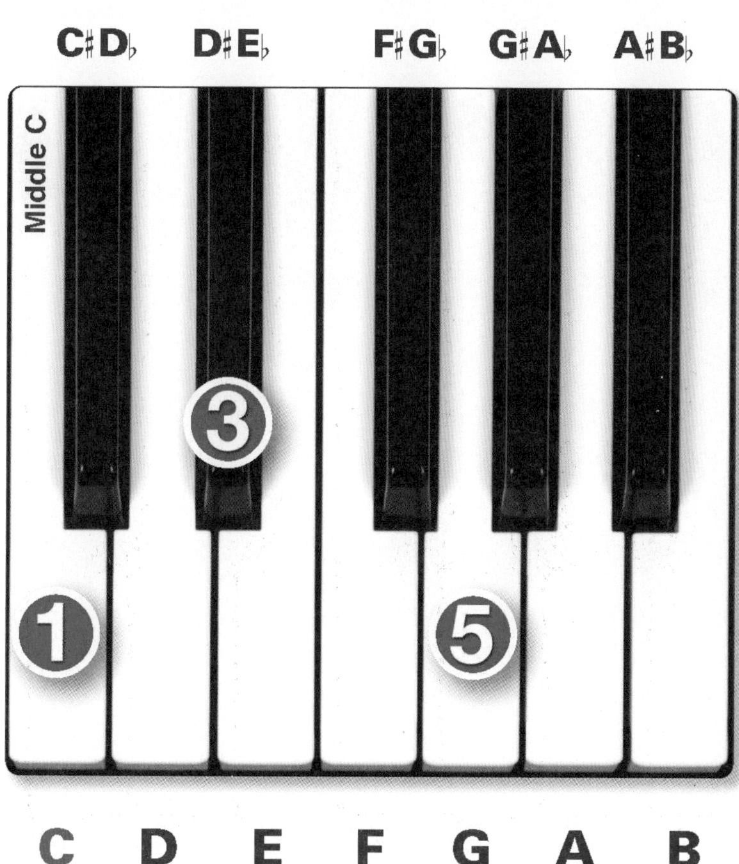

1 = thumb 2 = index finger 3 = middle finger 4 = ring finger 5 = little finger

Chord Spelling

1st (F), ♭3rd (A♭), 5th (C), ♭7th (E♭), 9th (G)

FREE ACCESS on smartphones including iPhone & Android  Using any QR code app scan and **HEAR** the chord

F♯/G♭
Major

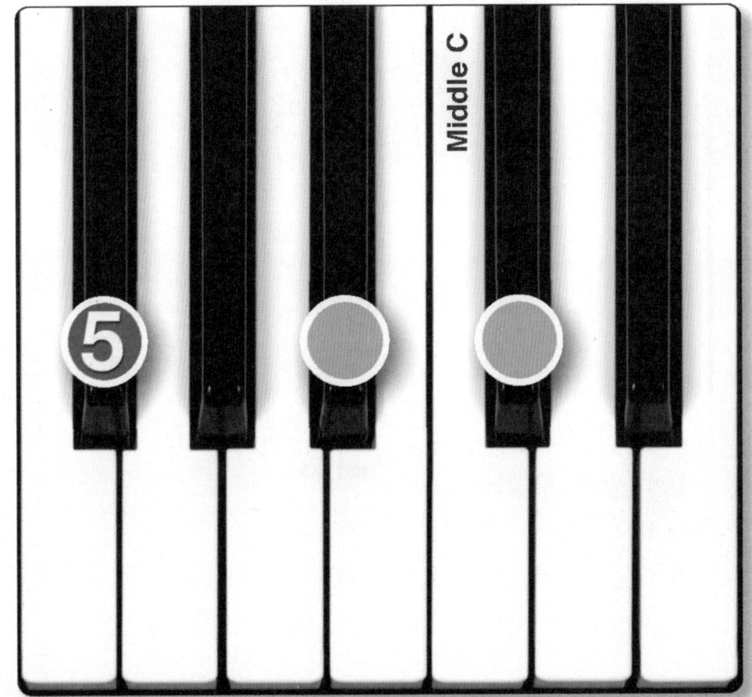

5 = little finger 4 = ring finger 3 = middle finger 2 = index finger 1 = thumb

Chord Spelling

1st (F♯), 3rd (A♯), 5th (C♯)

FREE ACCESS on smartphones including iPhone & Android

Using any QR code app scan and **HEAR** the chord

Right Hand

F♯/G♭
Major

1 = thumb 2 = index finger 3 = middle finger 4 = ring finger 5 = little finger

Chord Spelling

1st (F♯), 3rd (A♯), 5th (C♯)

FREE ACCESS on smartphones including iPhone & Android

Using any QR code app scan and **HEAR** the chord

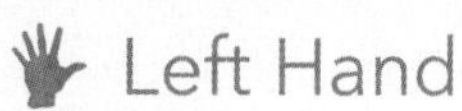

A
A♯/B♭
B
C
C♯/D♭
D
D♯/E♭
E
F
F♯/G♭
G
G♯/A♭

F♯/G♭m
Minor

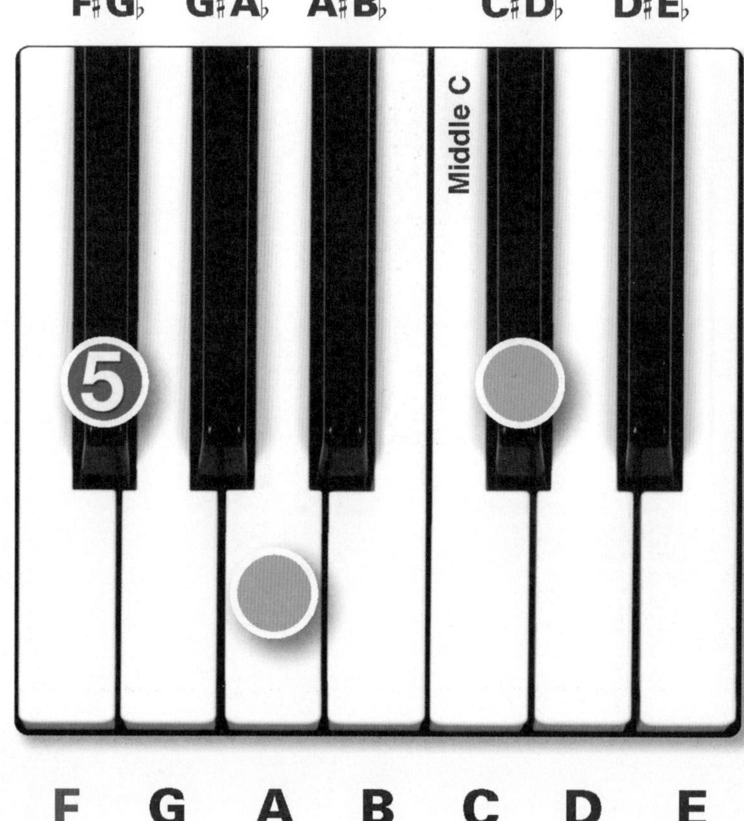

5 = little finger 4 = ring finger 3 = middle finger 2 = index finger 1 = thumb

Chord Spelling

1st (F♯), ♭3rd (A), 5th (C♯)

FREE ACCESS on smartphones including iPhone & Android

Using any QR code app scan and **HEAR** the chord

F♯/G♭m
Minor

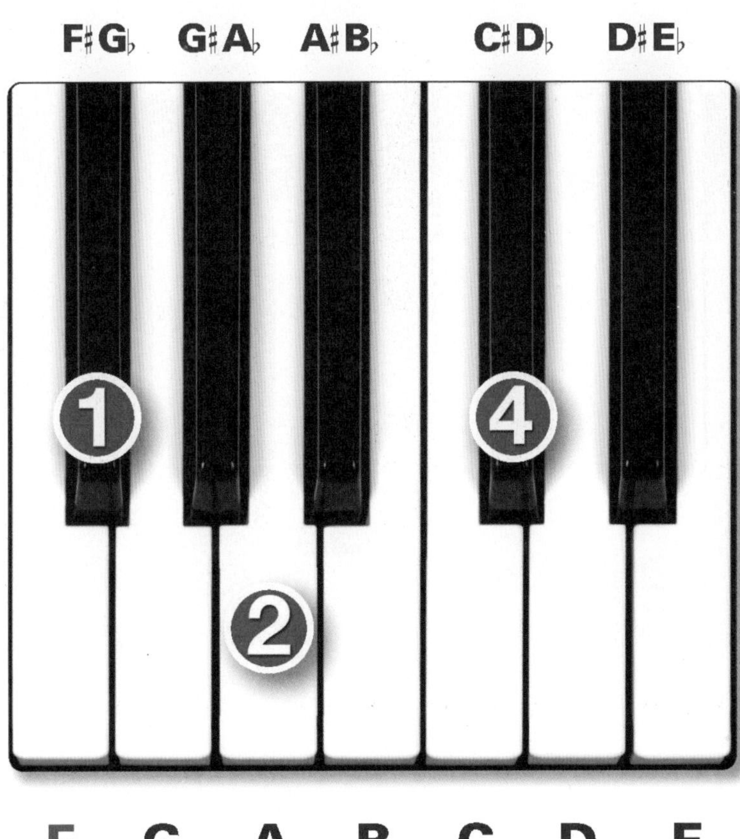

1 = thumb 2 = index finger 3 = middle finger 4 = ring finger 5 = little finger

Chord Spelling

1st (F♯), ♭3rd (A), 5th (C♯)

FREE ACCESS on smartphones including iPhone & Android  Using any QR code app scan and **HEAR** the chord

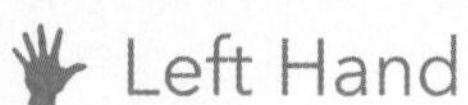

A

A♯/B♭

B

C

C♯/D♭

D

D♯/E♭

E

F

F♯/G♭

G

G♯/A♭

F♯/G♭+

Augmented Triad

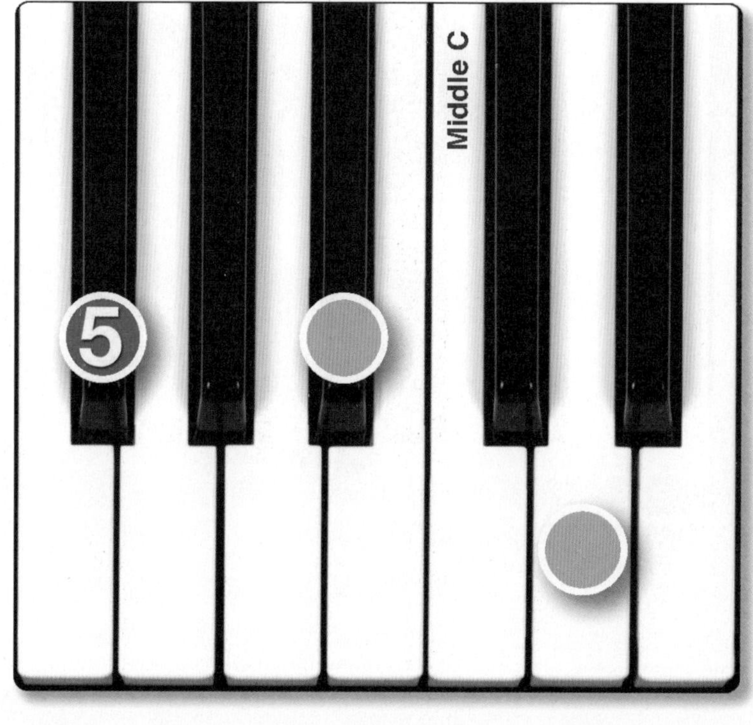

5 = little finger 4 = ring finger 3 = middle finger 2 = index finger 1 = thumb

Chord Spelling

1st (F♯), 3rd (A♯), ♯5th (Cx)

FREE ACCESS on smartphones including iPhone & Android

Using any QR code app scan and **HEAR** the chord

F♯/G♭+

Augmented Triad

1 = thumb 2 = index finger 3 = middle finger 4 = ring finger 5 = little finger

Chord Spelling

1st (F♯), 3rd (A♯), ♯5th (Cx)

FREE ACCESS on smartphones including iPhone & Android

Using any QR code app scan and **HEAR** the chord

A

A♯/B♭

B

C

C♯/D♭

D

D♯/E♭

E

F

F♯/G♭

G

G♯/A♭

F♯/G♭°

Diminished Triad

F G A B C D E

5 = little finger 4 = ring finger 3 = middle finger 2 = index finger 1 = thumb

Chord Spelling

1st (F♯), ♭3rd (A), ♭5th (C)

FREE ACCESS on smartphones including iPhone & Android

Using any QR code app scan and **HEAR** the chord

F♯/G♭°
Diminished Triad

Right Hand

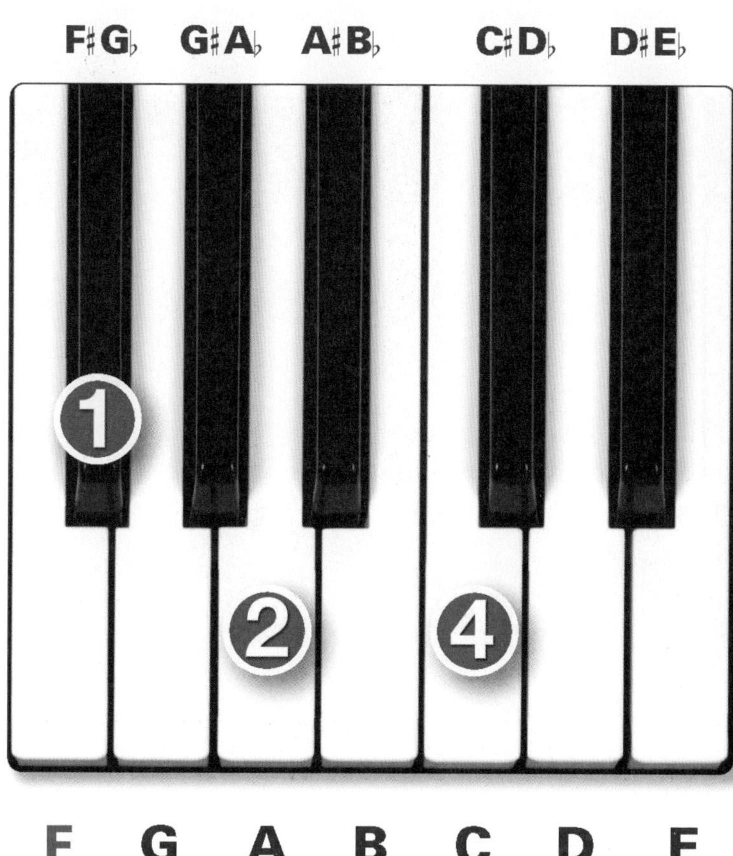

1 = thumb 2 = index finger 3 = middle finger 4 = ring finger 5 = little finger

Chord Spelling

1st (F♯), ♭3rd (A), ♭5th (C)

FREE ACCESS on smartphones including iPhone & Android

Using any QR code app scan and **HEAR** the chord

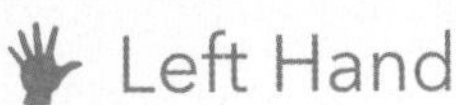

A
A♯/B♭
B
C
C♯/D♭
D
D♯/E♭
E
F
F♯/G♭
G
G♯/A♭

F♯/G♭6
Major 6th

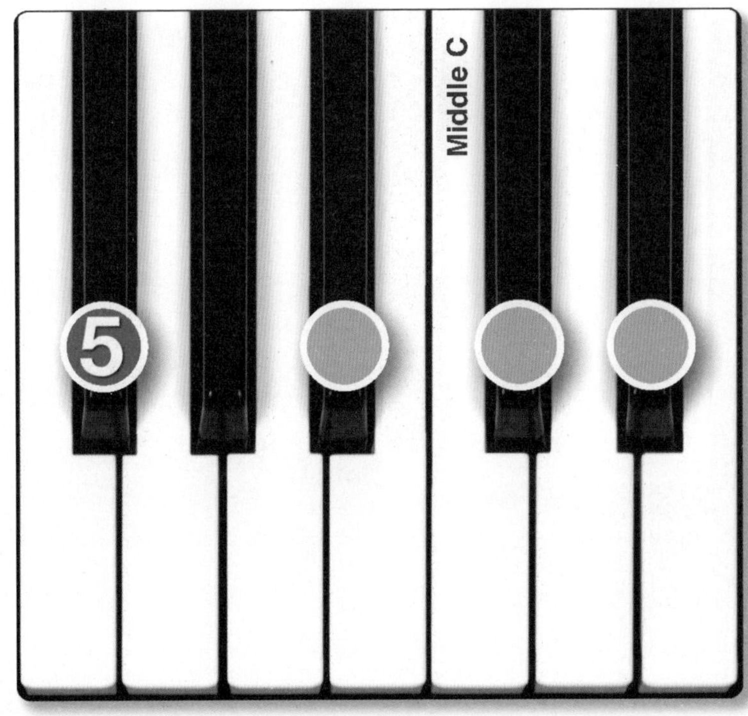

5 = little finger 4 = ring finger 3 = middle finger 2 = index finger 1 = thumb

Chord Spelling

1st (F♯), 3rd (A♯), 5th (C♯), 6th (D♯)

FREE ACCESS on smartphones including iPhone & Android

Using any QR code app scan and **HEAR** the chord

F♯/G♭6
Major 6th

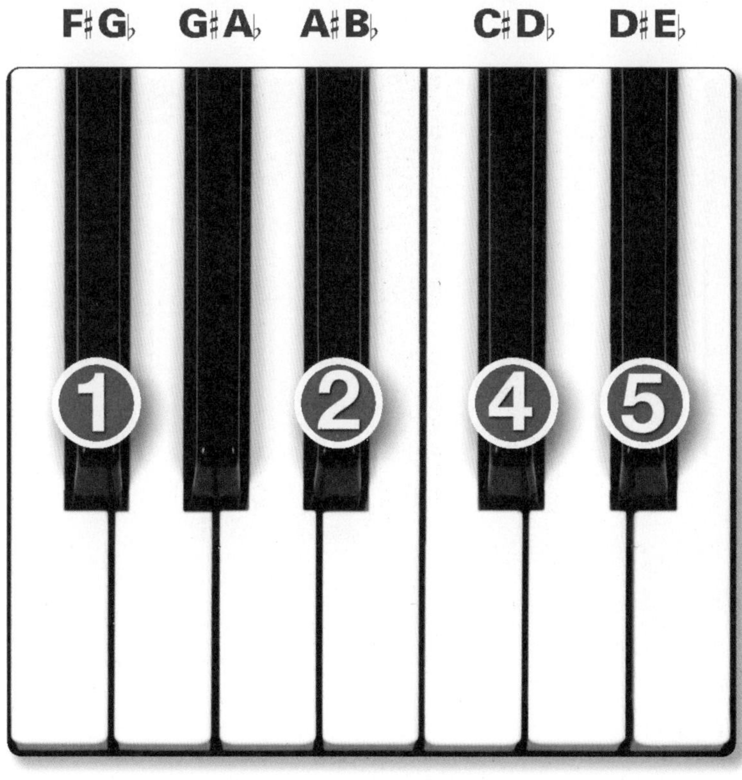

1 = thumb 2 = index finger 3 = middle finger 4 = ring finger 5 = little finger

Chord Spelling

1st (F♯), 3rd (A♯), 5th (C♯), 6th (D♯)

FREE ACCESS on smartphones including iPhone & Android  Using any QR code app scan and **HEAR** the chord

Left Hand

A
A♯/B♭
B
C
C♯/D♭
D
D♯/E♭
E
F
F♯/G♭
G
G♯/A♭

F♯/G♭m6

Minor 6th

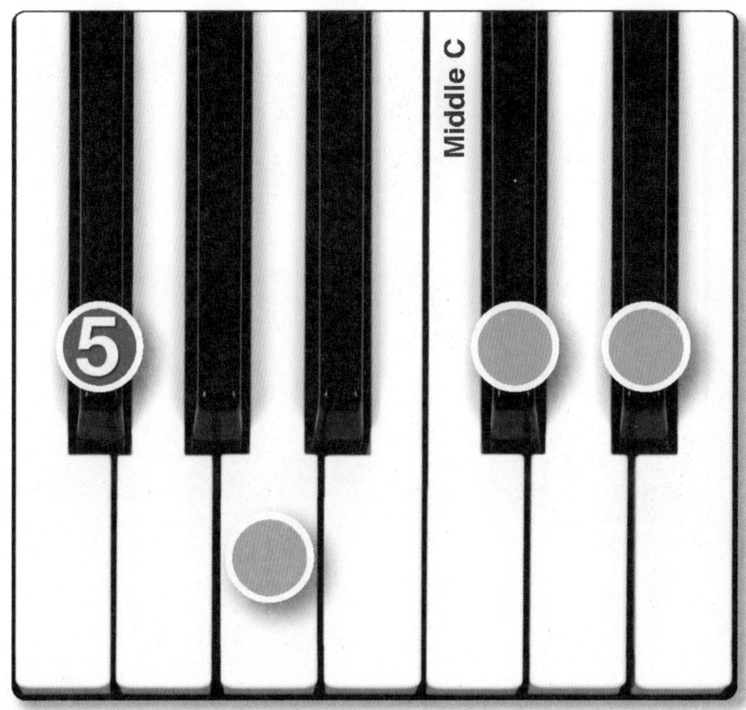

5 = little finger 4 = ring finger 3 = middle finger 2 = index finger 1 = thumb

Chord Spelling

1st (F♯), ♭3rd (A), 5th (C♯), 6th (D♯)

FREE ACCESS on smartphones including iPhone & Android  Using any QR code app scan and **HEAR** the chord

F♯/G♭m6
Minor 6th

Right Hand

F♯G♭ G♯A♭ A♯B♭ C♯D♭ D♯E♭

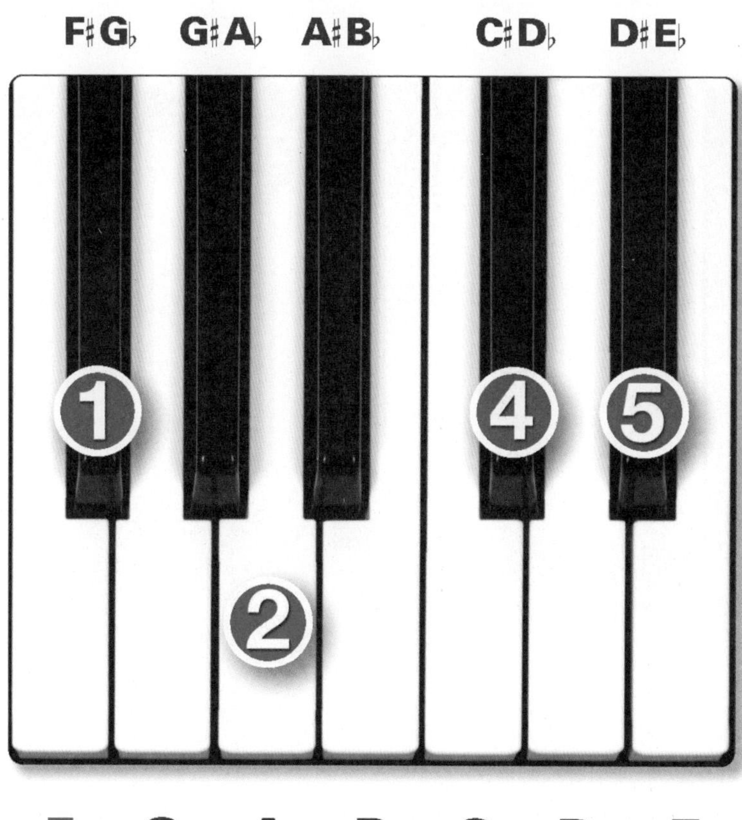

F G A B C D E

1 = thumb 2 = index finger 3 = middle finger 4 = ring finger 5 = little finger

Chord Spelling

1st (F♯), ♭3rd (A), 5th (C♯), 6th (D♯)

FREE ACCESS on smartphones including iPhone & Android

Using any QR code app scan and **HEAR** the chord

F♯/G♭maj7

Major 7th

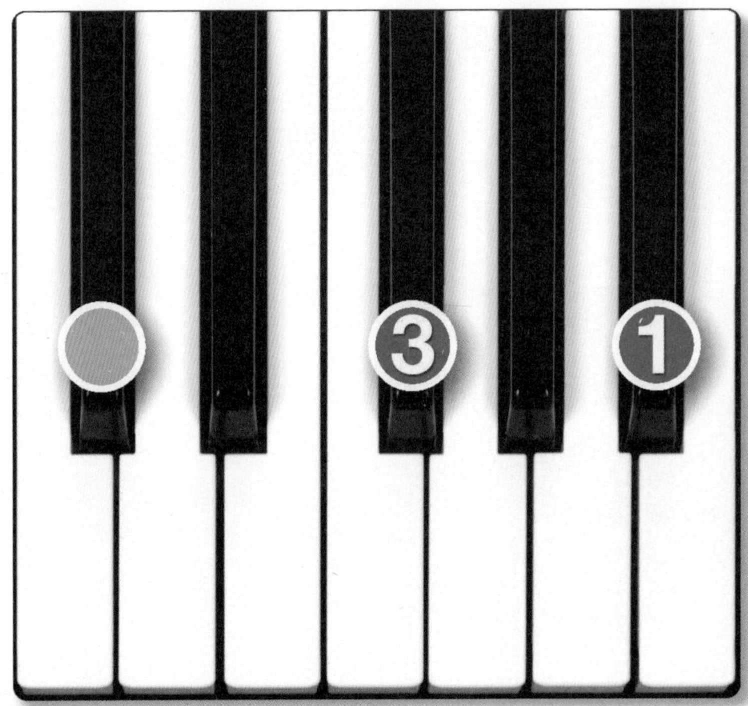

5 = little finger 4 = ring finger 3 = middle finger 2 = index finger 1 = thumb

Chord Spelling

1st (F♯), 3rd (A♯), 5th (C♯), 7th (F)

FREE ACCESS on smartphones including iPhone & Android

Using any QR code app scan and **HEAR** the chord

F♯/G♭maj7

Major 7th

Right Hand

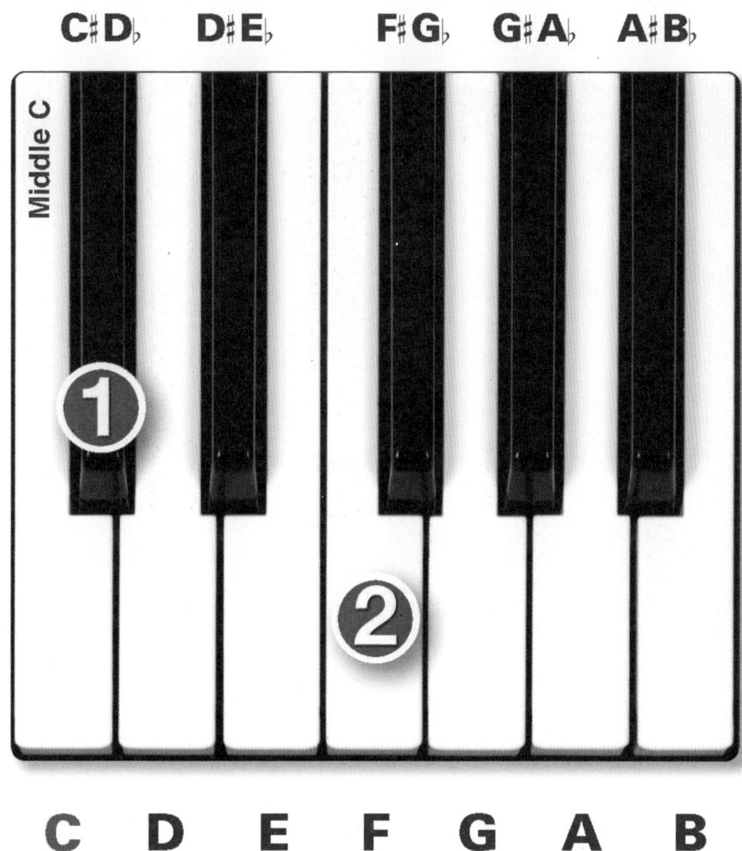

1 = thumb 2 = index finger 3 = middle finger 4 = ring finger 5 = little finger

Chord Spelling

1st (F♯), 3rd (A♯), 5th (C♯), 7th (F)

FREE ACCESS on smartphones including iPhone & Android

Using any QR code app scan and **HEAR** the chord

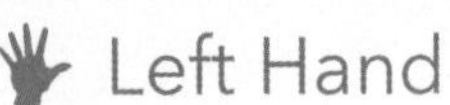

A
A♯/B♭
B
C
C♯/D♭
D
D♯/E♭
E
F
F♯/G♭
G
G♯/A♭

F♯/G♭m7

Minor 7th

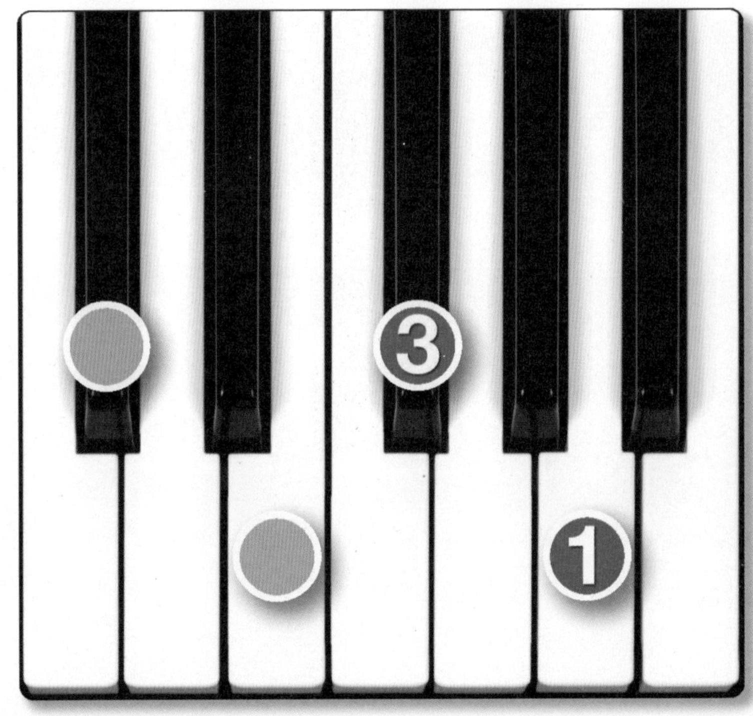

5 = little finger 4 = ring finger 3 = middle finger 2 = index finger 1 = thumb

Chord Spelling

1st (F♯), ♭3rd (A), 5th (C♯), ♭7th (E)

FREE ACCESS on smartphones including iPhone & Android  Using any QR code app scan and **HEAR** the chord

F♯/G♭m7
Minor 7th

1 = thumb 2 = index finger 3 = middle finger 4 = ring finger 5 = little finger

Chord Spelling

1st (F♯), ♭3rd (A), 5th (C♯), ♭7th (E)

FREE ACCESS on smartphones including iPhone & Android

Using any QR code app scan and **HEAR** the chord

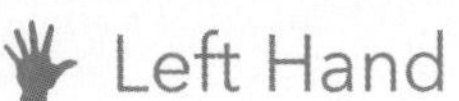

F♯/G♭maj9

Major 9th

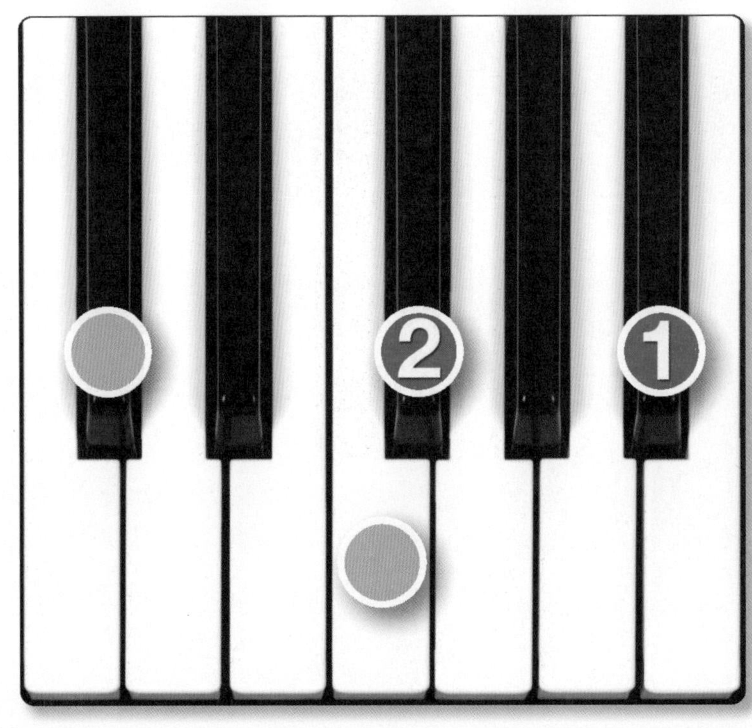

5 = little finger 4 = ring finger 3 = middle finger 2 = index finger 1 = thumb

Chord Spelling

1st (F♯), 3rd (A♯), 5th (C♯), 7th (E♯), 9th (G♯)

FREE ACCESS on smartphones including iPhone & Android

Using any QR code app scan and **HEAR** the chord

F♯/G♭maj9
Major 9th

Right Hand

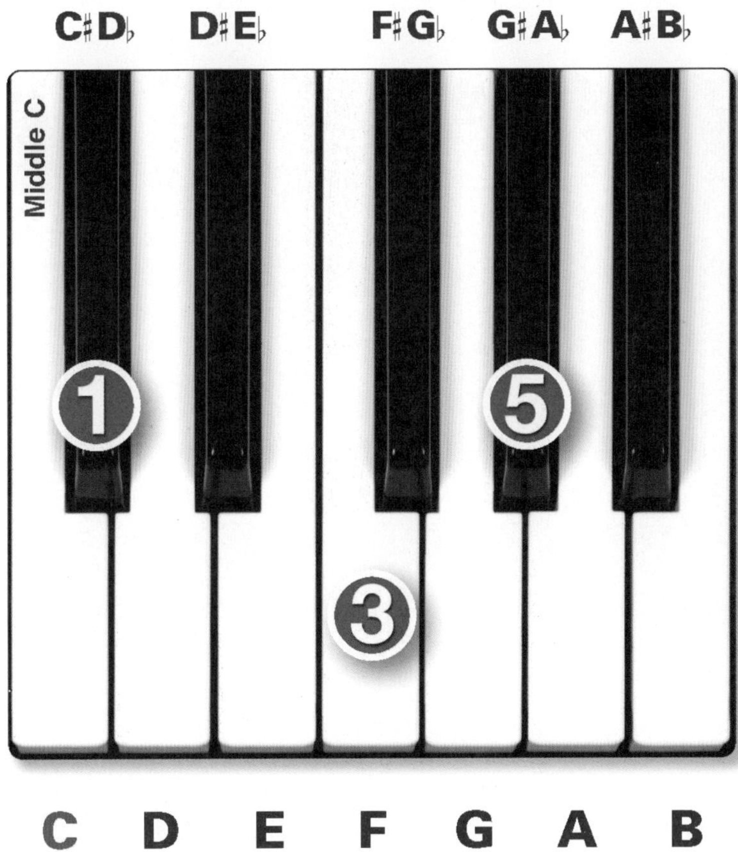

1 = thumb 2 = index finger 3 = middle finger 4 = ring finger 5 = little finger

Chord Spelling

1st (F♯), 3rd (A♯), 5th (C♯), 7th (E♯), 9th (G♯)

FREE ACCESS on smartphones including iPhone & Android

Using any QR code app scan and **HEAR** the chord

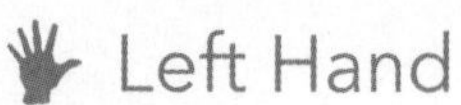

F♯/G♭m9

Minor 9th

C♯D♭ D♯E♭ F♯G♭ G♯A♭ A♯B♭

2

1

C D E F G A B

5 = little finger 4 = ring finger 3 = middle finger 2 = index finger 1 = thumb

Chord Spelling

1st (F♯), ♭3rd (A), 5th (C♯), ♭7th (E), 9th (G♯)

FREE ACCESS on smartphones including iPhone & Android

Using any QR code app scan and **HEAR** the chord

F♯/G♭m9

Minor 9th

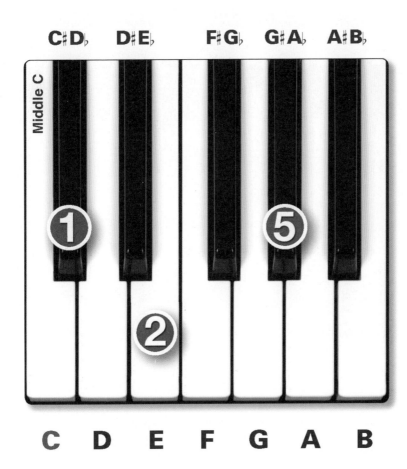

Right Hand

C♯D♭ D♯E♭ F♯G♭ G♯A♭ A♯B♭

Middle C

1 5 2

C D E F G A B

1 = thumb 2 = index finger 3 = middle finger 4 = ring finger 5 = little finger

Chord Spelling

1st (F♯), ♭3rd (A), 5th (C♯), ♭7th (E), 9th (G♯)

FREE ACCESS on smartphones including iPhone & Android

Using any QR code app scan and **HEAR** the chord

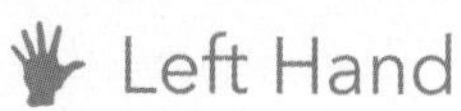

G
Major

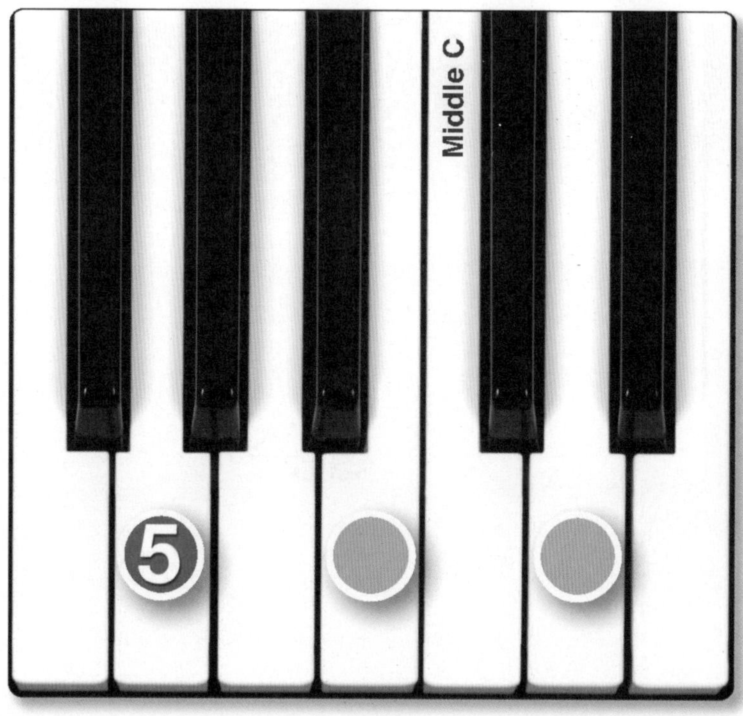

5 = little finger 4 = ring finger 3 = middle finger 2 = index finger 1 = thumb

Chord Spelling

1st (G), 3rd (B), 5th (D)

FREE ACCESS on smartphones including iPhone & Android

Using any QR code app scan and **HEAR** the chord

G

Major

F♯G♭ G♯A♭ A♯B♭ C♯D♭ D♯E♭

1 2 4

F G A B C D E

1 = thumb 2 = index finger 3 = middle finger 4 = ring finger 5 = little finger

Chord Spelling

1st (G), 3rd (B), 5th (D)

FREE ACCESS on smartphones including iPhone & Android  Using any QR code app scan and **HEAR** the chord

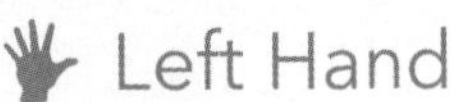

Gm

Minor

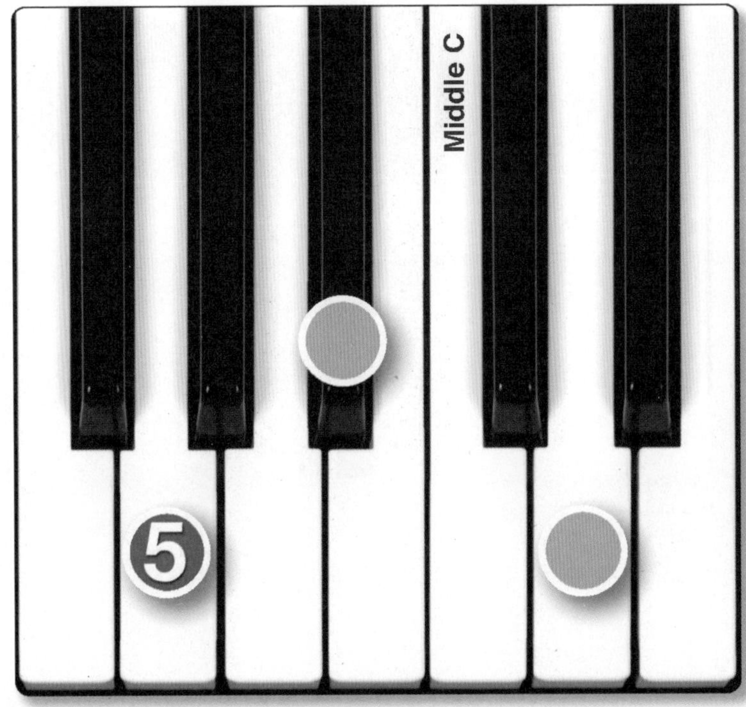

5 = little finger 4 = ring finger 3 = middle finger 2 = index finger 1 = thumb

Chord Spelling

1st (G), ♭3rd (B♭), 5th (D)

FREE ACCESS on smartphones including iPhone & Android  Using any QR code app scan and **HEAR** the chord

Right Hand 

Gm

Minor

F♯G♭ G♯A♭ A♯B♭ C♯D♭ D♯E♭

1 2 4

F G A B C D E

1 = thumb 2 = index finger 3 = middle finger 4 = ring finger 5 = little finger

Chord Spelling

1st (G), ♭3rd (B♭), 5th (D)

FREE ACCESS on smartphones including iPhone & Android  Using any QR code app scan and **HEAR** the chord

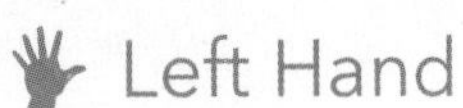

G+

Augmented Triad

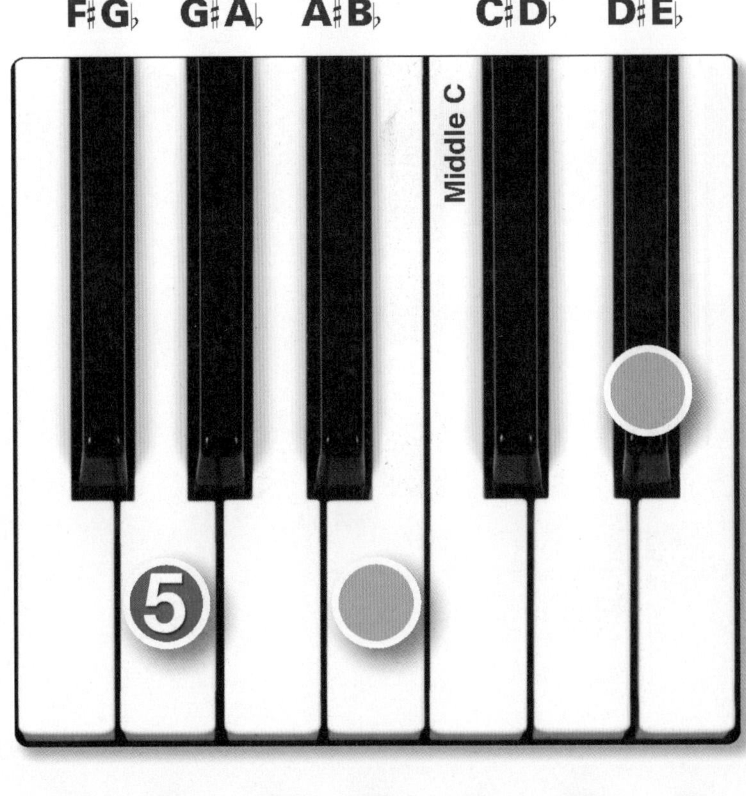

F G A B C D E

5 = little finger 4 = ring finger 3 = middle finger 2 = index finger 1 = thumb

Chord Spelling

1st (G), 3rd (B), ♯5th (D♯)

FREE ACCESS on smartphones including iPhone & Android

Using any QR code app scan and **HEAR** the chord

G+

Augmented Triad

1 = thumb 2 = index finger 3 = middle finger 4 = ring finger 5 = little finger

Chord Spelling

1st (G), 3rd (B), ♯5th (D♯)

FREE ACCESS on smartphones including iPhone & Android

Using any QR code app scan and **HEAR** the chord

G°

Diminished Triad

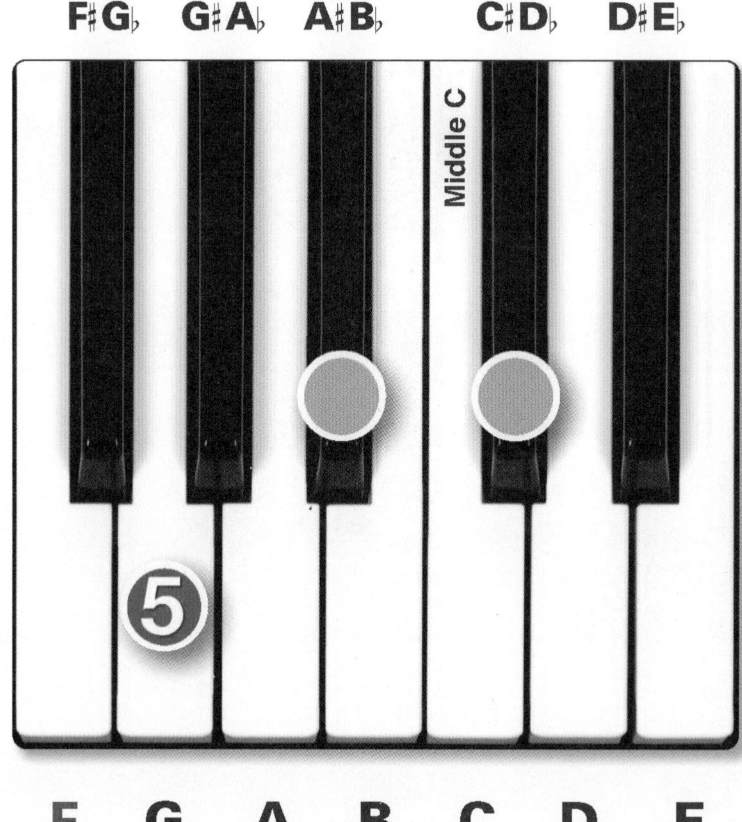

5 = little finger 4 = ring finger 3 = middle finger 2 = index finger 1 = thumb

Chord Spelling

1st (G), ♭3rd (B♭), ♭5th (D♭)

FREE ACCESS on smartphones including iPhone & Android

Using any QR code app scan and **HEAR** the chord

G°

Right Hand 

Diminished Triad

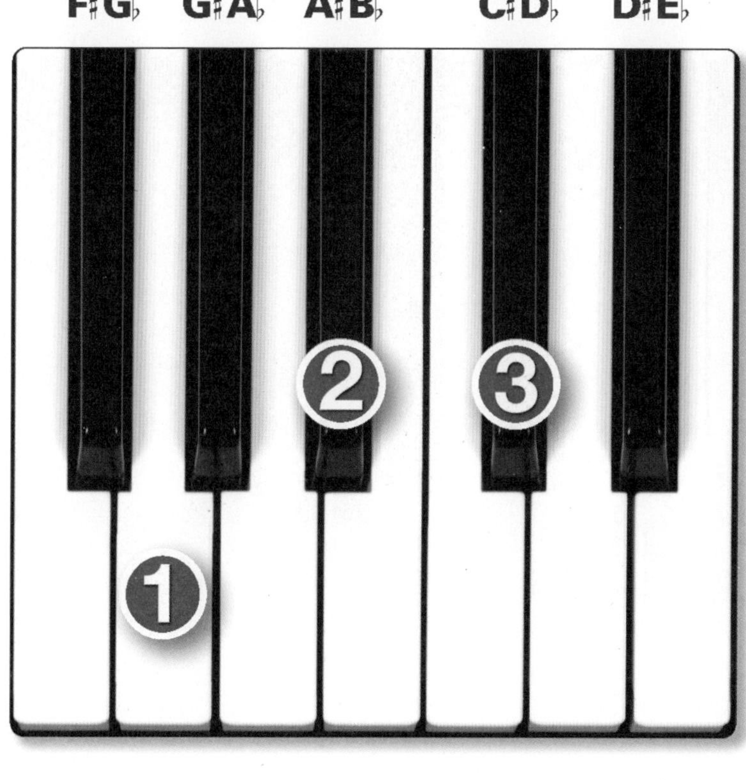

1 = thumb 2 = index finger 3 = middle finger 4 = ring finger 5 = little finger

Chord Spelling

1st (G), ♭3rd (B♭), ♭5th (D♭)

FREE ACCESS on smartphones including iPhone & Android

Using any QR code app scan and **HEAR** the chord

Left Hand

A
A♯/B♭
B
C
C♯/D♭
D
D♯/E♭
E
F
F♯/G♭
G
G♯/A♭

G6

Major 6th

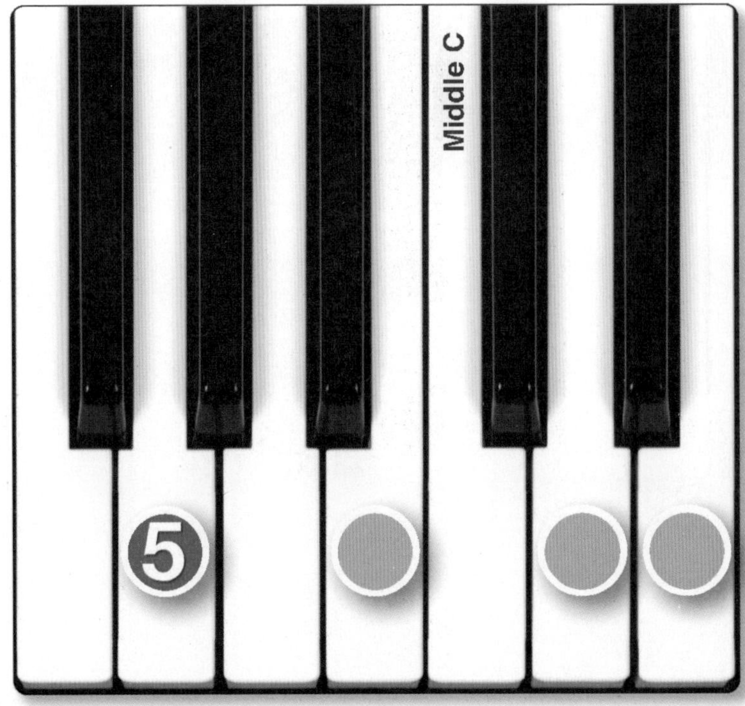

5 = little finger 4 = ring finger 3 = middle finger 2 = index finger 1 = thumb

Chord Spelling

1st (G), 3rd (B), 5th (D), 6th (E)

FREE ACCESS on smartphones including iPhone & Android  Using any QR code app scan and **HEAR** the chord

G6
Major 6th

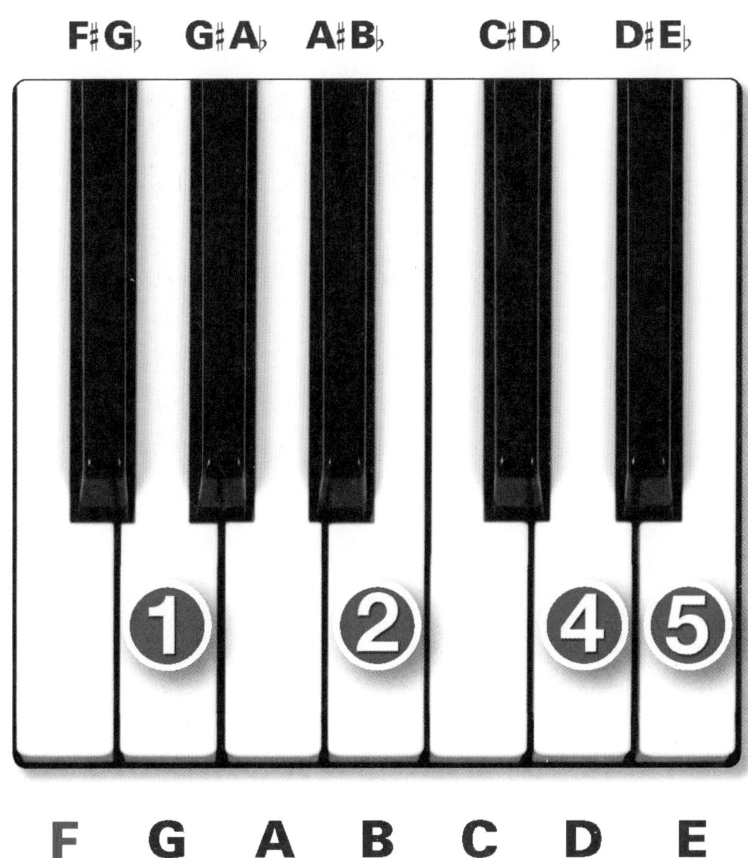

1 = thumb 2 = index finger 3 = middle finger 4 = ring finger 5 = little finger

Chord Spelling

1st (G), 3rd (B), 5th (D), 6th (E)

FREE ACCESS on smartphones including iPhone & Android

Using any QR code app scan and **HEAR** the chord

Gm6

Minor 6th

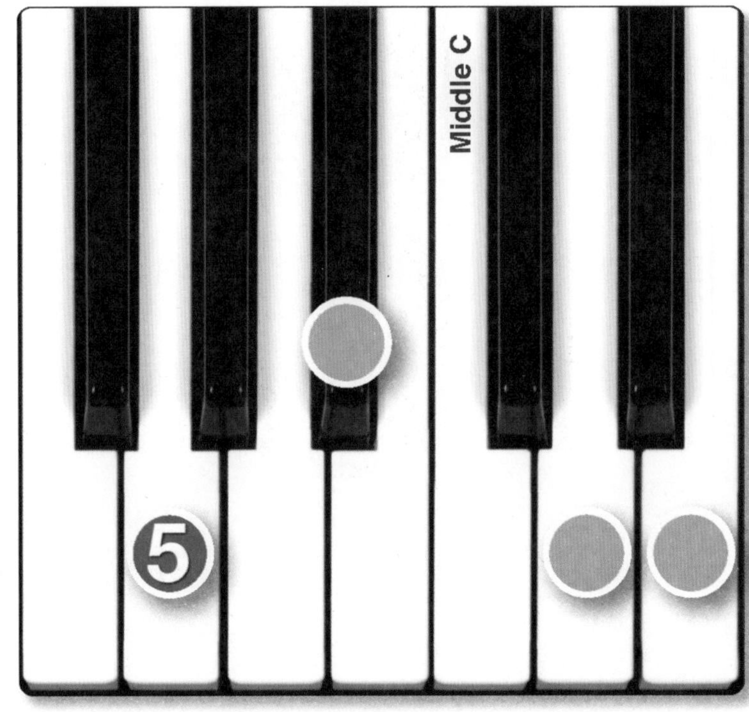

5 = little finger 4 = ring finger 3 = middle finger 2 = index finger 1 = thumb

Chord Spelling

1st (G), ♭3rd (B♭), 5th (D), 6th (E)

FREE ACCESS on smartphones including iPhone & Android

Using any QR code app scan and **HEAR** the chord

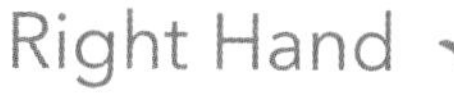

Gm6

Minor 6th

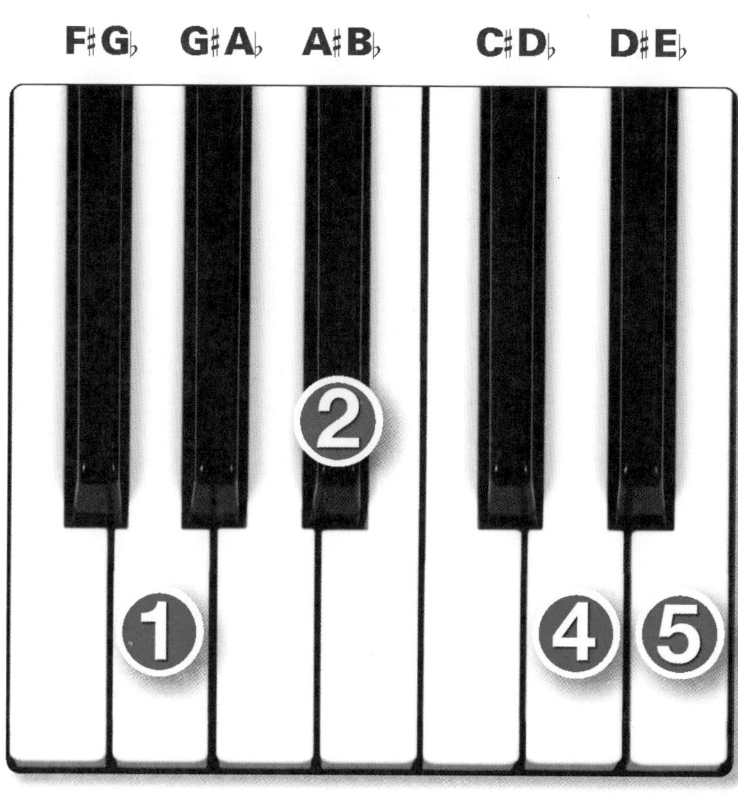

1 = thumb 2 = index finger 3 = middle finger 4 = ring finger 5 = little finger

Chord Spelling

1st (G), ♭3rd (B♭), 5th (D), 6th (E)

FREE ACCESS on smartphones including iPhone & Android

Using any QR code app scan and **HEAR** the chord

Gmaj7

Major 7th

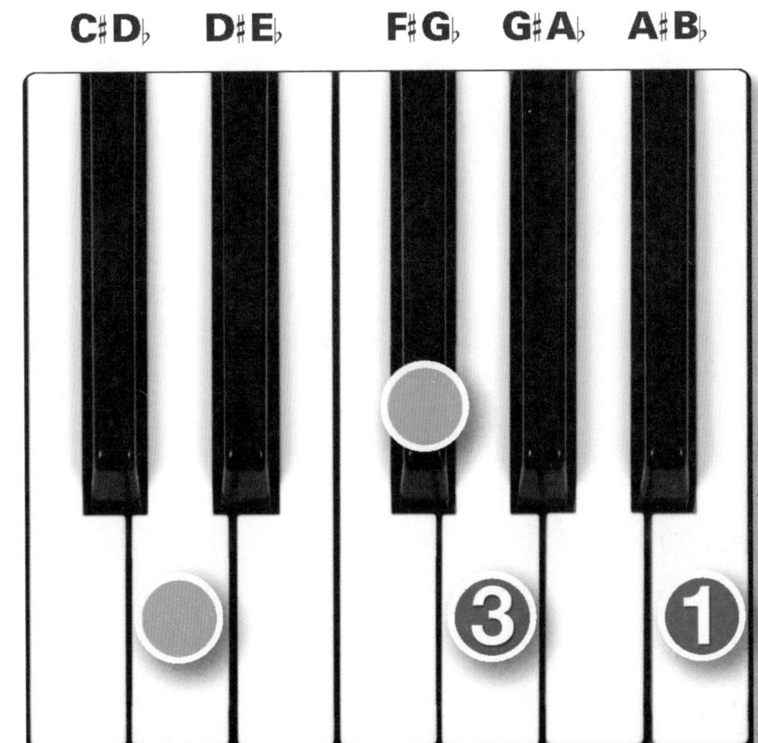

5 = little finger 4 = ring finger 3 = middle finger 2 = index finger 1 = thumb

Chord Spelling

1st (G), 3rd (B), 5th (D), 7th (F♯)

FREE ACCESS on smartphones including iPhone & Android

Using any QR code app scan and **HEAR** the chord

Right Hand 

Gmaj7

Major 7th

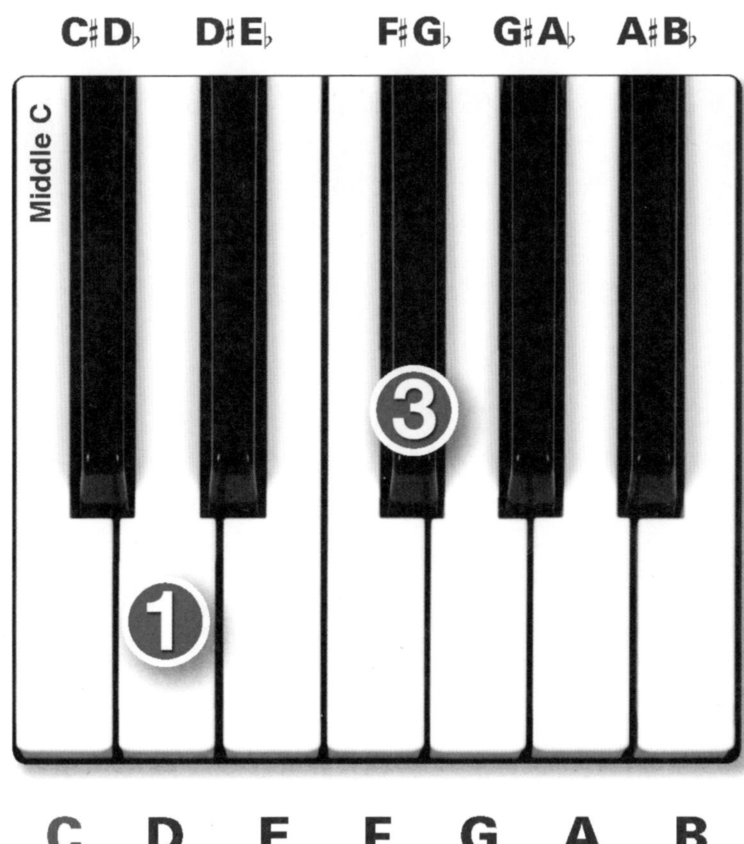

1 = thumb 2 = index finger 3 = middle finger 4 = ring finger 5 = little finger

Chord Spelling

1st (G), 3rd (B), 5th (D), 7th (F♯)

FREE ACCESS on smartphones including iPhone & Android  Using any QR code app scan and **HEAR** the chord

Left Hand

A
A♯/B♭
B
C
C♯/D♭
D
D♯/E♭
E
F
F♯/G♭
G
G♯/A♭

Gm7

Minor 7th

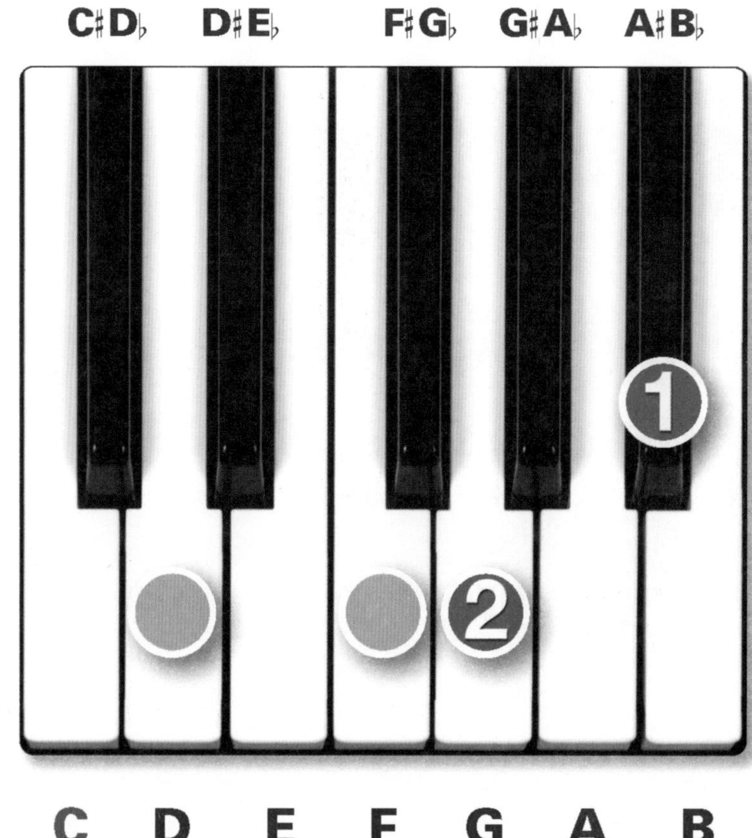

5 = little finger 4 = ring finger 3 = middle finger 2 = index finger 1 = thumb

Chord Spelling

1st (G), ♭3rd (B♭), 5th (D), ♭7th (F)

FREE ACCESS on smartphones including iPhone & Android

Using any QR code app scan and **HEAR** the chord

Gm7

Minor 7th

Right Hand 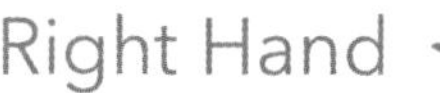 

C D E F G A B

1 = thumb 2 = index finger 3 = middle finger 4 = ring finger 5 = little finger

Chord Spelling

1st (G), ♭3rd (B♭), 5th (D), ♭7th (F)

FREE ACCESS on smartphones including iPhone & Android  Using any QR code app scan and **HEAR** the chord

A
A♯/B♭
B
C
C♯/D♭
D
D♯/E♭
E
F
F♯/G♭
G
G♯/A♭

Gmaj9

Major 9th

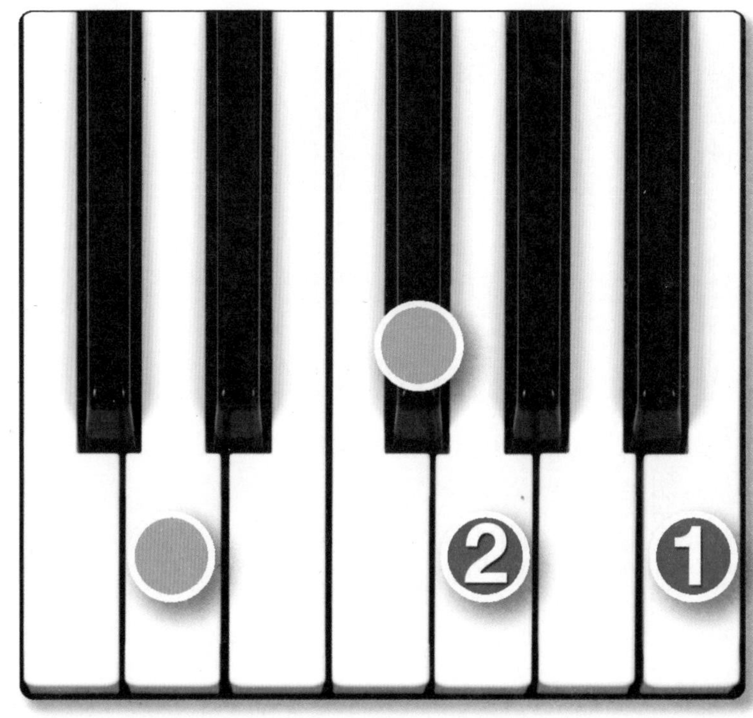

5 = little finger 4 = ring finger 3 = middle finger 2 = index finger 1 = thumb

Chord Spelling

1st (G), 3rd (B), 5th (D), 7th (F♯), 9th (A)

FREE ACCESS on smartphones including iPhone & Android

Using any QR code app scan and **HEAR** the chord

Right Hand 

Gmaj9
Major 9th

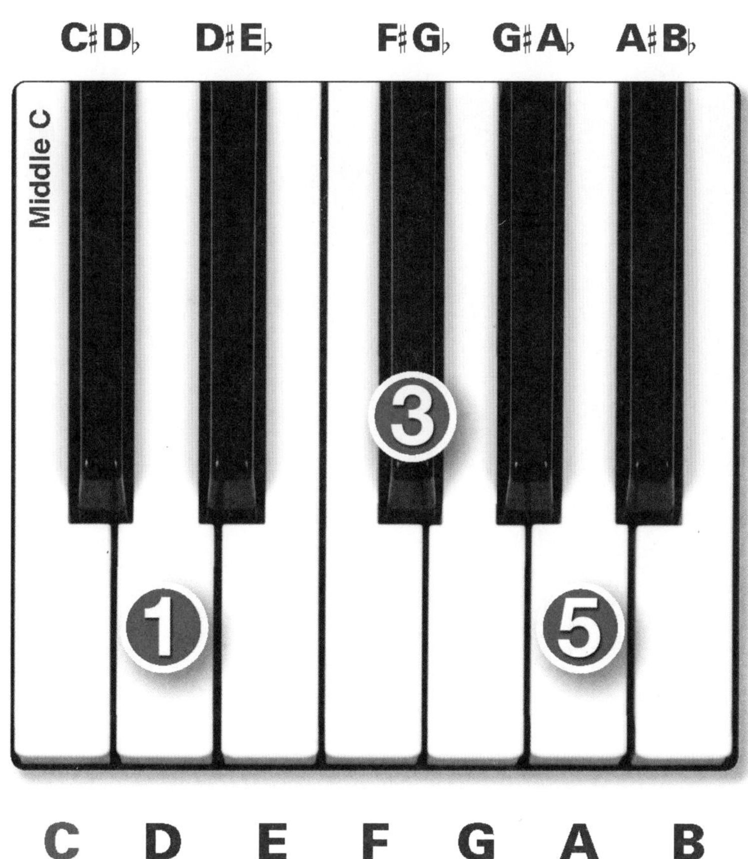

1 = thumb 2 = index finger 3 = middle finger 4 = ring finger 5 = little finger

Chord Spelling

1st (G), 3rd (B), 5th (D), 7th (F♯), 9th (A)

FREE ACCESS on smartphones including iPhone & Android  Using any QR code app scan and **HEAR** the chord

Left Hand

Gm9

Minor 9th

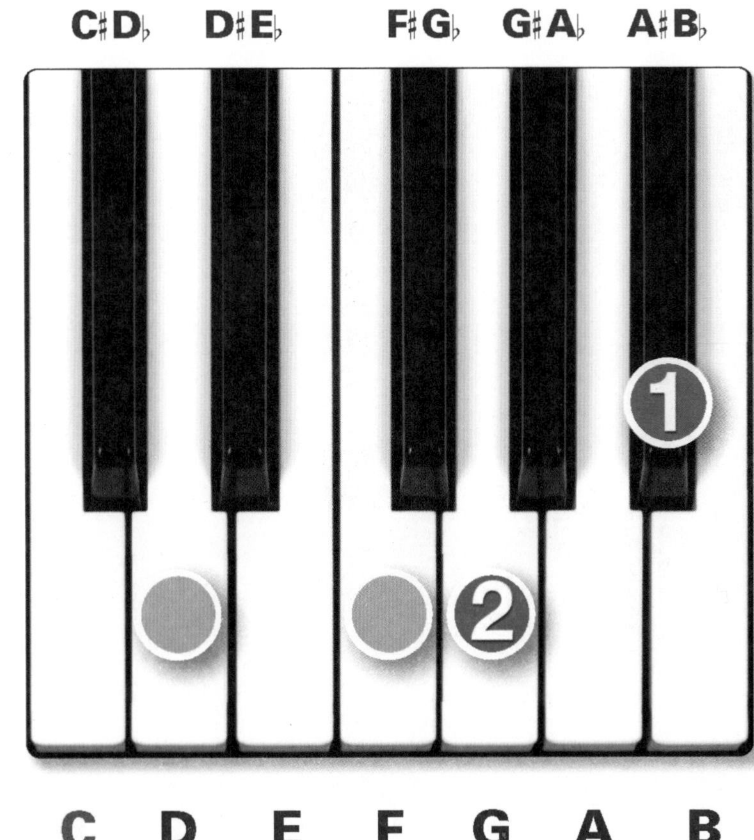

5 = little finger 4 = ring finger 3 = middle finger 2 = index finger 1 = thumb

Chord Spelling

1st (G), ♭3rd (B♭), 5th (D), ♭7th (F), 9th (A)

FREE ACCESS on smartphones including iPhone & Android

Using any QR code app scan and **HEAR** the chord

Gm9

Minor 9th

Right Hand 

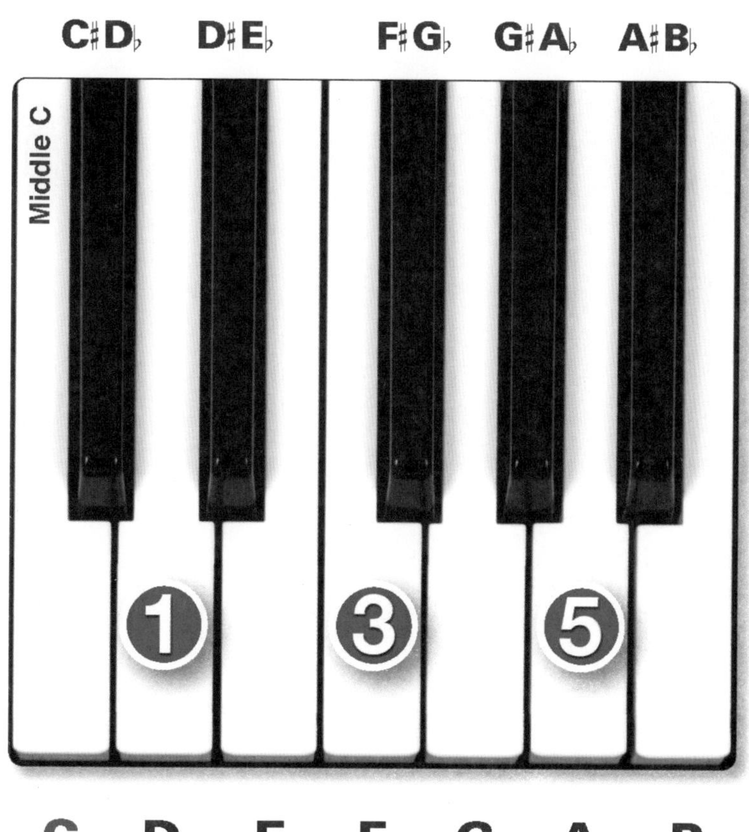

C D E F G A B

1 = thumb 2 = index finger 3 = middle finger 4 = ring finger 5 = little finger

Chord Spelling

1st (G), ♭3rd (B♭), 5th (D), ♭7th (F), 9th (A)

FREE ACCESS on smartphones including iPhone & Android  Using any QR code app scan and **HEAR** the chord

G♯/A♭ Major

F♯G♭ G♯A♭ A♯B♭ C♯D♭ D♯E♭

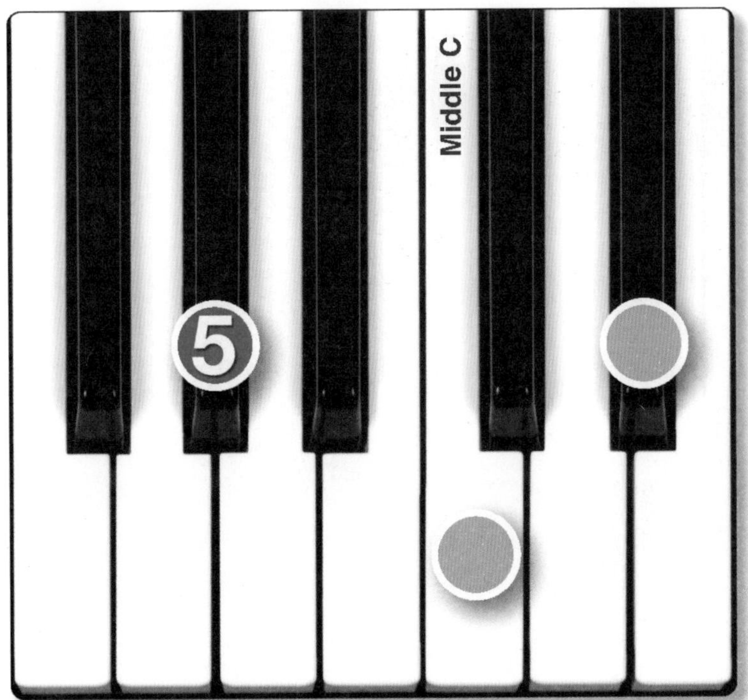

F G A B C D E

5 = little finger 4 = ring finger 3 = middle finger 2 = index finger 1 = thumb

Chord Spelling

1st (A♭), 3rd (C), 5th (E♭)

FREE ACCESS on smartphones including iPhone & Android

Using any QR code app scan and **HEAR** the chord

G♯/A♭
Major

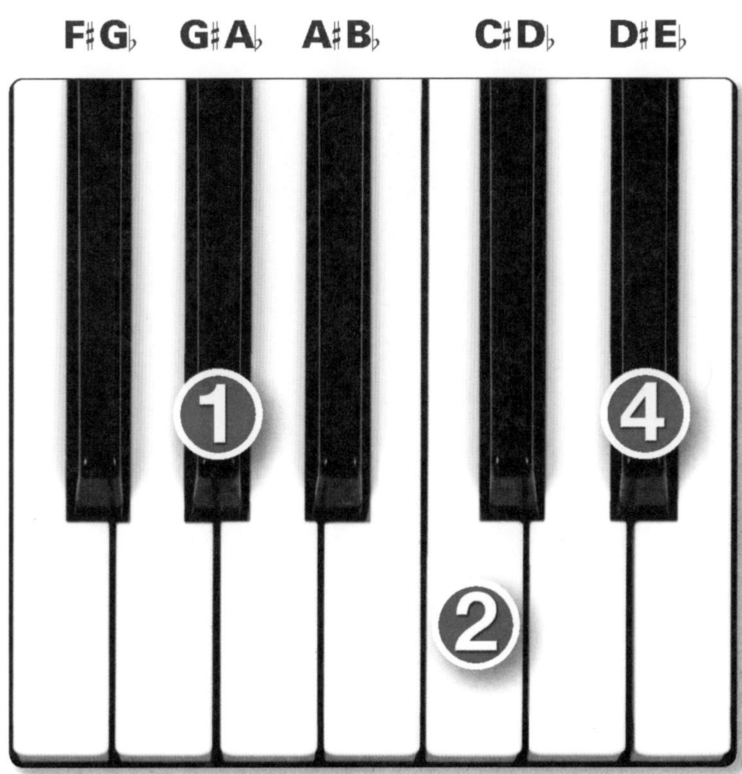

1 = thumb 2 = index finger 3 = middle finger 4 = ring finger 5 = little finger

Chord Spelling

1st (A♭), 3rd (C), 5th (E♭)

FREE ACCESS on smartphones including iPhone & Android

Using any QR code app scan and **HEAR** the chord

G♯/A♭m
Minor

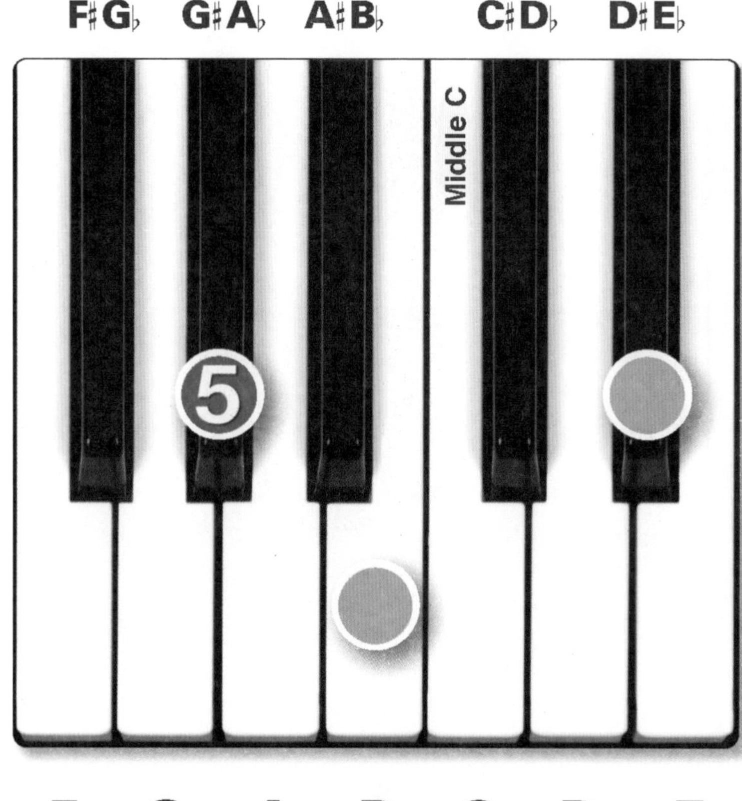

5 = little finger 4 = ring finger 3 = middle finger 2 = index finger 1 = thumb

Chord Spelling

1st (A♭), ♭3rd (C♭), 5th (E♭)

FREE ACCESS on smartphones including iPhone & Android

Using any QR code app scan and **HEAR** the chord

G♯/A♭m
Minor

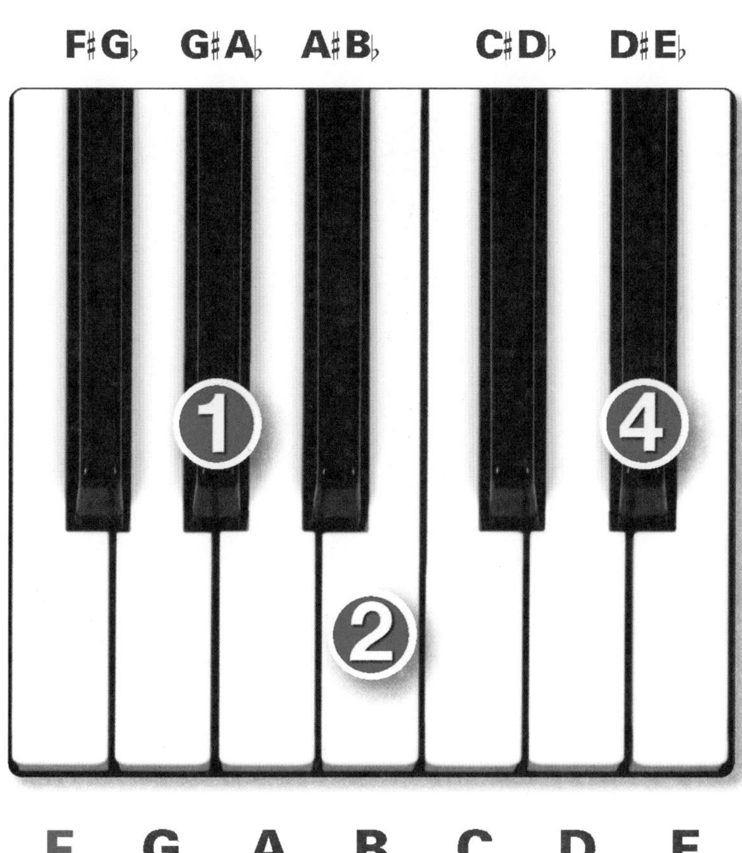

1 = thumb 2 = index finger 3 = middle finger 4 = ring finger 5 = little finger

Chord Spelling

1st (A♭), ♭3rd (C♭), 5th (E♭)

FREE ACCESS on smartphones including iPhone & Android  Using any QR code app scan and **HEAR** the chord

G♯/A♭+
Augmented Triad

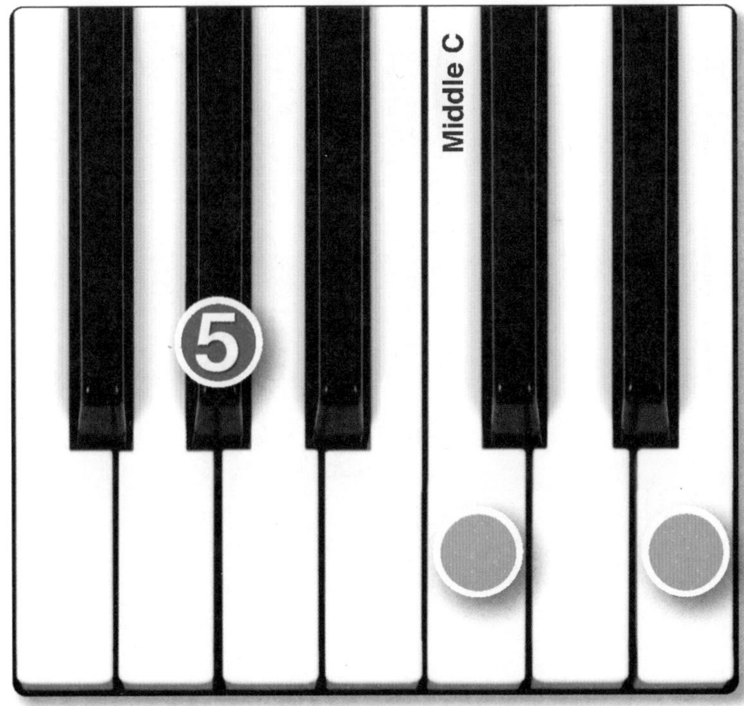

F G A B C D E

5 = little finger 4 = ring finger 3 = middle finger 2 = index finger 1 = thumb

Chord Spelling

1st (A♭), 3rd (C), #5th (E)

FREE ACCESS on smartphones including iPhone & Android

Using any QR code app scan and **HEAR** the chord

G♯/A♭+
Augmented Triad

F♯G♭ G♯A♭ A♯B♭ C♯D♭ D♯E♭

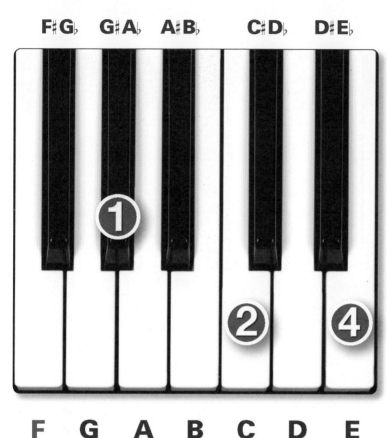

1

2 4

F G A B C D E

1 = thumb 2 = index finger 3 = middle finger 4 = ring finger 5 = little finger

Chord Spelling

1st (A♭), 3rd (C), #5th (E)

FREE ACCESS on smartphones including iPhone & Android  Using any QR code app scan and **HEAR** the chord

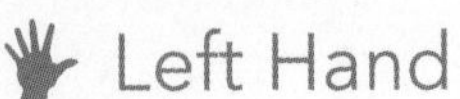

A

A♯/B♭

B

C

C♯/D♭

D

D♯/E♭

E

F

F♯/G♭

G

G♯/A♭

G♯/A♭°

Diminished Triad

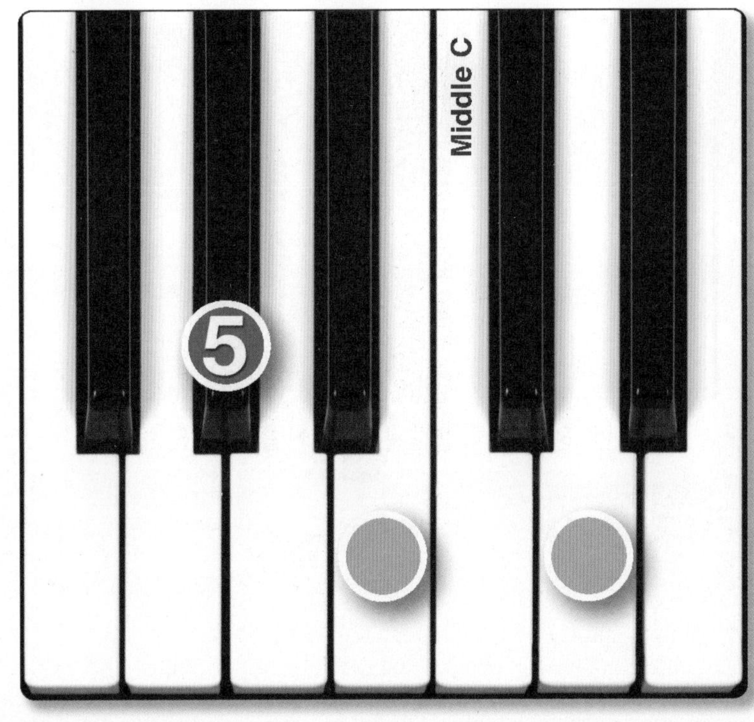

5 = little finger 4 = ring finger 3 = middle finger 2 = index finger 1 = thumb

Chord Spelling

1st (A♭), ♭3rd (C♭), ♭5th (E♭♭)

FREE ACCESS on smartphones including iPhone & Android

Using any QR code app scan and **HEAR** the chord

G♯/A♭°

Diminished Triad

Right Hand 

F♯G♭ G♯A♭ A♯B♭ C♯D♭ D♯E♭

1 2 4

F G A B C D E

1 = thumb 2 = index finger 3 = middle finger 4 = ring finger 5 = little finger

Chord Spelling

1st (A♭), ♭3rd (C♭), ♭5th (E♭♭)

FREE ACCESS on smartphones including iPhone & Android  Using any QR code app scan and **HEAR** the chord

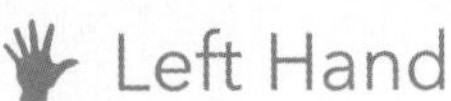

G♯/A♭6
Major 6th

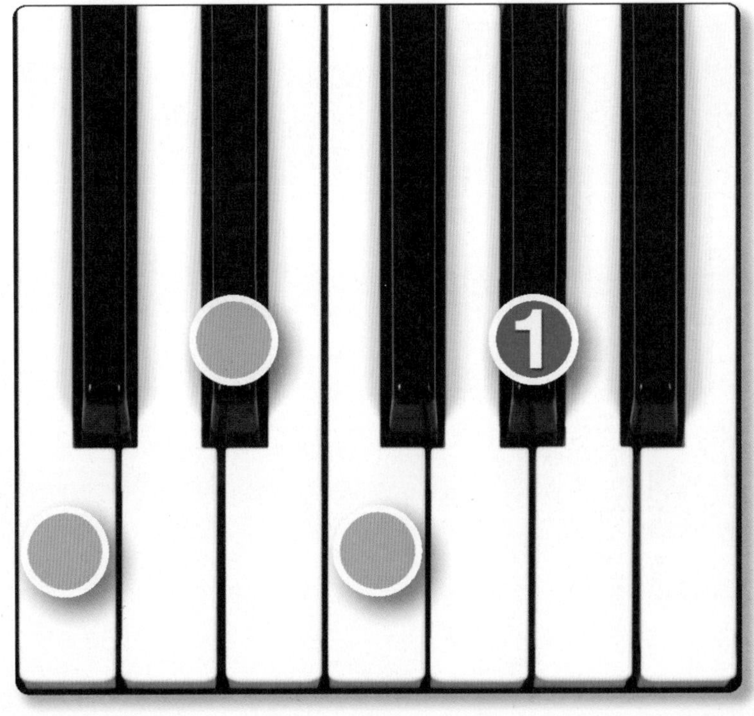

5 = little finger 4 = ring finger 3 = middle finger 2 = index finger 1 = thumb

Chord Spelling

1st (A♭), 3rd (C), 5th (E♭), 6th (F)

FREE ACCESS on smartphones including iPhone & Android

Using any QR code app scan and **HEAR** the chord

G♯/A♭6
Major 6th

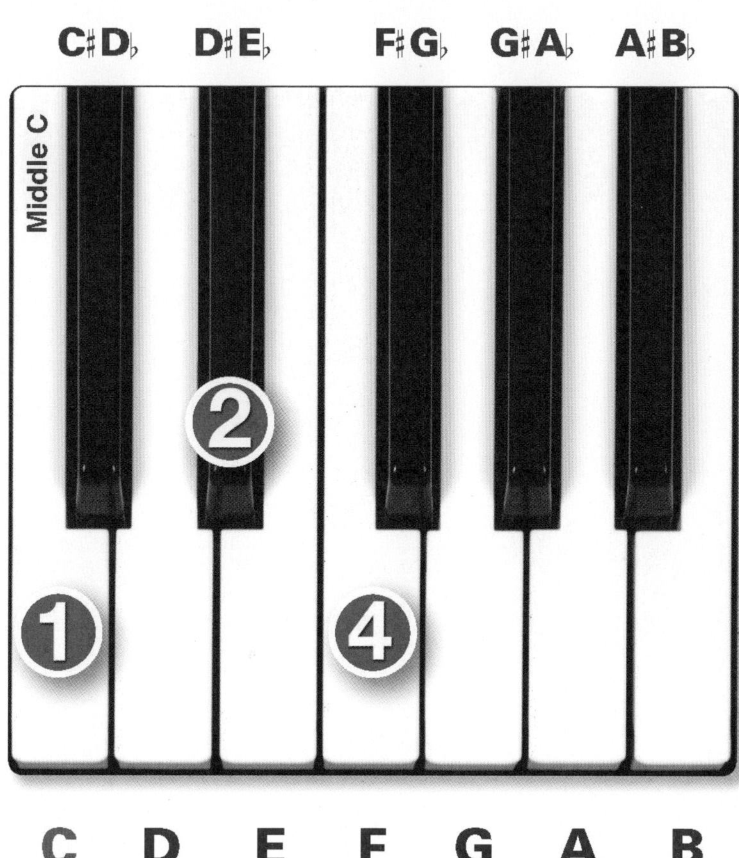

1 = thumb 2 = index finger 3 = middle finger 4 = ring finger 5 = little finger

Chord Spelling

1st (A♭), 3rd (C), 5th (E♭), 6th (F)

FREE ACCESS on smartphones including iPhone & Android  Using any QR code app scan and **HEAR** the chord

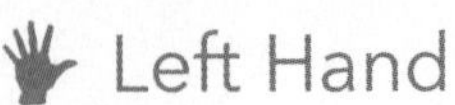

G♯/A♭m6
Minor 6th

C♯D♭ D♯E♭ F♯G♭ G♯A♭ A♯B♭

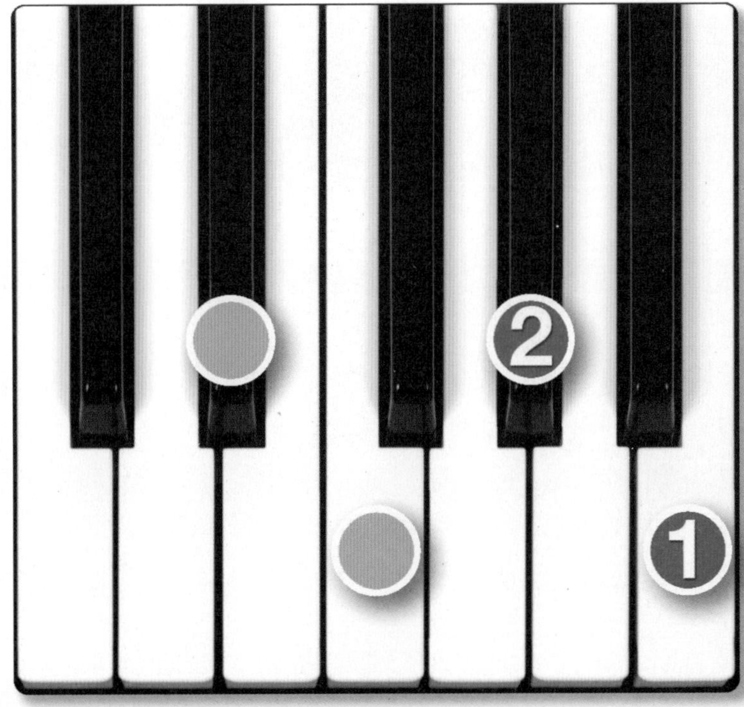

C D E F G A B

5 = little finger **4** = ring finger **3** = middle finger **2** = index finger **1** = thumb

Chord Spelling

1st (A♭), ♭3rd (C♭), 5th (E♭), 6th (F)

FREE ACCESS on smartphones including iPhone & Android

Using any QR code app scan and **HEAR** the chord

Right Hand

G♯/A♭m6

Minor 6th

1 = thumb 2 = index finger 3 = middle finger 4 = ring finger 5 = little finger

Chord Spelling

1st (A♭), ♭3rd (C♭), 5th (E♭), 6th (F)

FREE ACCESS on smartphones including iPhone & Android

Using any QR code app scan and **HEAR** the chord

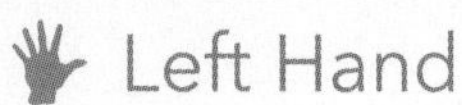
Left Hand

G♯/A♭maj7
Major 7th

C♯D♭ D♯E♭ F♯G♭ G♯A♭ A♯B♭

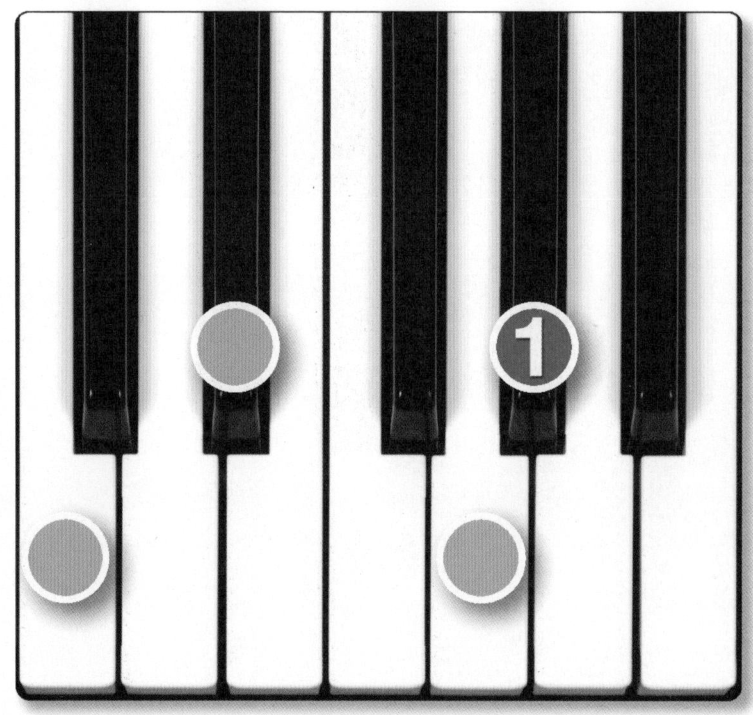

C D E F G A B

5 = little finger 4 = ring finger 3 = middle finger 2 = index finger 1 = thumb

Chord Spelling

1st (A♭), 3rd (C), 5th (E♭), 7th (G)

FREE ACCESS on smartphones including iPhone & Android

Using any QR code app scan and **HEAR** the chord

G♯/A♭maj7

Major 7th

1 = thumb 2 = index finger 3 = middle finger 4 = ring finger 5 = little finger

Chord Spelling

1st (A♭), 3rd (C), 5th (E♭), 7th (G)

FREE ACCESS on smartphones including iPhone & Android

Using any QR code app scan and **HEAR** the chord

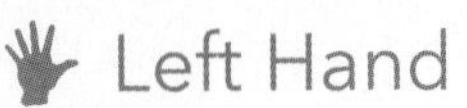

G♯/A♭m7
Minor 7th

C♯D♭ D♯E♭ F♯G♭ G♯A♭ A♯B♭

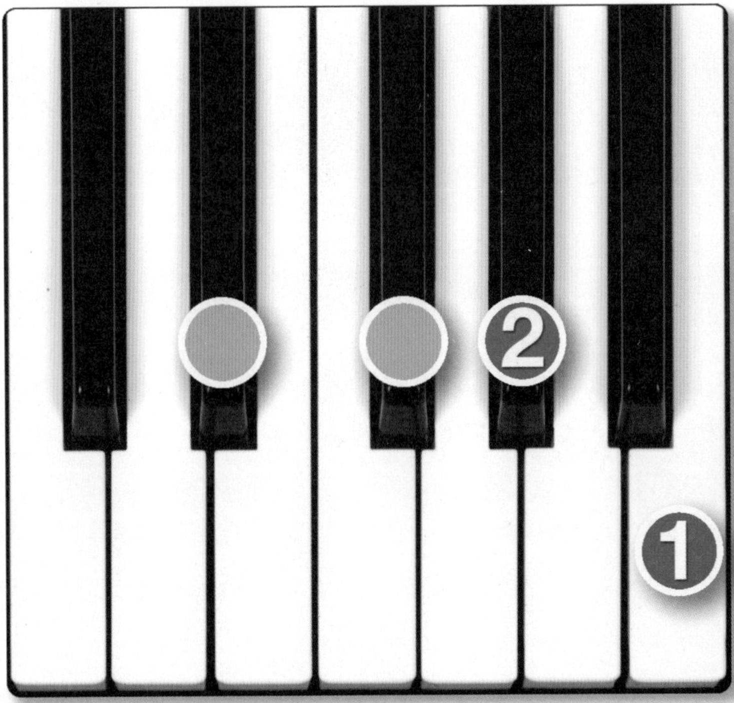

C D E F G A B

5 = little finger 4 = ring finger 3 = middle finger 2 = index finger 1 = thumb

Chord Spelling

1st (A♭), ♭3rd (C♭), 5th (E♭), 7th (G♭)

FREE ACCESS on smartphones including iPhone & Android

Using any QR code app scan and **HEAR** the chord

Right Hand 

G♯/A♭m7
Minor 7th

1 = thumb 2 = index finger 3 = middle finger 4 = ring finger 5 = little finger

Chord Spelling

1st (A♭), ♭3rd (C♭), 5th (E♭), 7th (G♭)

FREE ACCESS on smartphones including iPhone & Android  Using any QR code app scan and **HEAR** the chord

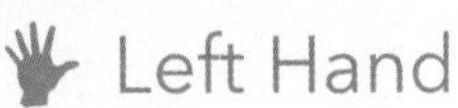

G♯/A♭maj9

Major 9th

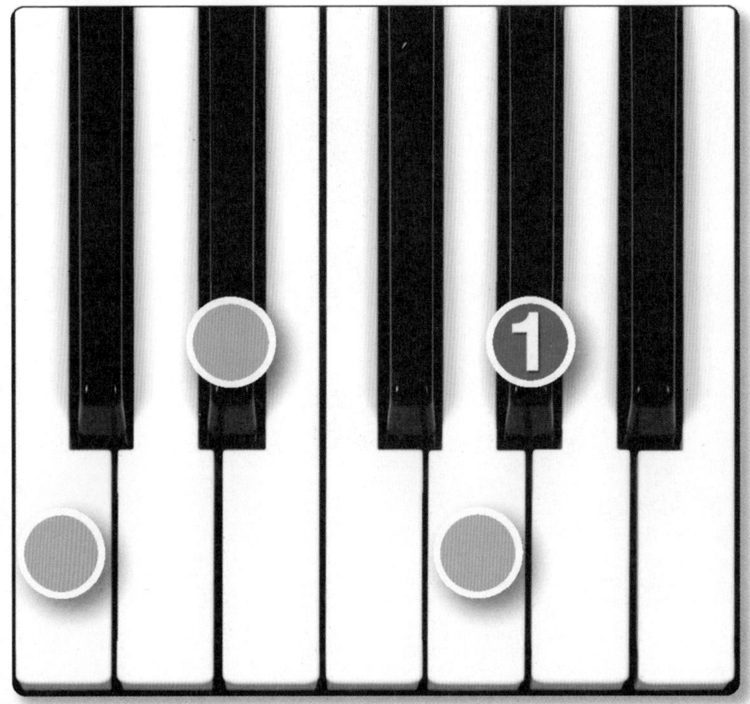

5 = little finger 4 = ring finger 3 = middle finger 2 = index finger 1 = thumb

Chord Spelling

1st (A♭), 3rd (C), 5th (E♭), 7th (G), 9th (B♭)

FREE ACCESS on smartphones including iPhone & Android  Using any QR code app scan and **HEAR** the chord

G♯/A♭maj9

Major 9th

1 = thumb 2 = index finger 3 = middle finger 4 = ring finger 5 = little finger

Chord Spelling

1st (A♭), 3rd (C), 5th (E♭), 7th (G), 9th (B♭)

FREE ACCESS on smartphones including iPhone & Android

Using any QR code app scan and **HEAR** the chord

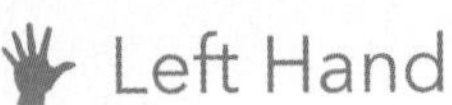

G♯/A♭m9

Minor 9th

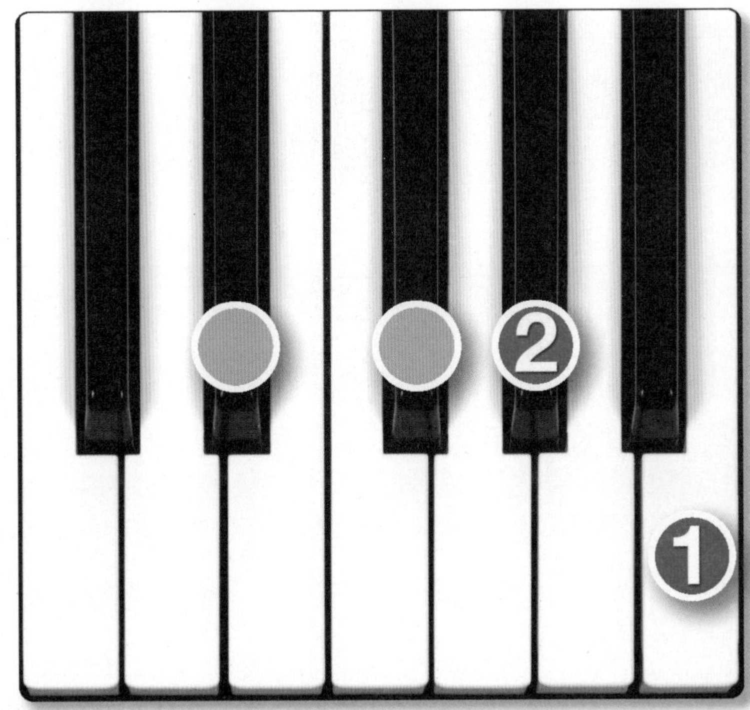

C D E F G A B

5 = little finger 4 = ring finger 3 = middle finger 2 = index finger 1 = thumb

Chord Spelling

1st (A♭), ♭3rd (C♭), 5th (E♭), ♭7th (G♭), 9th (B♭)

FREE ACCESS on smartphones including iPhone & Android

Using any QR code app scan and **HEAR** the chord

Right Hand 

G♯/A♭m9
Minor 9th

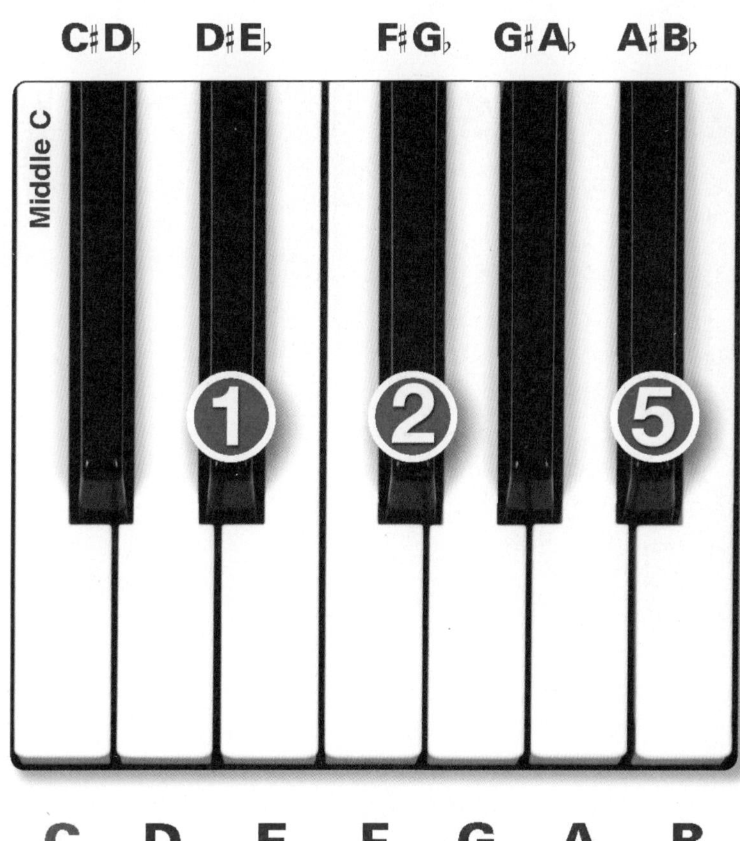

1 = thumb 2 = index finger 3 = middle finger 4 = ring finger 5 = little finger

Chord Spelling

1st (A♭), ♭3rd (C♭), 5th (E♭), ♭7th (G♭), 9th (B♭)

FREE ACCESS on smartphones including iPhone & Android

Using any QR code app scan and **HEAR** the chord

PIANO & KEYBOARD CHORDS MADE EASY

A new title in our best-selling series, designed for players of all abilities and ages. Created for musicians by musicians, these books offer a quick and practical resource for those playing on their own or with a band. They work equally well for the rock and indie musician as they do for the jazz, folk, country, blues or classical enthusiast.

The MUSIC MADE EASY series

See it and Hear it! Comprehensive sound links

Guitar Chords Made Easy, Piano and Keyboard Chords Made Easy, Scales and Modes Made Easy, Reading Music Made Easy, Learn to Play Piano Made Easy, Learn to Play Guitar Made Easy.

The SPIRAL, EASY-TO-USE series

Advanced Guitar Chords, Advanced Piano Chords, Guitar Chords; Piano & Keyboard Chords; Chords for Kids; Play Flamenco; How to Play Guitar; How to Play Bass Guitar; How to Play Classic Riffs; Songwriter's Rhyming Dictionary; How to Become a Star; How to Read Music; How to Write Great Songs; How to Play Rock Rhythm, Riffs & Lead; How to Play Hard, Metal & Nu Rock; How to Make Music on the Web; My First Recorder Music; Piano Sheet Music; Brass & Wind Sheet Music; Scales & Modes, Beginners' Guide to Reading Music

For further information on these titles please visit our trading website:
www.flametreepublishing.com

www.flametreemusic.com

Practical information on chords, scales, riffs, rhymes and instruments through a growing combination of traditional print books and ebooks. Features over **1800 chords**, with **sound files** for notes and strummed chords.

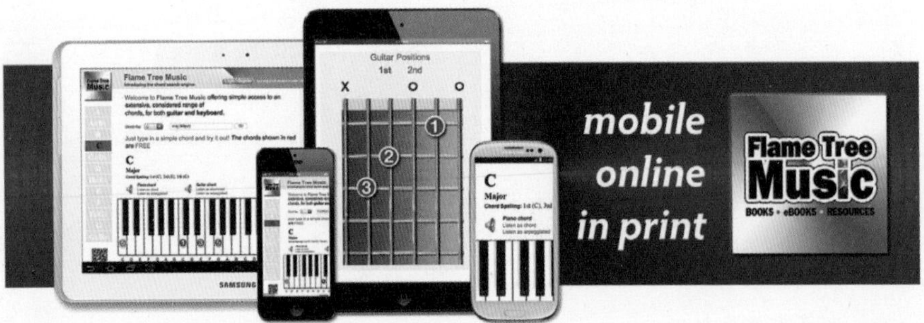